Understanding psychology as a science

101 778 492 2

ONE WEEK LOAN

Also by Zoltán Dienes

IMPLICIT LEARNING: Theoretical and Empirical Issues (*Berry, D. C. & Dienes, Z. (1993), Psychology Press*).

Understanding psychology as a science

An introduction to scientific and statistical inference

Zoltán Dienes
University of Sussex

First published 2008 by
PALGRAVE MACMILLAN
Houndmills, Basingstoke, Hampshire RG21 6XS and
175 Fifth Avenue, New York, N.Y. 10010
Companies and representatives throughout the world

PALGRAVE MACMILLAN is the global academic imprint of the Palgrave
Macmillan division of St. Martin's Press, LLC and of Palgrave Macmillan Ltd.
Macmillan® is a registered trademark in the United States, United Kingdom
and other countries. Palgrave is a registered trademark in the European
Union and other countries.

ISBN-13: 978–0–230–54231–0 paperback
ISBN-10: 0–230–54231–X paperback
ISBN-13: 978–0–230–54230–3 hardback
ISBN-10: 0–230–54230–1 hardback

This book is printed on paper suitable for recycling and made from fully
managed and sustained forest sources. Logging, pulping and manufacturing
processes are expected to conform to the environmental regulations of the
country of origin.

A catalogue record for this book is available from the British Library.

A catalog record for this book is available from the Library of Congress.

10   9   8   7   6   5   4
15 14 13 12 11 10 09

Printed and bound by Thomson Litho, East Kilbride, Scotland

To Mr. Mallenson, who lent me Magee's 'Popper' when I was in Imberhorne's Sixth Form, and to Jonck, whose witty and profound comments on this manuscript I could sadly never hear.

Contents

Preface

The aim of the book is to address those issues in the philosophy of science, including the conceptual basis of statistical inference, that have a direct bearing on the practice of psychological research. The book will enable lecturers teaching critical thinking, research methods or the new British Psychological Society's core area 'conceptual and historical issues' to cover material that every psychology undergraduate should know, but does not. The book will also be valuable for masters students, PhD students and experienced researchers.

The book is organized around influential thinkers whose admonitions and urgings are heard in the head of every research psychologist. The core arguments surrounding Popper, Kuhn, Lakatos, Fisher, Neyman and Pearson and Bayes are still live, heated, important and potentially within the grasp of every psychology undergraduate. Further, key points of the Neyman–Pearson approach are deeply misunderstood even by seasoned researchers in ways that can reflect badly on their research decisions. The best place to uproot these misconceptions is right at the undergraduate level, but I found no other existing book suitable for this purpose. Further, there is a live debate on whether psychologists even should be following the orthodoxy of Neyman–Pearson. Few psychologists have an opinion on this matter (which has important consequences for how research is conducted and evaluated) because they have not been exposed to the issues (and mostly do not realize there are any issues). There is a large and growing literature on the confusions and misuse of orthodox statistics, and what the alternatives might be. But the clarifications have not percolated through to ground level. The reason is that the literature is largely technical and read only by the aficionado. The very people who need to know it are just the people who do not read it. What has been missing is a simple (though not simplistic) introduction showing conceptually how the characteristics of the different approaches arise from first principles. There has been a gap in our education that has existed far too long. To paraphrase Phil Johnson Laird's famous quip, I hope the current book helps fill this much unwanted gap. (I leave the task of my writing books filling much *needed gaps* to other occasions.) In any case, if my role in all this is to start corrupting undergraduates at a young age, the cat will be let out of the bag. I think the sooner the conceptual issues underlying inference form a part of the undergraduate's education in research methodology, the better.

The first two chapters cover classic philosophy of science (Popper, Kuhn, Lakatos) in a way accessible to psychologists while avoiding the normal textbook caricatures. The aim is to appreciate the depth of these authors so that their ideas provide real tools for thinking about research. Examples are drawn from psychology and practical advice is given.

The next three chapters motivate the reasoning behind statistical thinking. Chapter 3 covers the Neyman–Pearson approach, that is the logic meant to underlie the statistics in every textbook for psychology students. It is a sad fact – indeed, a scandal – that few undergraduates, PhD students or lecturers actually understand the logic of hypothesis testing (with or without Fisherian twists). The Neyman–Pearson logic will not be fully grasped until alternatives are also presented. Many people instinctively believe that they are getting Bayesian or likelihood answers to Neyman–Pearson statistics. This basic confusion more than any other probably underlies the widespread misuse of significance testing. So Chapter 4 shows the logic of Bayesian inference, the opposite of Neyman–Pearson in fundamental ways. The book's website (http://www.lifesci.sussex.ac.uk/home/Zoltan_Dienes/inference/) includes a program that can be used for analysing data in a Bayesian way. Finally, the logic of the third major school of statistical inference, likelihood inference, is presented and motivated in Chapter 5. Chapter 5 shows how to use likelihood inference in practice and how it leads to different research decisions than the other schools. The book's website also includes programs for conducting likelihood analyses.

None of the chapters on statistics assume mathematics beyond that necessary for an undergraduate course in statistics as run in an average psychology department. The chapters aim only to provide foundational concepts and link them to practical research decisions. The arguments for each school are presented conceptually, so for the first time the average user of statistics can start making informed decisions – and accept or reject orthodoxy on a rational basis.

I wish to warn the psychology undergraduate reader that the material may at first appear daunting, as it will require thinking in new ways. Persistence will bring reward. Do not deride your own intellectual reactions; the interesting thing about philosophy is that whatever view you hold on a topic, there is bound to be some very eminent philosopher who holds a similar view. In many cases, I am not giving you settled answers. Be confident in thinking through your own arguments. However, the multiplicity of views does not mean that nothing has been achieved in philosophy nor that all views are acceptable. On the contrary, having understood the issues discussed in this book, you will evaluate and practise research in ways you could not have done before. Whatever decisions you come to on the open issues, you will become a far better researcher and evaluator of research having thought about the issues in this book.

If in reading this book you feel confused at times, that is a very good sign. Confusion means you have found a way to arrive at a deeper understanding. Value that feeling. Confusion is not the end goal of course, it is a sign-post for what to think about and a spur to think it through now because your mind is ripe. While I hope to confuse you, I also hope I have given you what you need to subsequently gain clarity. Any confusion caused by errors or omissions on my part is not good, and I will endeavour to correct them in any future editions. You can contact me on dienes+inference@sussex.ac.uk.

Thanks to the Cognitive Science Society for allowing reproduction of Figures 1.4 and 1.5, for which they hold the copyright. Many thanks to Robert Clowes, Bruce Dienes, Alan Garnham, Nomi Olsthoorn, Ryan Scott and Dan Wright, and also the four anonymous reviewers, for their valuable comments on previous versions of the manuscript. Many thanks also to the students I taught this material to over the last two years without whom truly this book would not have been possible. I am indebted to Leiming He and Xiaolong Zhang for the excellent cartoons. Finally, I very much appreciate the patience of my wife Mina and my son Harry over the past year.

Zoltán Dienes
Brighton, UK, 2007

1 Karl Popper and demarcation

Philosophy, they say, cannot by its very nature have any significant consequences, and so it can influence neither science nor politics. But I think that ideas are dangerous and powerful things, and that even philosophers have sometimes produced ideas.

Popper (1963, p. 6)

Box 1.1 Questions

What is science?

What is the difference between science and pseudo-science?

What is the difference between good science and bad science?

On what grounds should papers submitted to scientific journals be rejected or accepted?

Are Christian Science, Creation Science, Scientology, astrology, traditional Chinese medicine, or chiropractic sciences? Why or why not and why does it matter?

Is psychology a science? Good science or bad science?

How does knowledge grow?

We are constantly faced by choices concerning what to believe, choices of great practical and personal importance (Box 1.1). Will taking an anti-depressant pill help me if I am depressed? Should I prefer the use of these herbs or those drugs for my hay fever? Are the economic policies for controlling inflation of one political party more effective than those of another? Are some forms of exercise rather than others more effective for losing weight, gaining muscle or excelling in sporting performance? What methods might help me overcome anxiety? What are the best methods for learning a second language? What principles might enable different groups of people to live together more harmoniously, or a given group to work more smoothly, or a relationship to run better?

The choice of what to believe is not just a practical matter. A desire to understand the world seems intrinsic to homo sapiens. I remember as a teenager being fascinated to find

I needed only my high-school algebra to follow arguments concerning the fundamental nature of space and time as portrayed by special relativity. The sheer fact that such elegant and counter-intuitive laws had survived severe tests counted for me as amongst mankind's greatest achievements. (It still does.) Further, the details of how evolution works, of how genetics work, of how the brain works, of how the mind works are surely worth knowing for no other reason than we gain understanding of ourselves and the universe. The burgeoning popular science section of bookshops attests to people's simple desire to understand, that is, to know the best explanations around. But what counts as a satisfactory explanation of phenomena in the world? When is one such explanation better than another? This is a philosophical problem, but not an empty one, it is a problem of real substance regardless of whether our aim is practical or it is understanding itself.

The Austrian Karl Popper (1902–1994) formulated the problem in terms of what distinguishes science from non-science (including pseudo-science). He called it the problem of demarcation. He was not interested in merely categorizing or labelling something as science or not, he was interested in the substantial problem of how we can best pursue knowledge of the world. His works inspired many scientists, including various Nobel Laureates, who publicly declared how beneficial Popper's philosophy had been to them as scientists. For most of his academic career Popper held a chair in logic and scientific method at the London School of Economics. He was also a highly influential political and social philosopher. He continued producing work right up until his death at age 92. For his achievements, Sir Karl was knighted in 1965.

Background: logical positivism

Popper was born in Vienna in 1902, then an intellectual and cultural centre of the Western world. A prominent philosophical movement during Popper's time in Vienna was the so-called 'Vienna Circle' (Wiener Kreis), a group of scientists and philosophers who met regularly to discuss the implications of the major revolutions in science happening at that time, especially those triggered by Einstein's work (see Edmonds and Eidinow, 2001, for a very readable biographical account). The discussions were led by Moritz Schlick (1882–1936); attendance required his personal invitation.[1] Among the members were mathematician Kurt Gödel (of Gödel's theorem fame) and philosophers like Rudolf Carnap and Carl Hempel, and the economist Otto Neurath. They formulated a philosophical approach called *logical positivism*. It is worthwhile knowing a little bit about logical positivism to understand what Sir Karl was partially opposing.

Logical positivism was itself a reaction against a style of philosophy then popular in the German world which emphasized pompous, difficult and obscure writing. In fact, members of the Vienna Circle wondered whether such writing actually said anything at all. In order to sort meaningful statements from meaningless nonsense, the logical positivists proposed that meaningful statements were either definitions, and thus necessarily true (like 'a triangle has three sides'); or else *verifiable* empirical statements (statements about the world). Empirical statements were only meaningful if they satisfied the *verification criterion*, that is, if one could specify the steps that would verify whether the statement was true.

---

1. Schlick had an early death because of a vengeful and mentally unstable student. Schlick had failed the student and later slept with his wife. The student confronted Schlick on the steps of the University and shot him in the chest. Although Schlick was not a Jew, the killer was subsequently hailed as a Jew killer in the popular press.

For example, the statement 'my desk is three foot tall' can be verified by measuring its height with a ruler, so the statement is meaningful. But how could one verify that 'The essence of Spirit is freedom'? Or 'The world does not really exist, it is just an idea'? Or 'The world really does exist'? Or 'Free will is an illusion'? Or 'God exists'? Or 'God is loving kindness'? For the logical positivists such unverifiable statements were just *metaphysical* nonsense. Much conventional philosophy could be swept away as dealing with pseudo-problems! One could get on with the real work of developing mathematics and logic (which deal with statements which are necessarily true) and natural science. Science could be construed as sets of empirical statements, dealing only with possible observations that could be directly verified, and theoretical statements which acted as definitions linking theoretical terms (like 'electron') to observations. If you have ever read a lot of old German texts (or indeed many things written today in English – e.g. see Sokal and Bricmont, 1998), you may have some sympathy with the urge to throw much in the dustbin labelled 'gibberish' (Box 1.2).

Box 1.2 Operational definitions

A notion inspired by logical positivism, and used extensively in modern psychology, is the idea of an *operational definition*, introduced by the Nobel Laureate physicist Percy Bridgeman in 1927. An operational definition defines the meaning of a concept in terms of the precise procedures used to determine its presence and quantity. For example, an operational definition of intelligence could be the score obtained on a certain IQ test. An operational definition of unconscious knowledge could be above baseline performance on a knowledge test when the person verbally claims they are guessing. An operational definition of the degree of penis envy in women could be the number of pencils returned after an exam. Experimental psychologists habitually produce operational definitions. They are invaluable but often the 'definition' is actually not a definition at all but rather a way to measure more-or-less imperfectly the thing we want to measure. More-or-less imperfectly measuring is different from defining; if the measurement is a definition the outcome is never imperfect. Defining being 'successfully anaesthetized' as 'having received a standard dose of anaesthetic' might strike some unfortunate people as having completely missed the point. When a psychologist has his back against the wall in an argument to the effect he is not measuring what he claims, there is the temptation for him to say, for example, 'But what I MEAN by emotional intelligence is a score on this test'. (The word 'mean' is always emphasized in this tactic.) The temptation should normally be resisted in psychology. It is rarely the case that what we *mean* by a concept is exhausted by some particular way of measuring it. An operational definition should not be an excuse to stop thinking critically about the validity of one's measure.

The logical positivists had two problems in determining whether a sentence was verifiable. There is the problem of how to verify statements about specific individuals and their observable properties, like 'Emma the swan is white'; and there is the problem of verifying generalizations like 'All swans are white'. The first problem was meant to be solved by direct observation, and the second by a putative logical process called *induction*. Induction can be contrasted with *deduction*. Deduction is the process of drawing inferences such that if the premises are true the conclusion is guaranteed to be true. For example:

> All swans are white
> Sam is a swan
> _____
> Conclusion: Sam is white

Induction is the process of inferring universal rules given only particular observations:

> Sam the swan is white;
> Georgina the swan is white;
> Fred the swan is white;
> . . .
> Emma the swan is white
>
> _____
>
> Conclusion: All swans are white (?)

The conclusion here cannot be guaranteed to be true, hence the inference is not deductive. But still one instinctively feels the conclusion has increased in plausibility by the repeated particular observations. We feel very sure the sun will rise tomorrow for no other reason than it has done so repeatedly in the past. You might say, we also have a theory of gravitation that predicts the sun will continue to rise. But why do we feel confident in that theory other than for the fact that it has worked on so many particular occasions in the past? Inductivists, including logical positivists, believe that science proceeds by induction. Science is objective because it is based on actual observations rather than just speculation, and it goes from those particular observations logically – inductively – to general rules.

With the Second World War and Hitler's dismantling of the university system in Germany and neighbouring countries, many Jewish intellectuals, including members of the Vienna Circle, sought refuge in the United States. In fact, logical positivism went from being a minority philosophical position in Europe before the war to being the dominant force in American philosophy by about 1960 (see Giere, 1999, Chapter 11). Since then many people have defined their philosophy of science either as being in the same tradition or as reacting against logical positivism. Popper, however, is the person who credits himself with killing it off (Box 1.3).

Box 1.3

Consider the following theory: In human beings, the hippocampus is required for spatial navigation.

You find Sam who, due to a recent unusual viral illness, has destruction of all his hippocampus and no other brain structure. His spatial navigation is very bad.

Have you established the theory is true?

What about if you found eight teenage drivers who all destroyed their hippocampi (and no other brain structure) in car accidents. Their spatial navigation is very bad.

Have you established the theory?

Your ninth teenage driver with complete destruction of the hippocampus has excellent spatial navigation.

What can you conclude about the theory?

The problem of induction

Popper denied all aspects of logical positivism just described. The positivists rejected metaphysics as meaningless; Popper argued that metaphysics could be not only meaningful but also important. The positivists wished to view science as a method of moving towards certain knowledge: knowledge based on a firm foundation of observation and induction. Popper denied that either observation or induction provided means for moving towards certain knowledge. He denied further that certainty was even the goal of science. The core feature of Popper's philosophy was fallibilism: we may be wrong in anything we believe. We will see how this principle can be turned into a practical philosophy of science that allows knowledge to progress!

Induction had received a crippling, if not fatal, attack earlier by the Scottish philosopher David Hume (1711–1776). Hume argued that we are never justified in reasoning from repeated instances of which we have experiences (e.g. different swans being white) to other instances of which we have had no experience yet (other swans we are yet to observe the colour of). Induction is never justified. No matter how often we have seen a white swan, it never follows that the next swan we see will be white, yet alone that all swans are white. (A famous example because when the British went to Australia they finally found swans that were black!) A common response is to accept that, yes, from particular observations no generalization follows with certainty – but surely the *probability* of the generalization is increased with each supporting observation. Each time we see a white swan, is it not more likely that all swans are white? Hume pointed out that this does not follow. No matter what observations up to now support a generalization, it may be the case that every instance after *now* fails to support it. No matter how often your car has started early in the morning, one day it will not, and one day will mark the point that the car never starts again. Indeed, you might feel that the more days your car has started, the *less* likely it is it will start the next day, because that is the effect of age on cars! One morning the chicken at the Colonel's ranch is greeted by someone who is not offering breakfast. But surely, you might reply, induction has empirically proved itself because using induction in the past to infer generalizations has often been successful. This argument, Hume pointed out, assumes that induction is true in order to argue for it: No matter how often induction has worked in the past, there is no reason to think it will work ever again. Not unless you already assume induction, that is.

Popper (e.g. 1934, 1963, 1972) accepted all these arguments. The claim that an explanatory universal theory is true is never justified by assuming the truth of any number of observation statements. One stunning intellectual event happening during Popper's formative years was the replacement of Newtonian physics by relativity and quantum physics. No theory had received more 'inductive support' – over several hundred years – than Newtonian physics. But in the space of a few years it went from a theory widely regarded as being the established truth to one recognized as literally false. The moral for Popper was clear: We can never actually establish the truth of our theories. Establishing truth is not what science does. No matter how strongly we or others believe a theory, the theory is and always remains just a guess, even if it is our best guess. Induction does not exist.

What is the problem that people wished to explain by postulating induction? Typically, Popper points out, the situation is that we have several theories which compete as explanations and we must choose between them. Bertrand Russell (1872–1970), the grandfather of the logical positivists, thought that without working out how induction could be valid we could not decide between a good scientific theory and the 'mere obsession of a madman'. Popper argued that we do not need induction to solve the problem of theory choice. He pointed out that while assuming the truth of a particular observation or test statement never allows us to justify the claim that a universal theory is *true*, it sometimes allows us to justify the claim that the universal theory is *false*. For example, accepting that 'Sam the Swan is black' allows us to conclude that the universal claim 'All swans are white' is false. Although we cannot *establish* our theories, we may be able to successfully criticize them. There is a genuine asymmetry here in our ability to falsify versus establish a theory, given we accept singular observations. Popper exploits that asymmetry to the full in developing his philosophy of science. Rationality consists in critical discussion, trying to find the weaknesses in a theory or argument, weaknesses that may be shown by, for example, observations – observations used to criticize the theory.

The role of critical discussion

How does knowledge grow? According to Popper, there is only one practicable method: critical discussion. Knowledge does not start from unprejudiced pure observation. There is no such thing: All observation involves some theory, some prejudice. Consider the ridiculous nature of the task of just telling someone: 'Observe!'. Observe what? For what purpose? Science is not built from naked observations. One starts with a theory, a conjecture. Then one tries to refute it. If the theory resists refutation, new lines of criticism can be attempted. In the light of a successful refutation, a new conjecture can be proposed to deal with the new problem situation.

Popper points out that in most societies in human history and around the world we find schools of thought which have the function not of critical discussion but to impart a definite doctrine and preserve it, pure and unchanged. Attempting to change a doctrine is heresy and will probably lead to expulsion from the school. In such a tradition, the successful innovator insists that he is just presenting what the master's original doctrine really was before it was lost or perverted! The critical tradition, in contrast, was founded by explicitly establishing the method of proposing a conjecture then asking your students, after having understood it, to try to do better by finding the weaknesses in the proposal. In the critical tradition, the aim is not to preserve a doctrine but to improve it. Popper (1994) suggests that remarkably this method was invented only once in human history. Whether or not Popper's historical conjecture is true is irrelevant for his main point, though it remains an intriguing speculation. Popper suggests that it was Thales (c.636–c.546 BCE) who established the new tradition of free thought in ancient Greece. The students of Thales openly criticized him and presented bold new ideas to overcome those criticisms (for details, see Popper, 1963, Chapter 5). The growth in knowledge in the space of a few years was breathtaking. Xenophanes (570–480 BCE) spread the critical tradition, expressing the philosophy that all our knowledge is guess work in this poem (Popper's translation, in his e.g. 1963):

> But as for certain truth, no man has known it
> Nor will he know it; neither of the gods,
> Nor yet of all the things of which I speak.
> And even if by chance he were to utter
> The perfect truth, he would himself not know it;
> For all is but a woven web of guesses

Though we can never know if we have the truth, we can always try to improve on what we have. This critical tradition died in the West, according to Popper, when an intolerant Christianity suppressed it. It smoldered in the Arab East, from where it finally migrated and ignited the Renaissance and modern science. Once again there was an explosion in knowledge. The scientific tradition just is this critical tradition.[2]

---

2. In developing your own critical skills, bear in mind the advice of Donald Broadbent: Stand on the shoulders of those who have gone before you and not on their faces.

Popper's historical conjecture about the critical tradition arising only once is a reminder not to take the tradition for granted. It would be easy to see claims of the importance of criticism as platitudes. But participating in a tradition of one's students and colleagues criticizing oneself is not psychologically easy. Further, regardless of the intrinsic difficulties, external attacks and erosions are all around, from religious, party political and corporate authoritarianism. To take an extreme example, in 1957, Mao said, 'Let a hundred flowers bloom; let the hundred schools of thought contend', meaning let everyone voice their opinions so the best ideas may survive. Those who voiced opinions critical of Mao were silenced.

What is science?

Popper rejected the logical positivists' attempt to distinguish meaningful statements from nonsense but instead sought to distinguish science from non-science, or metaphysics. But that does not mean that Popper believed in a scientific method as a specifiable formula to be followed for developing knowledge. 'As a rule, I begin my lectures on Scientific Method by telling my students that scientific method does not exist. I add that I ought to know, having been, for a time at least, the one and only professor of this non-existent subject within the British Commonwealth' (1983, p. 5). Popper despised compartmentalizing knowledge into subjects in any case. What is really important is just interesting problems and attempts to solve them. For example, there is the problem (which I find interesting) of explaining why hypnotized people behave as they do. Solving that problem may involve thinking about it in ways typical of the subjects of philosophy, cognitive and social psychology, or neuroscience. But none of *those* 'subjects' has any separate reality (beyond being useful administrative divisions for organizing a university); I may blend their ideas in my own conjectures concerning hypnosis. All relevant knowledge should be brought to bear on interesting problems. Nonetheless, 'Scientific Method holds a somewhat peculiar position in being even less existent than some other non-existent subjects' (p. 6).

There is according to Popper no method of discovering a scientific theory, no method of inferring a theory from 'pure' observation. Science consists of freely, creatively *inventing* theories: Science is made by people. There is also according to Popper no method – like induction – of determining the truth of a theory, no method of verification. There is not even any method of determining whether a theory is probably true. This follows from Hume's critique of induction. Many philosophers refuse to accept this conclusion (see e.g. Salmon, 2005, for a defense of the Popperian thesis, see Miller, 1994, Chapter 2. For an accessible introduction to arguments concerning induction, see Chalmers, 1999, Chapter 4). We will see later in the book that there is an approach, the Bayesian approach, aimed precisely at determining the probability of a hypothesis. But the Bayesian approach never actually answered Hume's critique as such; instead, the argument is *assuming that the world follows a certain specified type of model* (i.e., *assuming* generalizations of a certain type hold and will continue to hold), *then the probabilities of different versions of the model can be calculated*. Popper rejected such approaches, not only because he accepted Hume's critique but also because he rejected the relevance of the subjective probabilities the Bayesians used. This issue is very much a current live debate and is explained further in Chapter 4.

Popper thought how people invent their theories is not relevant to the logic of science. The distinction between the process of conceiving a new idea (which Popper, 1934, called the psychology of knowledge) and the process of examining it logically (the logic of knowledge) is more commonly known as the distinction between the *context of discovery* and the *context of justification*. These latter terms were introduced by Hans Reichenbach (1891–1953) in 1938. Reichenbach had founded the 'Berlin Circle' and a type of logical positivism. He had been dismissed from the University of Berlin in 1933 due to Nazi racial laws and eventually established himself in the United States. Reichenbach illustrated the distinction between the context of discovery and the context of justification by the distinction between psychological and historical facts concerning Einstein the man, on the one hand, and the logical relation of his theory of general relativity to relevant evidence, on the other (see Giere, 1999). Giere suggests that Reichenbach was motivated by the cultural climate at the time to deny that the characteristics of a person, such as being a Jew, has anything to do with the scientific validity of a hypothesis proposed by the person. The hypothesis stands or falls on its own logical merits independently of who thought it up or how they thought it up (see Box 1.4).

Box 1.4 Is there a distinction between the contexts of discovery and justification?

The distinction between the context of discovery and the context of justification has good face validity. For example, Kekule is said to have thought of the idea of a ring of carbon atoms as the structure of benzene by dreaming of snakes biting their tails. The process of dreaming is part of the context of discovery or the psychology of knowledge and irrelevant to the evaluation of his hypothesis. It is the hypothesis itself – of a ring of atoms – and its relation to laboratory evidence that belongs to the logic of knowledge or the context of justification. Nonetheless, the usefulness of the distinction between the contexts of discovery and justification has been controversial. Thomas Kuhn (1969), for example, rejected the distinction. He did not believe that there was a special logic of scientific knowledge to make a distinctive context of justification. Kuhn also thought the processes by which a particular scientist within a discipline comes to discover new knowledge is an integral part of what makes the practice scientific. We will discuss Kuhn's position in more detail in the next chapter. Even within Popper's philosophy the distinction can sometimes be blurred. As we will see, central to Popper's account of science is that scientists adopt a 'falsificationist attitude'. Such an attitude is surely as much part of the psychology of knowledge as its logic. The psychological problem of what factors facilitate scientific discovery is a theoretically interesting and educationally important problem on which progress has been made; for example, in the work of Peter Cheng on the role of diagrams (e.g. Cheng & Simon, 1995) and of Roger Shepard on thought experiments (Shepard, 2001). Diagrams and images aid *psychologically* by embodying the underlying *logic* of the scientific problem. However, while the contexts of discovery and justification can be intertwined, Salmon (2005, Chapter five) believes that the distinction is still 'viable, significant, and fundamental to the philosophy of science' (p. 85) if not to scientists themselves. As scientists, we are concerned with the logical relations between theory and evidence, stripped of accidental irrelevancies concerning the discovery of the theory or of the evidence. Just what is relevant and what is irrelevant to these logical relations is an issue every chapter of this book will bear on.

There are no set methods for creating theories and there are no methods at all for showing a theory to be true. According to Popper, theory testing is not inductive, but deductive: Accepting certain observation statements can show a theory is false (the one black swan showing that not all swans are white). This is how observations make contact with theories; this is how, therefore, our knowledge acquires its empirical character. Science can only work in this way if a theory is falsifiable to begin with: The theory says certain things cannot happen. Non-science or metaphysics is, by contrast, non-falsifiable. That is a logical property distinguishing science from metaphysics. This distinction does not render metaphysics meaningless in any way; it just is not science. Metaphysical knowledge can still grow by critical discussion; but scientific knowledge can also grow by the feedback provided by actual observations as part of that critical discussion. In sum, falsifiability is Popper's demarcation criterion between science and metaphysics.

Popper sees science as the process of proposing falsifiable theories then rigorously attempting to falsify them. It is only when theories are falsified that we get feedback from Nature and a chance to improve our knowledge. But one must be clear: Theories that survive rigorous attempts at falsification are NOT proved or established. They are 'corroborated' as Popper puts it; they survive and prove only their mettle not their truth. They can be held only tentatively. Because they are held only tentatively, in a genuine scientific tradition, the researchers will have a 'falsificationist attitude'. That is, on Popper's view, it is not enough for empirical knowledge to grow that the theories be simply falsifiable as such; the community as a whole must be actively trying different ways of falsifying the proposed theories. In this way, the community becomes part of the critical tradition.

Box 1.5 Why do people often prefer the food they were brought up on, but not always?

Consider the following two factor theory of liking:

Factor 1: We are programmed to like familiar things (e.g. foods, people, animals, tools, etc.) because our knowledge and skills are likely to apply to them. They are not dangerous, we can deal with them. Thus, there is a mechanism that automatically makes us like things as we come across them more often.

Factor 2: But we also get bored with familiar things, because there is little to learn from them and we have a drive to learn.

These two factors act in opposition to each other.

So increasing people's exposure to a new thing can

1. Increase people's liking because the familiarity means it is safe (first factor operating)
2. Decrease peoples liking because they get bored (second factor operating)
3. First increase then decrease liking because the first factor operates initially before boredom becomes stronger
4. First decrease then increase liking because boredom operates initially before the first factor becomes stronger

The theory is a good one because it explains all these outcomes.

Discuss.

Psychoanalysis, Marxism and Relativity

Popper was impressed by two opposing types of experiences in 1919: on the one hand, with Marxism and psychoanalysis; on the other hand, with Einstein. As Popper puts it,

Admirers of Marx, Freud and Adler [a student of Freud's] were impressed by the ability of the theories to explain everything that happened within their domain. They saw confirming instances everywhere; whatever happened always confirmed it. Its truth appeared manifest; people who did not see the truth refused to because of their class interest or

Popper believed that there were genuine problems in philosophy, and that he, Popper, had even solved some (including the problem of demarcation between science and non-science). Yet, he comments, 'nothing seems less wanted than a simple solution to an age-old philosophical problem' (Popper 1976, pp. 123–124). Wittgenstein held there were no genuine philosophical problems only puzzles created by the inappropriate use of language. In their one and only meeting at a seminar at Kings College Cambridge, 5 October 1946, a meeting lasting 10 minutes, Popper gave a list of what he considered to be genuine philosophical problems, including the problem of the validity of moral rules.

Different people attending the seminar had different memories of their impassioned exchange, culminating in Wittgenstein storming out of the room (see Edmonds and Eidnow, 2001, for the full story).

because of their repressions which were crying out for treatment. A Marxist could not open a newspaper without finding on every page confirming evidence for his interpretation of history (Popper, 1963, p. 45).

The method of looking for verifications is unsound; indeed, it seemed to Popper to be the typical method of pseudo-science. 'All swans are white' is equivalent to 'All non-white things are non-swans'. Thus every time you see a non-swan you *verify* both statements. Verifications can come cheaply if you are interested in just any old verification. By contrast, knowledge will progress most rapidly by the method of criticism, by the method of looking for falsifying instances in order to improve one's theory.

Popper briefly worked for Alfred Adler and describes a related anecdote.

Once in 1919 I reported to [Adler] a case which did not seem particularly Adlerian, but which he found no difficulty in analyzing in terms of his theory of inferiority feelings, although he had not even seen the child. Slightly shocked, I asked him how could he be so sure. 'Because of my thousand-fold experience' he replied; whereupon I could not help saying, 'And with this new case, I suppose, your experience has become one thousand-and-one-fold' (Popper, 1963, p. 46).

What do these confirmations mean if every conceivable case could be interpreted in the light of Adler's (or Freud's) theory? How would Adler or Freud or Marx ever get any indication that they were wrong? If any behaviour by a person can be 'explained', the theory cannot be criticized by the use of observations; it loses its empirical character. Consider an analyst giving a patient an interpretation. If the patient accepts the interpretation, this analyst may conclude that it was the right one. But if a patient rejects the interpretation, particularly with some vigor, the analyst might conclude that the interpretation hit pretty close to home. What would give the analyst the slightest inkling that she were wrong? And if we cannot learn from our mistakes, how can we improve our theories? Popper's attempt at demarcation between science and non-science was not a mere attempt at classification, but an analysis of how knowledge can best grow.

As an example, Popper (1983, pp. 159–174) discusses Freud's approach to dealing with objections to Freud's theory of dreams and whether it illustrates the critical attitude. For example, consider Freud's central tenant that the content of dreams represents in a disguised way the fulfillments of wishes. An apparent objection to this theory is that some dreams are nightmares. Nightmares do not seem to represent the fulfillment of wishes at all. Does this count as a falsification? Popper has always insisted that the difference between falsifiable and unfalsifiable is not sharp, nor need it be. In terms of the growth of knowledge the point is whether the theory was used to motivate falsifiable predictions which are in turn used to improve the theories. In fact, on Popper's analysis, Freud does not show this critical approach; he attempts to evade rather than use criticism. Freud points out that disguised wish fulfillment *could* occur in the context of an anxiety dream or nightmare, and leaves the matter there. On Popper's analysis, what is important to Freud is possible verifications of the theory. A means for knowledge about the problem of dream meaning to genuinely grow is sadly sidestepped.

Grünbaum (1984; see also 1986) argued that Freudian psychoanalysis is actually falsifiable, contra Popper. Part of the problem is Popper's equivocation on falsifiability as a purely syntactic property (i.e. what matters is the literal form of the statements of the theory) and falsifiability as depending on the attitude of the community of people using the theory (which we discuss below). Grünbaum focused on the fact that clear predictions *can* be derived from the statements of psychoanalysis. For example, therapeutic outcomes should be better for people undergoing psychoanalysis rather than other therapies. (On these grounds, Grünbaum argued that psychoanalysis was both falsifiable and falsified.) Further, if other therapies do remove symptoms, then because they do not address the actual causes, new symptoms should appear (this prediction is also largely falsified). Freudian theory can also make epidemiological predictions: For example, because paranoia is theorized to be due to repressed homosexual desires, an increase in tolerance to homosexuality should lead to a decrease in paranoia in the community (a possible example alluded to by Popper, 1983). But Popper's point still remains: Were such predictions used to test and develop the theory? In general, was every hypothesis formulated such that it could be subjected to severe tests and then subjected to those tests whenever it could be? The ability to generate some predictions does not situate the approach within the critical tradition and it does not imply the falsificationist attitude of its practitioners, an attitude which is essential to rendering the theoretical claims actually falsifiable. [3]

In 1919, Popper went to a lecture by Einstein which impressed him greatly. Einstein said if in a particular situation (viewing a star close to the sun during a solar eclipse) light were not observably bent, his general theory of relativity would be untenable. (The prediction was tested in May 1919 by Eddington and the effect was found.) Einstein, in contrast to either Freud, Adler or Marx, was willing to put his theory on the line by specifying in advance what observations would falsify his theory. Likewise, Popper advised in general that if someone proposes a scientific theory they should answer, as Einstein did, 'Under what conditions would I admit that my theory is untenable?'

A philosopher strongly influenced by Popper was the Hungarian Imre Lakatos (1922–1974). Lakatos reported,

> I used to put this question to Marxists and Freudians: 'Tell me what specific social and historical events would have to occur in order for you to give up your Marxism?'. I remember this was accompanied by either stunned silence or confusion. But I was very pleased with the effect (1999, p. 26).

In fact, Lakatos later considered the question as such too simple and a more sophisticated version was needed; we will consider the subtleties in the next chapter. Nonetheless, the question is always one worth asking yourself for any theory you hold. It is regarded as a key question in experimental psychology; if you do not consider it thoroughly with respect to your own views, someone else certainly will. The more clearly specified the conditions are that would falsify a theory, the more highly such a theory is now regarded in experimental psychology. Whenever you read an explanation someone else has proposed, ask yourself: How could I find out if the theory were wrong?

To be clear, Popper believed that the relative non-falsifiability of Freudian and other views was perfectly consistent with them often seeing things correctly. Popper (1963) regarded much of what Freud and Adler said to be of considerable importance and as one day potentially forming the basis of a proper psychological science (see Erdelyi, 1985, for an attempt to relate psychoanalysis to ideas in experimental psychology). In fact, according to Popper, almost all scientific theories originate from something like myths. Starting from myths and metaphysics is perfectly fine, if not unavoidable. Eventually though, we want those myths to generate empirical sciences wherever that is possible. As Popper said, 'Those among us who are unwilling to expose their ideas to the hazard of refutation do not take part in the game of science' (1934/1959, p. 280).

Degrees of falsifiability

A potential falsifier of a theory is any potential observation statement that would contradict the theory (e.g., 'Peter the swan is black' is a falsifier of the hypothesis that 'all swans are white'). One theory is *more falsifiable* than another if the class of potential falsifiers is larger. Popper urges us to prefer theories which are more falsifiable. For example, one needs fewer

---

3. On my reading of Popper, see section below on Falsifiability. If the purely syntactic reading is taken, Popper contradicts himself regularly and often within the space of a sentence. Hence, I do not believe the common reading captures Popper's meaning.

Figure 1.1

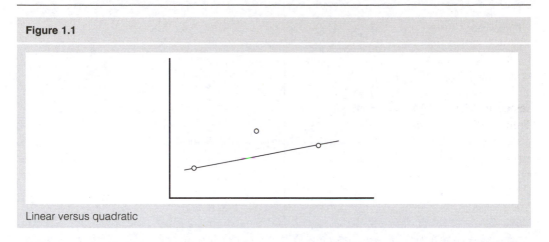

Linear versus quadratic

data points to rule out a straight line relationship than a quadratic. The three observations in Figure 1.1 are sufficient to falsify a proposed linear relation between the two variables, but cannot even in principle falsify a postulated quadratic relation. Put another way, a quadratic function can fit more data patterns than a linear function can; the latter has more falsifiers.

Scientists prefer simple theories. But what is simplicity? Simple theories are better testable. Straight lines are simpler than curves. There is no doubt more to simplicity than this, but perhaps falsifiability captures part of what it is for a theory to be simple.

'A is positively correlated with B' allows all the positive regression lines (Figure 1.2) and just rules out all the negative ones; that is, 50% of possible lines are excluded. 'A is correlated with B' rules out practically nothing. All positive and negative regression lines are permitted (Figure 1.3). 'A is positively correlated with B' has more falsifiers than 'A is correlated with B'. The former is more falsifiable and would constitute a better form of theory than the latter. The latter appears to be not falsifiable at all and hence incapable of being a scientific hypothesis according to Popper! This may strike you as odd given scientific psychology is packed full of hypotheses of the form 'A is correlated with B'. In a famous paper, Meehl

Figure 1.2

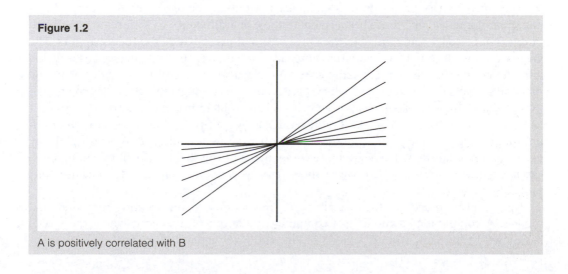

A is positively correlated with B

Figure 1.3

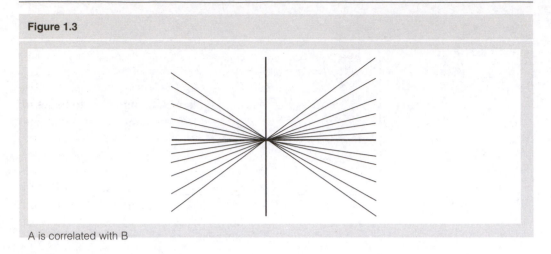

A is correlated with B

(1967) powerfully criticized much psychology on just these grounds (Meehl's arguments are discussed further in Chapter 3).

Similarly, 'Group A will score differently from Group B' also rules out virtually nothing; it is a very weak theory. 'Group A will score higher than B' is better: It rules out 50% of the possible difference scores. 'Group A will perform 30% better than Group B' rules out a lot! It would be a prediction of a very falsifiable theory.

One style of theorizing in psychology is to predict simply that the score of one group will be higher than that of another group. This appears very weak on Popperian grounds, and indeed it is. But psychological theories can redeem themselves by making predictions for contrasts between a range of conditions and experiments. For example, a theory that predicts simply the score for condition A will be greater than that for B is less falsifiable than a theory that predicts not only that the score for condition A will be greater than that for condition B, but also the score for condition C will be less than that for D, and the score for condition E greater than that of either condition A or B. Further, a theory that makes predictions not only about behaviour but also about brain regions gains in falsifiability; as does a theory that makes predictions not only about learning to read but also about learning social norms. A theory can gain in falsifiability not only by being precise (e.g. predicting a particular numerical difference between conditions, or a difference to within a smaller band of error) but also by being broad in the range of situations to which the theory applies. The greater the universality of a theory the more falsifiable it is, even if the predictions it makes are not very precise. In fact, Popper (e.g. 1983) warned social scientists of trying to ape the physical sciences by being 'precise' when it is uncalled for. He suggested the following moral: 'Never aim at more precision than is required by the problem in hand' (p. 7).

Revisions to a theory may make it more falsifiable by specifying fine-grained causal mechanisms. As long as the steps in a proposed causal pathway are testable, specifying the pathway gives you more falsifiers: There are more components of the theory which, by failing tests, can falsify the theory. But a theory with more verbiage is not for that reason more falsifiable; probably the reverse is true.

Psychologists sometimes theorize and make predictions by constructing computational models. A computational model is a computer simulation of a subject, where the model is exposed to the same stimuli subjects receive and gives actual trial-by-trial responses. For example, neural networks (or 'connectionist models') are simulated collections of artificial neurons connected together in a certain way, which can learn according to specified learning rules (see Plunkett et al., 1998, for an introduction). A computational model has a number of 'free parameters', that is, numbers that have to be fixed, like the number of artificial neurons used, the learning rate determining the size of the change between the connections on each learning trial, and so on. In order for the model to perform, the free parameters have to be set to particular values. But we cannot directly observe the values of these parameters by looking in the brain of the subject. However, one can choose a full range of values for each parameter then measure the performance of the network on each combination of parameter values.

For example, Boucher and Dienes (2003) contrasted two models, trained on the same stimuli as subjects were. (The models differed in terms of the way in which they learned.) In Figure 1.4, the axes are dependent variables in an experiment people participated in; specifically, the performance on two different tests measuring different aspects of what had been learned. Performance on these two tests for each model was determined for the full range of allowable parameter values. Each mark in the graph is the actual performance of a model with a certain combination of parameter values (e.g. with 20 artificial neurons, a learning rate of 0.5, and so on). For one model, its performance for each combination of parameter values is marked with a black cross; different black crosses correspond to different parameter values. Call this the black model. The performance of the other model for each combination of parameter values is marked with a grey x. Call this the grey model. Notice that the models occupy different size regions of the space. The grey model occupies less area than the black model. The grey model is easier to falsify.

Figure 1.5 shows the performance of people superposed on Figure 1.4. The people were given the same learning phase and the same two tests as the models. The five dots making a square represent people's data, with the central dot indicating the mean of all people on both tests. (The four other dots define limits called the 95% confidence intervals; this is explained in Chapter 3). In fact, the human data fell in the region of space occupied by the

Figure 1.4

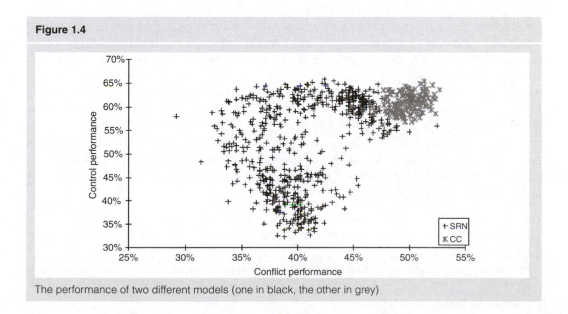

The performance of two different models (one in black, the other in grey)

Figure 1.5

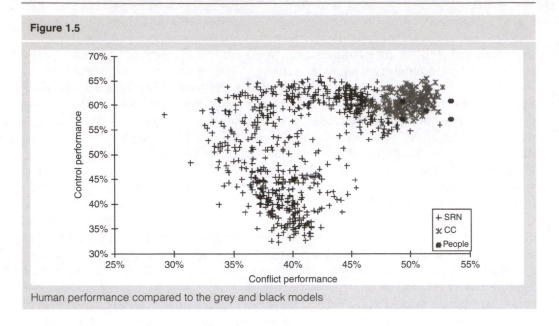

Human performance compared to the grey and black models

grey model: The grey model was easy to falsify, but it survived this attempt at falsification. The grey model was not proven true but it was corroborated: It proved its mettle.

With computational models it can be difficult to predict how the model will do just by thinking about it. The model has to be run and its behaviour observed and analysed. Let us say two models, A and B, happen to produce data schematically as illustrated in Figure 1.6. The figure also shows where the hypothetical human data fell. Notice the human data does not falsify either model; either model can reproduce the human data, given a suitable combination of parameter values. However, model B is more falsifiable than model A. As the human data is consistent with both models, model B is to be preferred. The point is obvious but often disregarded: Often modellers just try to find any set of parameter values that fits the data (i.e. such that model performance reproduces human performance). A typical procedure – showing a verificationist attitude – would be to report the exact parameter values that allowed model B to fit the human data as closely as possible and the same for model A. If the best-fitting model of each fitted about as well, the modeler may conclude that there is no reason to prefer one model than another. Popper's ideas – as relevant today as they were in 1934 – indicate the inadequacy of simply finding best-fit models. One needs to see what if any observations would rule the model out.

In order to express our preference for more falsifiable theories, Popper would say that even though both models A and B pass the test in Figure 1.6, model B has been more strongly *corroborated*. Model B has passed a more severe test than model A because it was more falsifiable to begin with.[4]

4. The degree of corroboration depends on the severity of the test passed. Popper suggested that test severity could be determined by working out the probability of the evidence obtained given the combination of theory and background knowledge compared to the probability of the evidence given background knowledge alone. In Figure 1.6 the data are more probable given model B than model A: Model A allows anything so any particular data region is not very likely. If the data are very likely given the model and unlikely otherwise, the test is a good one. This notion is very close to the notion of the 'likelihood', which is the topic of Chapters 4 and 5. Likelihood and Bayesian theorists would also prefer model B to model A for the data illustrated in Figure 1.6.

Figure 1.6

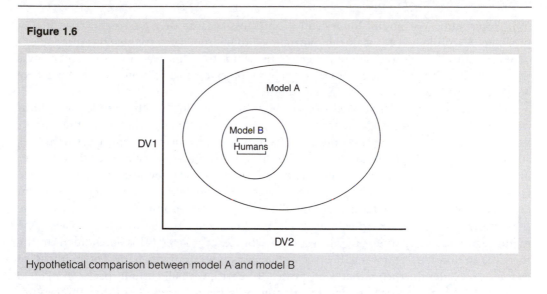

Hypothetical comparison between model A and model B

Figure 1.7

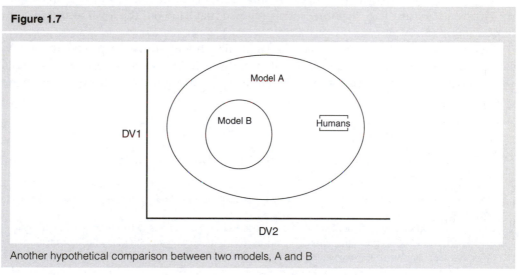

Another hypothetical comparison between two models, A and B

Of course, if the data were inconsistent with model B, model B would have to be rejected (as in Figure 1.7). Model A would be tentatively accepted until a better (more simple, more falsifiable) theory could be discovered. Notice that model A in Figure 1.7 does not rule out very much; it does not really *explain* why people behaved as they do. *A theory that allows everything explains nothing.* If model A, much like psychoanalysis in its domain, was consistent with any behaviour, it would give us no explanation at all for why people behaved as they did. In short, *the more a theory forbids, the more it says about the world. The 'empirical content' of a theory increases with its degree of falsifiability*. A theory that allows almost anything has very little content. Such phrases of Popper ring in the ear of every experimental psychologist.

The more falsifiable a theory is, the more open it is to criticism. So the more falsifiable our theories are, the faster we can make progress, given progress comes from criticism. We also should prefer more falsifiable theories, according to Popper, because they are bold and more interesting. We are not interested in truths just because they are true or even highly probable. A tautology (i.e. a statement guaranteed to be true like 'a triangle has three sides') or a near tautology ('People cannot remember the words that they were told to forget *because* there is a "forget" label on the word representation blocking recall') is precisely not what we are after in science, even if the statement is true.[5]

Popper (1934) argued that good science shows itself not just by the simple literal form of its theories, but also by the nature of the history of its theories leading to the current proposals. Science aims at the maximum falsifiability it can achieve; hence successive theories should be successively more falsifiable, either in terms of universality or precision. Popper urged the methodological rule: Only revise theories, introduce new theories, or introduce those auxiliary hypotheses that increase the degree of falsifiability of the system. A revision or addition that decreases falsifiability is called 'ad hoc'. For example, one starts with the hypothesis that 'All swans are white'. Then one finds Peter the Swan who is black. One might revise one's hypothesis to 'All swans are white except Peter'. This amendment to the theory is ad hoc, it decreases the theory's falsifiability and so is unsatisfying. For an historical example, consider the theory that 'God created the Earth, with all current species in it, 6000 years ago'. The fossil record provides apparently falsifying evidence. So in the 19th century the clearly ad hoc auxiliary hypothesis was proposed that 'God put the fossil record there to test our faith' (Box 1.6).

Popper proposed that revisions and amendments should always increase falsifiability. Clearly, this is desirable, if possible, but often unrealistic in the short term. For example, simply not diminishing falsifiability is obviously a step forward if the theory is no longer

---

Box 1.6   The function of female orgasm

Theory of researcher 1: Female orgasm makes the female lie down and perhaps sleep, increasing sperm retention. This leads to greater female fertility.

Theory of researcher 2: Female orgasm causes suction into the uterus from the vagina. Such 'upsuck' increases female fertility.
  But a Cosmo survey of new couples found that those women who regularly have intercourse orgasms have only a tiny and non-significant increase in fertility above those women who rarely have orgasms.
  (Imaginary results. I don't know what the real figures are.)

Response by Researcher 1:
The effect on sperm retention is small and hard to detect but still real. Also it may be small or non-existent for the young, say for people less than 25 or so.

Response by researcher 2:
Upsuck doesn't increase the number of children but their genetic variety.
When the orgasm occurs seconds before to minutes after the male orgasm, it sucks up sperm leading
  to a greater chance of fertilization.
If the orgasm occurs more than a minute before male ejaculation, acidic vaginal mucus is sucked up,
  acting as contraceptive.
Upsuck is used by a woman in a pair bond to make sure her partner sires at least one child, and her illicit
  lover sires another. (For discussion of real data, see Baker and Bellis, 1994, and Lloyd, 2005.)
A research council only has enough money to fund one of the researchers.
Which one should it give its money to and why?

---

5. This is one reason why Popper rejected the Bayesian approach discussed in Chapter 4: Many Bayesians assumed scientists pursue the most probable hypotheses; Popper argued they do exactly the reverse.

actually falsified. Even more strongly, if data rule out, for example, a straight line, surely one can accept a curve. Nature may be simple, but she is only so simple! In any case, it may often be impossible to say whether falsifiability has increased or decreased. But there is a maxim that can always be followed: Make sure that any revision or amendment to theory can be falsified. That way theory development is guaranteed to keep its empirical character. (The amendment 'God put the fossil record there to test us' is not falsifiable at all.) For example, a theory may improve not because of an increase in falsifiability, but because our choice of observation statements is better motivated, for example we use measures with better construct validity. The claim that the new measure has better construct validity should itself be falsifiable and severely tested. Consider a researcher with a good falsificationist attitude, declaring his theory would be falsified if such and such is observed using measure X. Having dutifully falsified and rejected the theory, he could be later criticized for using measure X. Such criticism might not involve an increase in falsifiability, because it just recommends a different measure, but it may represent scientific progress if the claim that the new measure is a better measure that has survived severe tests.

In psychology, attempts to save theories in ways that do not suggest new tests are often called 'post hoc' ('ad hoc' is not typically used in the psychology literature). Whenever you propose a revision or an amendment to your theories to account for your data always ask yourself, 'How could I test this idea?'. If you cannot think of a way of testing your idea in principle, you should think harder about how to explain the data. Of course, one always strives for the simplest most falsifiable revision or amendment one can (Box 1.7).

Box 1.7 Marriage guidance therapy

Therapist A can predict whether or not a couple argues in any 5-minute period of observation based on whether one or both people felt insecure in the preceding 5 minutes. He finds some cases where couples argue but neither rated feeling insecure beforehand. He concludes that his theory is still correct, but these apparently discrepant cases arise when the insecurity is unconscious.

Allowing for unconscious insecurity, he finds all data from a further 20 couples fit his theory: On 80% of the occasions they argue that they state being insecure before the argument, and thus the remaining 20% can be attributed to unconscious insecurity.

Has A established his theory?

Therapist B can predict arguments based on style of conversation just beforehand. He divides conversational style into two types and proposes that one type invariably precedes an argument. He finds a number of cases that do not fit. He devises a new way of categorizing conversational styles: 30 styles, roughly equiprobable across all 20 couples in his sample. He proposes one and only one of the 30 styles always precedes an argument. This new generalization holds true for a further 20 couples.

Has B established his theory?

A's therapy is based on increasing feelings of security. B's therapy is based on changing the conversational style that precedes arguments. If you had to choose between them, which therapy would you choose and why?

Popper's early view of scientific progress as specifically the replacement of one falsified theory by another theory even more falsifiable (but not yet falsified) is just one, somewhat ideal, path that progress could take (see e.g. Feyerabend, 1975, for the argument that often science should *not* proceed in this way). We will consider Popper's later and more flexible view of scientific progress in discussing Verisimilitude below.

Falsifiability

Is it actually possible to distinguish falsifiable from non-falsifiable systems? A problem arises because, according to Popper (1934/1959), observations are always 'theory impregnated'. Thus, falsification is not so simple as pitting theory, on the one hand, against observation, on the other. Theories are needed to determine what an observation is. Even when making the simplest observation, of length or of time, there is the question of whether it is an accurate clock or a rigid rod. One can only refer to our theories to answer this. Consider a measurement of how extroverted a participant is in testing the theory that extroverts are more alert during the evening rather than the morning. We need a theory of extroversion and also of why our scale measures extroversion. Similarly, a measurement of working memory span depends on a theory of working memory. A measurement of how 'anxious' a rat is (in testing a drug for treating human anxiety) depends on a theory relating the rat's behaviour to human anxiety.

Popper (1934/1959) pointed out that a theoretical system can always escape falsification by doubting the observations ('The extroversion scale has limited validity'), or changing a definition ('a non-white swan is not a swan', 'an extrovert who is alert in the morning is no extrovert'). This is possible because observation statements are never given directly from experience. Every statement uses universal names; thus, every statement has the character of a theory. To use an example of Popper's, 'Here is a glass of water' uses the universal terms 'glass' and 'water'. We rely on theories, prejudices and expectations in describing our experience with these terms. Thus, the statement cannot strictly be verified or justified by any observational experience. Experiences, however, clearly can *motivate* observation statements. According to Popper, observation statements are finally accepted only by decision or agreement. Finally, there comes a point where everyone concerned feels the observation statement is sufficiently motivated that no one wishes to deny it. Considerable work may be needed to reach that point; and even then the decision to accept an observation may be overturned by new considerations. For example, in accepting a questionnaire as a good measure of a personality dimension, we might consider whether we accept a statistical tool called 'factor analysis' as a useful tool in isolating a personality dimension, whether past factor analyses have been conducted in an optimal way, whether the scale has been sufficiently tested for its reliability (e.g. stability over time) and whether its validity has been appropriately tested (e.g. whether it has been shown to correlate with other more direct measures of the personality dimension).

In the end we must *decide* which observation statements we will accept. The decision is fallible and amounts to tentatively accepting a low-level empirical hypothesis which describes the effect: For example, accepting an observation statement amounts to accepting a hypothesis that 'Peter is an extrovert', or 'This extrovert was asleep at 7 am' and so on.

Given these considerations, Popper (1934/1959) argued that the question of whether a theoretical system as a set of statements is strictly falsifiable or not is 'misconceived' (p. 82). It is only with regard to the methods applied in examining or testing the theory that we can ask whether it is falsifiable or not. That is, the good scientist will consider carefully under what conditions an observation statement will be sufficiently well motivated that it would constitute a falsification of his theory. There should be no attempt to avoid this task. The decision is fallible, so the feedback from nature is noisy, but at least we are exposing ourselves to feedback! We are giving ourselves a chance to learn from our mistakes! Contrast Freud's attitude as described by Popper in the previous section.

Consider also astrology. Astrology can be used to make falsifiable predictions. But astrologers as a community do not seek to test and falsify theories, let alone do this in order to improve both specific and more general theory. Thus, astrology does not constitute a science. It is not part of the critical tradition.

Given you have accepted an actual observation statement, you are logically committed to rejecting any theory that forbade the statement. (You are not logically committed to accepting any general theory as true though; there is still this asymmetry even though basic statements are fallible and falsifications never certain.) The early Popper (i.e. 1934/1959) held that the honest scientist would not reverse this decision; to be honest, scientists must decide to avoid excuses for saving a theory.

Falsifiability: too strong a criterion or too weak?

In this section, we consider two criticisms of Popper's approach. The first is that no theory is falsifiable at all and the second is that all theories are falsified anyway. In a subsequent section, we consider the problem of theories that do not make strictly universal claims true but only probabilistic ones (i.e. like most theories in psychology).

The fact that no system of statements is falsifiable as such has just been considered in the previous section, but Popper's critics often raise the issue. Critics often focus on the fact that accepting an observation statement involves accepting various levels of theory as well as the theory under test. There is no general method of determining which of the theories should be rejected when an apparent falsification occurs. Theory at the most general level (e.g. Newton's law of gravitation; Eysenck's theory that extroversion is related to low cortical arousal) needs to make contact with a particular observational or experimental set-up. Contact is made by auxiliary hypotheses. For example, one might test Eysenck's theory that extroversion is related to low cortical arousal by testing introverts and extroverts with a memory task sensitive to arousal. Already we need at least three theories in addition to the proposal nominally under test: one theory that specifies our measurement of extroversion is actually measuring extroversion; another that specifies that our measurement of memory really is measuring the sort of memory we think it is; and then the auxiliary hypothesis linking such memory to cortical arousal. If the results come out the wrong way round, why not keep Eysenck's theory but reject, say, the theory specifying the relationship between memory performance and arousal? Maybe it was the auxiliary hypothesis that got things the wrong way round? One can only falsify the system of reasoning as a whole, including auxiliary hypotheses, theories of measurement, and also any prior observations used in generating predictions in the current case (e.g. we may need scale norms to determine what counts as a reasonable spread of extroversion scores). Given a falsification, how do we know which component of the system to reject? This widely recognized problem of scientific inference is called the Duhem–Quine problem.

Popper's answer to this problem appears in his earliest work. In order for criticism to occur at all, some part of our knowledge must be accepted for current purposes as unproblematic. Popper calls such knowledge 'background knowledge'. For example, we may take as background knowledge the claim that memory depends on cortical arousal in a certain way. That is, we must make a methodological decision, we must accept at least some of past research in order to make progress. Then we are in a position to test other proposals, for example that extroversion involves low cortical arousal. Isolating the right component of the system of knowledge to reject depends on hunches and critical discussion. Popper suggested that such discussion can involve, for example, the outcome of different tests in which we can vary what is being taken as background knowledge. It is widely acknowledged that such converging evidence with different background assumptions is very important in science, a process Whewell (1840) called consilience. Further, any part of the background knowledge involved in a test may be opened up to critical scrutiny later.

There need not be a general algorithm for how to solve the Duhem–Quine problem; each case can be taken on its own merits, which is precisely what scientists seem to do. In the end, experience motivates us to accept some test statements, and some theories are sufficiently well corroborated that we find ourselves with no reason to doubt them for current purposes. Once we accept some beliefs, we can criticize other beliefs. Popper's methodology does not say how this is done; it only accepts the obvious fact that we do do it. In sum, the Duhem–Quine problem does not obviously threaten the Popperian argument for the importance of the falsificationist attitude to the growth of knowledge. Nonetheless, there remains an interesting and fundamental problem: Can more be said in general about what parts of a system of knowledge people do or should find hard to reject or easy to give up? We will revisit this question in Chapter 2 in discussing the philosophy of Thomas Kuhn and Imre Lakatos.

Kuhn (1962), Lakatos (1970) and Feyerabend (1975) also delivered what is generally taken to be a fatal critique of Popper by pointing out that in the history of science 'all theories have been born falsified' (Lakatos, 1978). Even Newtonian mechanics, all through its history, had applications that did not quite work out. The precise motion of the moon was a major problem for almost 100 years before it was substantially solved (Kuhn, p. 39). The precise motion of the planet Mercury was a completely unsolved problem within Newtonian physics. Yet few took these anomalies as reasons to reject the theory. Every falsifiable theory in psychology that has been around for any length of time has no doubt been challenged by recalcitrant data.

At no time did Popper state that any apparent falsification of a theory be accepted uncritically. Just because one should state the grounds on which one would reject a theory, it does not follow one should accept any grounds whatsoever. (This point seems almost universally misunderstood by writers on Popper.) It is no criticism of Popper to point out that scientists do not immediately give up a theory when apparent falsifications are presented to them. However, a genuine criticism of the early Popper is that having laid out the conditions under which one would give up a theory and seen such a set of results, 'we must reject the theory and not work on it again on pain of being irrational', in the striking phrase of Lakatos (1978). Yet there seems no principled reason for why one must always stick to the first analysis that such results would falsify the theory nominally under test. Previously un-thought-of considerations thrown up by the pattern of results or by a colleague or by a random thought may make it more reasonable to keep the general theory and doubt the observations. Indeed, flexibility in deciding what to accept would be most consistent with the overall principle of Popper's philosophy, namely fallibilism and the in-theory openness of all aspects of one's beliefs to criticism. Despite the severe yet aesthetic simplicity of his earlier formulations, Popper did come to have a more flexible approach. The later Popper even argued that we might accept as our current best theory a theory we hold to be false, a point we consider next.

Verisimilitude

Popper argued that given two theories that are apparently false we can still prefer one of them to the other if we think in terms of how closely each approximates to the truth; that is in terms of its *verisimilitude* or *truthlikeness*. It is quite natural for scientists to regard their theories, even their best theories, as mere approximations to the truth with later theories being better approximations than earlier ones. For example, Popper (1963) argued that we should be inclined to say of a theory t2 that it is *closer* to the truth than t1 in some sense if, other things being equal, (a) t2 makes more precise assertions than t1; or (b) t2 explains more facts than t1; or (c) t2 has passed more tests which t1 has failed to pass. Thus, we can prefer t2 to t1 even if there are some facts neither can explain (this may at first pass seem obvious; for some difficult problems, see Popper 1979, pp. 367–374, and Miller, 1994, Chapter 10). Our goal is to move in the direction of increasing verisimilitude which we can do even if we happen to accept all current theories are false, that is, not completely true. Intuitively, Einstein's theory is a better approximation to the truth than Newton's, which is a better approximation than Kepler's, and so on. Similarly, Smolensky (1988) has argued that many connectionist models provide a closer approximation to the truth than their corresponding information processing theories.

Popper attempted to produce a more formal definition of verisimilitude but that attempt failed and will not be discussed here. In the end, Popper appeared happy with the common-sense or intuitive notion of closeness to truth (1983, pp. xxxv–xxxvii), though his initial work did spark some decades of intensive technical work by other philosophers on the question (Miller, 1994; Thornton, 2005).

While we can never know whether our theory is actually true, or even what degree of verisimilitude it possesses, the question is whether there is a method able to move us in the direction of increasing verisimilitude. Popper accepts that there is no method that can guarantee this. However, what we can do, and the best we can do, is subject the conjecture that we have moved closer to the truth to critical scrutiny and see if it survives. That is, just as Popper has always recommended, we should aim to construct theories of increasing falsifiability in the long run which can pass more and more severe tests. Whenever we have a theory more falsifiable than another and which has passed more severe tests than the other, then in the light of current discussion this theory is our best guess as the theory which is closest to the truth (even if it has also failed some test). The theory remains a guess of course, but the best current explanation for *why* it has fared so well is its closeness to the truth. And that explanation for why it has fared so well may easily be overturned at any time by a competing theory of the scientific problem that does better. Each successor theory specifies the way in which previous theories were close to the truth. And the best tentative explanation of why each successor theory does so well is *its* closeness to the truth. Of course, consistent with Popper's fallibilism, it follows that the process in no way *guarantees* that science will always actually move closer to the truth.

Objective knowledge

Popper (1972) made an important distinction between two different senses of the word 'knowledge'. Knowledge can be subjective, referring to the mental states of a particular person – what she knows and how strongly she believes it. But there can be knowledge that exists independently of anybody knowing it, that is, objective knowledge. Consider a theory someone has invented; naturally, it starts out life as something (partly) subjectively known by a person. But once invented it takes on a life of its own. The theory has properties that must be *discovered*, just like the properties of any physical object. Indeed, the theory might have properties that are the opposite of what people subjectively believe they are. The theory acquires its own independent reality, it is something people can be right or wrong about. It is real also because it can *affect* physical objects. Because theories do have certain properties, our mental states will change as we come to know those properties; and our mental states can change the world, for example in writing books expressing those theories, or starting a revolution based on the theories. Marx's ideas changed the world, as did Maxwell's equations. Popper used the term 'World 3' to indicate the world of ideas as objective entities, including not just scientific theories but also musical themes, plot developments, methods of arguing and the character of Homer Simpson, to name a few inhabitants. (World 1 is the world of the physical universe *per se* and World 2 is the world of conscious experience.)

Scientific knowledge belongs to World 3. The objective properties of theories include their relation to observation statements (do they contradict or are they consistent?), and the consequences and implications of the theory. The methods used by people in discovering the properties of a theory also have objective properties and belong to World 3 (e.g. the method of vigorously searching for falsifications). It can take some time to discover the properties of one's theory; hence, the later Popper urged scientists to have at least to some degree a 'dogmatic attitude', that is some persistence in sticking with a theory, despite initial problems, because it is only by such persistence one can fully explore the theory and decide whether to treat an apparent falsification as an actual one. Fully understanding whether or not a falsification has occurred may take years. This is a different way of answering the problem (of all theories in practice facing anomalies from the outset), raised by Kuhn, Lakatos and Feyerabend in the previous sections, a way that does not make use of the notion of verisimilitude. Note the dogmatism recommended by Popper still involves taking putative falsifications seriously; there should be a full recognition that they must be resolved.

Some dogmatism is not inconsistent with a critical attitude but necessary for it. Understanding a theory is based on the process of successively trying to criticize it and realizing why the criticisms do or do not work. When one sees why the initially obvious criticism does not work, one understands the theory better (Popper, 1972). Understanding the theory involves a process of conjecture and refutation repeated successively as one sticks with the theory. Current work in theoretical physics in string theory may be seen as trying to understand the theory as an objective entity in its own right as a preliminary to being able to test it against the world (see Greene, 1999 and Woit, 2006, for the Popperian complaint that such work has not yet rendered the theory falsifiable). Indeed, it is a satisfying aspect of a theory that its properties must be discovered. Part of the appeal of connectionist models is that predictions generated by a model cannot be produced by hand waving by the proponent of the model; the predictions have to be discovered by hard work. So some dogmatism is essential. It is when dogmatism is not accompanied by the critical attitude that knowledge will stagnate.

Probabilistic theories and falsification

One apparent problem for Popper is how to treat probabilistic hypotheses, that is almost all hypotheses in psychology. A probabilistic hypothesis does not state that a correlation will be perfect or that a person will always score greater in one condition than another; instead, the claim is that the correlation will be positive but middling, or that scores in one condition are more *likely* to be greater than scores in another condition. For example, we may predict that ginseng will on average improve running speed. But running speed depends on all sorts of factors. I may give ginseng to one person on one occasion and measure their running speed then compare to one other occasion without ginseng. If their speed was greater on the day without ginseng, I have not falsified the hypothesis at all. The hypothesis refers to the mean of a population – the set of ALL occasions we could be interested in measuring. A sample of one observation from the population does not definitely tell us what the mean of the population is. Nor does a sample of five. Or 20. Or a million. How can we ever falsify the hypothesis?

I may have the hypothesis that a coin is fair. I flip it 10 times and get 10 heads. Have I falsified my hypothesis? No, the hypothesis of a fair coin does not rule out a coin landing heads 10 times in a row; in fact, it predicts it will happen sometimes. Similarly, obtaining a million heads in a row does not strictly falsify the hypothesis that the coin is fair. In fact, the hypothesis predicts that sometimes (albeit extremely rarely) a fair coin will produce a million heads in a row. The hypothesis appears to have no falsifiers.

The problem though is no different from falsifying any theory. We have to set up a severe test and make a methodological decision. A test is severe if an outcome has very different probabilities assuming the hypothesis is true rather than false. We can conventionally decide that if the set-up allows an outcome very unlikely given the hypothesis, then the test is severe. Survival of the test then corroborates the hypothesis. Lakatos (1970) presumed that this Popperian analysis became the same as significance or hypothesis testing in statistics (see Chapter 3) as taught in most statistics textbooks for scientists. However, as we shall see in Chapter 3, the typical use of null hypothesis testing in the behavioural sciences has been roundly criticized for failing to be Popperian. The most natural application of Popper's thought to probabilistic hypotheses may in fact be a version of likelihood inference (see Chapter 5 for explanation of likelihood inference; and Taper and Lele, 2004, Chapter 16, for discussion with respect to Popper). For Popper the relative likelihood would not entail that hypotheses are supported in the sense of having increased probabilities (they are not inductively supported) but only in the sense that they are corroborated. (Popper himself was comfortable using the term 'support' provided by relative likelihood; see e.g. Section 2 of the Addenda to his 1963/2002.) Do not worry if these points do not make much sense to you now; revisit them after reading Chapters 3, 4 and 5 and decide for yourself what (if any) philosophy of statistical inference would fit in best with Popper's ideas.

Are theories in psychology falsifiable?

Popper often said that the falsifiability of a theory can be discerned from its linguistic or logical form. For example, the statement 'all x are y' is on the face of it falsifiable because finding a single accepted case of an x that was not a y would show the statement wrong. On the other hand, the statement 'some x are y' is not falsifiable, given we do not have access to all the x's. No matter how many xs we find that are not y, 'some x are y' could still be true. But then to what extent are theories in psychology falsifiable? We saw in the last section that many claims in psychology are probabilistic, that is, consist of statistical hypotheses ('The population means for the two groups differ by more than 5 units'). Statistical hypotheses are not of a form like 'all x are y', but we may, as Popper suggests, be able to set up conventions to apply a falsificationist methodology (see Chapters 3 and 5). What is really important is falsificationist attitude, rather than syntactic form.

A statistical hypothesis on its own is an impoverished psychological theory. To be satisfactory, a statistical hypothesis should be strongly motivated by a substantial theory, that is, a unifying idea from which many predictions could be drawn. For example, one might use the idea of cognitive dissonance (a substantial theory) to predict attitude change in a particular context (a specific statistical hypothesis). Often in psychology (and more generally in cognitive science, Boden, 2006, and in the life sciences, e.g. Bechtel, in press) substantial theories take the form of mechanistic explanation, that is by postulating a mechanism by which something is achieved. The specification of a mechanism may consist not of lists of propositions but of analogies or models (cf. Giere, 1999). While such representations can be far from the linguistic structures (e.g. 'all x are y') the logical positivists started with, and Popper continued his thinking with reference to, one can still apply a falsificationist attitude to such theories. There are consequences of mechanisms working in a certain way, consequences that may show in behaviour, reaction times, brain imaging or lesion studies. Despite what Popper himself has often said, the application of his philosophy, or the spirit of it, does not depend on psychological theories having a certain syntactic structure (cf. Lakatos, 1978). The better one can specify a mechanism such that possible observations can refute it, the more quickly we may learn about the actual mechanism in nature.

Indeed, psychologists rarely state their theories in terms of universals; but perhaps universals are sometimes implicit in how the theory is used. For example, universal statements are not explicitly used in the Boucher and Dienes (2003) paper that we discussed earlier despite the fact that the paper showed how the two models it considered differed in falsifiability. Maybe many theories in psychology could effectively be written in the form, 'In certain contexts, people *always* use this mechanism': 'When my experimental procedure is set up in this way, *all* learning involves this sort of neural network.' If predictions made by the network are falsified, either the specification of appropriate contexts or the model itself needs revision. That is, the practice of science can be Popperian regardless of explicit syntactic forms.

The strict description of scientific practice described by Popper may be regarded as an ideal in another way. In practice, scientists often do not either categorically accept or reject propositions (of theories or of observational claims). A scientist may hold a theory with a certain degree of conviction and likewise a statement of an experimental finding (and its relation to the theory) with some degree of conviction. He may believe to some degree both the theory and its apparently falsifying evidence. He can do this coherently because he believes neither completely. He may believe both with reasonable conviction yet also believe both are not simultaneously true. Of course, the more he believes the evidence (and the fact *that* it is falsifying) the less he believes the theory, and vice versa. Then, in practice, 'falsifying' evidence does not eliminate a theory in one hit; but the accumulation of different evidence may eventually drive conviction in the theory to low levels. Thagard (e.g. 1992) developed a computational model of theory choice in science involving such *continuous* degrees of acceptability as different constraints are satisfied or broken. The Bayesian approach to the philosophy of science can also directly capture these intuitions and is discussed in Chapter 4. Popper strongly rejected the Bayesian approach partly because the convictions of scientists (World 2) were not directly his concern; his concern was the logical relation between theory and evidence (World 3), what happens when scientists through critical discussion eventually do accept and reject relevant propositions. The Bayesians in turn believe that knowing how personal convictions in theories should be continuously altered is solving the logical problem of scientific inference. Lakatos, like Popper, rejected the Bayesian approach, but thought, like Bayesians, that theories were often gradually worn down by evidence and not directly falsified in one hit. We discuss Lakatos' approach and the Popperian reply in the next chapter.

Sociology of knowledge

Popper believed that the society and tradition in which scientists are embedded was very important. Science relies on not only a first-order tradition of particular myth and theory about the world, but most importantly a second-order tradition of free criticism about those myths, which is a social enterprise. The objectivity of science depends on this social aspect of scientific method: not on the attempt of any individual scientist to be objective but on the friendly hostile cooperation of many scientists (Popper, 1945, p. 241). Thus, Popper thought, the inevitable passion and prejudice of the individual scientist functioned as a *challenge* to other scientists to engage critically. This critical tradition is – or should be – supported by the institutions of science, but can be lost and needs to be actively maintained. Corporate, party political and religious culture is often inimical to the critical tradition, for example, and there is similarly no reason why the institutions of science will always perform their function of supporting it.

Our social traditions also provide us with frameworks for thinking, that is, unexamined assumptions that constrain us. But, as Popper points out, we are never trapped. Simply becoming conscious of a previously unrecognized assumption allows us to criticize it; and that allows us to keep it or to break out into a roomier framework. Popper (1994) regarded discussions between people with different frameworks as not only possible but particularly productive (contra Kuhn, see Chapter 2), even if difficult (and perhaps not so pleasant as discussions between people with the same framework).

Because theories are human inventions, they can show the characteristics of the cultures and societies of the people who proposed them. A theory is simply a stab at the truth or at truthlikeness and, although Popper did not emphasize it, there is no reason on Popper's philosophy (pace Giere, 1999) why there should not be cultural influences on their content. But such influences do not constitute the reason why science may move us towards the truth; they belong to the context of discovery. Nor is science *science* because of power struggles between scientists or between scientists and politicians (though such struggles exist) but because social institutions maintain the tradition of free criticism allowing the objective properties of theories to be understood and criticized. We discuss these issues in more detail in Chapter 2.

Truth, instrumentalism and realism

Even in his earliest writings Popper (1934/1959, p. 278) held that the search for truth is the strongest motive for scientific discovery. We wish to explain the world, and only true explanations explain. If you ask 'Why is the bridge in pieces?' and I say 'because an airplane dropped a bomb on it', I have only explained why the bridge is in pieces if my explanation is true. So it seems obvious we want truth, and truth that is interesting and relevant to us. Remarkably, some philosophers have denied that there is such a thing as truth (we will consider the post-modernists in Chapter 2) or have held that truth may apply to everyday descriptive statements but not to theories. According to one view, instrumentalism, theories are *nothing but* means for making predictions. On this view, theories can be more or less useful, but not, like descriptive statements, more or less true (for a clear up-to-date discussion of the concept of truth, see Lynch, 2005).

Popper (e.g. 1983) argued, in contrast, that theories aim at truth, in the sense of corresponding to the way the world is, and do not aim at just being instruments. If an instrument (like a thermometer) fails a test (e.g. it does not measure temperatures well at high altitudes) we do not reject the instrument; we just use it within its limits of application. But scientists are concerned if a theory fails to pass a test. Likewise scientists are concerned if theories are mutually incompatible (like general relativity and quantum physics), but there is no need to worry about this for instruments, as long as the appropriate domain is used for each. There is no problem with instruments becoming more and more specialized, which is their historical tendency; but scientists like theories that become more and more general, which is, according to Popper, their historical tendency. Importantly, scientists wish to *explain* phenomena, and simply making predictions does not allow explanation nor interpretation (consider a black box that always made the right predictions but we had no idea why: it would not constitute a good scientific theory). Further, given that instrumentalism needs to distinguish statements of theory from everyday observation statements, to the extent that there is no principled distinction between 'pure' observation statements and theoretical statements, instrumentalism founders.

Aiming at truth in Popper's sense means there is a real world about which statements can be true; that is, Popper was a *realist*. A contrasting view is *solipsism*, namely the view that only oneself exists. (Bertrand Russell once said he had received a letter from a lady who was surprised she had not met more solipsists like herself.[6]) Another view is *idealism*, namely the view that only ideas exist, there is no external world beyond ideas. Sometimes people (following Hume) argue against realism because it cannot be justified; how could I ever know that a real world exists? But, as Popper points out, this argument backfires; how could one ever know that idealism or solipsism is true? They are equally incapable of justification.

Further, Popper believed there were positive reasons for believing in the reality of other minds. Popper knew he could not have created Bach's music or Mozart's. (He tried to copy Bach's style once and found he could not.) He was 'even less able, if possible, to draw an average comic strip, or to invent a television advertisement, or to write some of the books on the justification of induction which I am compelled to read' (1983, p. 83). While acknowledging that the argument of his own apparent incapability is inconclusive, Popper was prepared to accept the reality of other minds. And by simple extension to the physical world, he also accepted its existence: he regarded himself as, for example, 'incapable of creating out of my imagination anything as beautiful as the mountains and glaciers of Switzerland' (p. 84). Popper mused perhaps that there are people with megalomania who think otherwise about themselves. However, the issue of realism and anti-realism is still hotly debated. For more discussion on realism in science, see Chalmers (1999, Chapter 15); see van Fraasen (1980) for the anti-realist position; and see Salmon (2005) for a realist position. Greene (1999) is an excellent accessible discussion for the lay reader about the implications of modern physics for what we should take to be real.

Psychologists, despite claims sometimes made to the contrary, also generally believe in the reality of the domain of their subject – of minds, and of brains, thoughts, images, networks, social pressures, social identities, psychological contexts and so on. However, saying what exactly a theory claims is real is an interesting question without a general answer. Sometimes hard work has to go into exploring why a theory or model works well in an attempt to conjecture what in the theory corresponds to reality.

Consider, for example, a connectionist model in which people's learning is being simulated with a neural network with a certain number of simulated neurons. The modeller will often have no commitment to there existing exactly that number of neurons in the person involved in learning the task in question. The modeller is not a realist about that aspect of the model. The modeller may be a realist only about something very abstract like 'the style of computation' used in the model. On the other hand, another neural network modeller may wish to model specific neurons in specific pathways in the brain, and may be a realist about each simulated neuron in the model as such (but not a realist about some of their details).

---

6. Quoted in Sokal and Bricmont (1998, p. 54)

Both are trying to say something about how the mind, the brain, human learning really is, and that goal is part of what makes them scientists.

The issue of realism crops up in a number of places in cognitive science. Do thoughts really exist? Some say yes (e.g. Searle, 2004) and a few say no (see e.g. Churchland, 1988, Chapter 2). (Popper was a realist about thoughts and conscious experience in general.) Almost all branches of psychology, especially cognitive psychology, postulate that the mind consists of representations. Are such representations conjectured to be real by the theorist or are they just devices for predicting how people will behave? There are realist theories of representation (see Perner and Dienes, forthcoming, for an overview) but also people who say whether a system has a representation is just a question of whether an onlooker wants to interpret the system that way (e.g. Dennett, 1987). Specifying what in the world and in the mind is real is an important task of the science of the mind in general and each theory in particular. In my view, a scientist who gives up the notion of some real world also gives up being a scientist – they cease to have a subject matter (Box 1.8).

Box 1.8 Revisiting Box 1

What is science?

What is the difference between science and pseudo-science?

What is the difference between good science and bad science?

On what grounds should papers submitted to scientific journals be rejected or accepted?

Are Christian Science, Creation Science, Scientology, astrology, traditional Chinese medicine, or chiropractic sciences? Why or why not and why does it matter?

Is psychology a science? Good science or bad science?

How does knowledge grow?

Using Popper's ideas to critically evaluate a psychology article

Ask yourself the following questions as you read any research report. The secret to critical analyses – and hence to being both a good researcher and a good evaluator of research – is to constantly ask questions as you read. Of course this takes effort, though the habit of asking certain questions will with practice become second nature. And that will make all the difference to your ability to evaluate research in a penetrating way rather than uncritically.

First determine if the paper has a clear substantial theory from which follow predictions (i.e. specific statistical hypotheses e.g. predicting a non-zero correlation, difference, etc.). Statistical hypotheses do not in themselves constitute a substantial theory; they follow from one. Make sure you distinguish the two. Further, in order to test the substantial theory, auxiliary hypotheses are necessary. Auxiliary hypotheses allow the substantial theory nominally under test to make contact with data. For example, in terms of the 'two factor theory' of liking in Box 1.5, the researcher may postulate that because the stimuli were new, liking should increase over exposures. That is, an auxiliary hypothesis is that the stimuli are new – and hence people will not get easily bored with them. (In this case, the substantial theory is two-factor theory, and a statistical hypothesis is that 'With this population of materials and subjects, liking will increase from trial one to trial three'.) Are you prepared to accept the auxiliary hypotheses as safe background knowledge? Might you be just as willing to accept different auxiliary hypotheses that lead to opposite predictions? For example, you may be just as willing to assume that the stimuli are simple and also very similar to familiar stimuli – so boredom will be easily induced. In other words, is there a plausible way of deriving opposite predictions from the theory? If so, then the theory is not being put to a strong test. Frequently in papers the predictions given in the introduction could be reversed with different plausible auxiliary hypotheses. (Could you independently test which auxiliary hypothesis to use?) This often happens because researchers see the results before they write the paper; then they can readily convince themselves of what auxiliaries must be true for the theory to make the 'right' predictions. One way to motivate your mind is to imagine opposite results: How would you fit those results with the theory? By being clear about the work done by the auxiliaries, you should then be able to devise conditions where clear predictions really do arise from the theory, because you have established which auxiliaries can be accepted. The auxiliaries should be safe enough that falsification of the predictions can be transmitted back to falsification of the theory under test.

Popper regarded a severe test as being one in which the prediction was unlikely given the rest of your background knowledge. If you did not accept the theory under consideration, what predictions would you make? Think of other well-established theories in psychology. Could they generate the predictions without assuming the theory under test? If so, the test is not a strong test of the theory: The prediction was not unlikely given background knowledge.

How many predictions were derived from the theory? The more predictions the theory makes, the more falsifiable it is. If the theory simply predicts that there will be a difference of any size in a comparison, then it is not really falsifiable at all. In practice, there should be background knowledge to specify what a minimally interesting difference would be. In that case, the test is severe to the extent that the test has sufficient power to detect the minimally interesting difference. The concept of power will be described in Chapter 3 (and see Chapter 5 for another take on test severity). If the test is powerful (in the technical sense to discussed in Chapter 3) then a null result falsifies the prediction of a difference. If the test is not powerful, or if power is not stated, then a null result does not falsify the prediction of a difference. This point is not well understood amongst researchers. Often low power null results are taken as disconfirming a prediction of difference: They do not. Predictions of a difference will only be falsifiable if the statistical test is powerful. Similarly, predictions of no difference will only be strongly corroborated if the test is powerful.

If the predictions come out as expected, the theory survives the tests. Popper would say, the theory is corroborated. He would also be happy for researchers to say the theory has been confirmed – we need not quibble over the exact words used. But on Popper's account the theory is not more probable as a result of this confirmation. Talk of the theory being proved would also not be appropriate.

If the theory failed one or more tests, was it modified in testable ways? Note that modifying a theory or introducing new auxiliary hypotheses in the light of falsifying evidence is perfectly acceptable – indeed, it is how knowledge grows. But the modifications should not be ad hoc.

Finally, think if you have other ways of explaining the results. How would you know if your favourite explanation were wrong?

Final note

Popper's ideas were well received by practising scientists, more so than by philosophers, and in fact his ideas, or versions of them, have become part of the background assumptions of scientists. Consider, for example, the description of science given by the great bongo-playing Nobel laureate Richard Feynman (1918–1988), one of the greatest theoretical physicists of last century:

> The scientist does not try to avoid showing that the rules are wrong; there is progress and excitement in the exact opposite. He tries to prove himself wrong as quickly as possible (p. 16)...The more specific a rule is, the more interesting it is (p. 19)...In science we are not interested in where an idea comes from. There is no authority that decides what is a good idea....there is no interest in the background of the author of an idea or his motive in expounding it. You listen and if it sounds like a thing worth trying...it gets exciting...(p. 22) (Feynman, 1998; see also Feynman, 1965 pp. 157–167 for a very Popperian account of how physics developed).

Feynman emphasized the fallibility of all scientific knowledge and the importance of doubt not certainty:

> If we did not doubt we would not get any new ideas...The freedom to doubt is an important matter in the sciences...it was born of a struggle. It was a struggle to be permitted to doubt, to be unsure...progress [is] made possible by such a philosophy, progress which is the fruit of freedom of thought. I feel a responsibility to proclaim the value of this freedom and to teach that doubt is not to be feared, but that it is to be welcomed as the possibility of a new potential for human beings (Feynman, 1998, pp. 27–28).

Review and discussion questions

1. What did the logical positivists believe?
2. Define the key terms of: induction, contexts of discovery and justification, demarcation criterion, falsifiability, ad hoc, auxiliary hypothesis, Duhem–Quine problem, and verisimilitude.
3. Does the existence of difficulties for theories that continue to be held pose a problem for Popper's philosophy of science?
4. Consider an empirical problem of interest to you. What is your favourite explanation for it? Under what conditions would you give up your theory?
5. If you are conducting any research, can you distinguish which of your beliefs relevant and valuable to that research are metaphysical and hence immune from the way data turn out, and which you hold ransom to the data, and hence are scientific properly speaking?
6. Is Darwin's theory of evolution scientific?

Further reading

For an example application of Popper's ideas in psychology, an analysis of the falsifiability of different theories of panic, see Roth et al. (2005). For a brief popular introduction to Popper's ideas, see Magee (1997). Chalmers' (1999) textbook on the philosophy of science, Chapters 5–7, deals with Popper in a clear way. Thornton (2005) gives a good concise summary of Popper's work and its criticisms. For more detail, Schilpp (1974) contains classic criticisms and a reply by Popper. Miller (1994) provides a detailed and robust defense of Popper's thought under the name of critical rationalism. For a discussion illustrating the social importance of a demarcation criterion, see Kitcher (1982). Finally, all of Popper's books are worth reading; his 1994 and 2001 publications are particularly accessible sets of essays.

2 Kuhn and Lakatos: paradigms and programmes

As a grad student at Harvard, I gazed abstractedly out my window – suddenly all at once the fragments fell into place, and I understood Aristotle's physics

Thomas Kuhn (2000, p. 16)

Popper urged that it was the *clash* between theory and observations that allowed knowledge to grow. We noted a problem in the previous chapter that a researcher always has to contend with in responding to the clash: Where in her network of beliefs should she change things to provide consistency? Or, the other way round, how can one orchestrate an experiment such that a clash would target one belief rather than some other? Popper did not say very much about this beyond pointing out its possibility.

Three of the most influential philosophers of science after Popper focussed on the way some beliefs were targeted more easily than a core set that provided an enduring relatively consistent paradigm (Kuhn), programme (Lakatos) or tradition (Laudan) of research. That is, they proposed that philosophy of science was best understood in terms of larger units of evaluation than the individual theory. Relatedly, given research programmes involved a core set of beliefs resistant to falsification, these philosophers naturally emphasized the extent to which apparent falsifications could in good conscience be ignored. Finally, they shifted the manner in which philosophy of science itself was evaluated, urging that philosophical theory be tested against a carefully examined historical record. Indeed, it was the historical record that suggested to them their different philosophies.

Like Popper, these writers were deeply insightful, providing phrases and images influencing the thinking if not the practice of scientists. We will consider the extent to which their ideas should influence one's day-to-day research. Remember no philosopher has yet provided the definitive account of either how science *has* proceeded or (the separate question) how it *should* proceed. Their role is to stimulate your own thinking on both issues. We will consider Kuhn (1922–1996) and Lakatos (1922–1974) in detail. Their confident assertions about the facts of history are bold and illuminating, but still conjectures with as yet minimal corroboration and plenty of contradictions.

Thomas Kuhn and the paradigm

Kuhn's (1962) *The structure of scientific revolutions* itself was a virtual revolution, achieving popularity that surprised Kuhn more than anyone. *Paradigm* and *paradigm change* became everyday buzz words almost over night. 'Paradigm' comes from the original Greek meaning 'pattern' or 'example'. Kuhn argued that science was learned by becoming familiar with particular examples of the successful application of theory. Scientific practice is then constituted by these examples ('paradigms' in Kuhn's narrow sense) being used to model attempted solutions to new problems. We do not learn to do science by learning a list of explicit rules. We learn by example, we learn like an apprentice learns a craft, whose practice, like most crafts, may be hard to explicate. Nonetheless, a community in accepting a shared list of examples of the best practice comes thereby to accept shared notions of what a tractable problem looks like and what counts as a solution, and thereby to accept common values. This is the shared 'paradigm' in a broad sense: A paradigm is the entire constellation of beliefs, values and techniques shared by members of a scientific community.

In psychology the word paradigm also has two main senses, directly based on Kuhn's narrow and broad senses. A paradigm can be a particular experimental technique: One can talk of the 'Deese–Roediger–McDermott paradigm' of false memory or the 'artificial grammar learning paradigm' for investigating implicit learning. These are canonical procedures to explore a particular question. A paradigm can also refer to a school of thought, like behaviourism, a broad commitment to a certain world-view. Though common usage does not really respect the requirement, Kuhn also meant a paradigm in the broad sense to be a world-view that eclipsed all others for a period of time, one without substantial competitors.

In academic psychology in and around the 1940s, behaviourism did dominate other schools of thought, in America at least (see Boden, 2006, for a history of cognitive science). A model problem and its solution was provided by, for example, Pavlov's analysis of dogs salivating to a bell in terms of classical conditioning. Students would learn psychology by studying such examples and thereby learn to *see* conditioning at work in new contexts, and to sense what problems were unlikely to succumb to such an analysis (and were thus outside the domain of a proper scientific understanding of the mind). Behaviourism as a paradigm in the broad sense thus involved a commitment to various beliefs and values; for example, the belief that all learning can be conceptualized as conditioning; that theories must only refer to stimuli and responses, not internal states and so on.

Kuhn argued that a science came to maturity when its research was firmly based on such a paradigm: This is *normal science*, an attempt to force nature into the preformed and rigid box that the paradigm provides. The aim is to stay within the box. This is, Kuhn argued, what mature science consists of most of the time. Before this stage is reached, in pre-normal science, there exists a range of different schools, not united by a common paradigm. A common paradigm frees the scientific community from exhausting its time on re-examining first principles; it is only when each scientist can take fundamentals for granted that the community is free to concentrate on the detailed application of those fundamentals to the world. 'To turn Sir Karl's view on its head, it is precisely the abandonment of critical discourse that marks the transition to a science' (Kuhn, 1970a, p. 6). A paradigm is similar to what Popper later called a metaphysical framework, except in a crucial respect that for Popper, one's metaphysical assumptions were always in principle open to criticism.

Kuhn's account was meant to be descriptive of the majority of actual scientific practice, but his argument was prescriptive as well. Feyerabend (1970, p. 198) objected,

More than one social scientist has said to me that at last he knows how to turn his field into a 'science' ... The recipe according to these people is to restrict criticism, to reduce the number of comprehensive theories to one, and to create a Normal science that has this one theory as its paradigm. Students must be prevented from speculating along different lines and the more restless colleagues must be made to conform and 'to do serious work'.

Kuhn was mortified by this comment; that was not his intention at all. But based on Kuhn's 1962 book it is hard to see why Kuhn should object to Feyerabend's colleagues. Later Kuhn (1970a, b and onwards) formulated an account of paradigm choice that answered this objection which we will come to below.

Kuhn himself used the metaphor of religion in understanding science: Both involve an uncritical faith. He regarded scientific education as narrow and rigid, 'probably more so than any other except in orthodox theology' (1962, p. 165). We will see later how he describes the process of becoming a normal scientist one of 'conversion', sometimes preceded by a 'crisis'. So where does the difference between science and religion lie? In science, the paradigm provides a means for identifying puzzles and likely solutions. Normal science is 'puzzle solving', specifically solving puzzles about the nature of the world. In fact, Kuhn (1970a) used puzzle solving as his demarcation criterion between science and non-science. Astrology, for example, made testable predictions at times, but its recognized failures did not create puzzles that could be solved. Failures were just explained as necessary consequences of the inevitable inaccuracies in knowing the exact state of the heavens at the moment of birth. Kuhn thought that puzzle solving required Popper's falsifiability criterion be satisfied in order for there to be relevant puzzles at all: There must be possible and actual mismatches between theory and data for there to be puzzles to work on. Although Kuhn required falsifiability just as Popper did, Kuhn thought, unlike Popper, that predictive failure would not challenge basic assumptions, only peripheral ones.

In normal science, if the puzzle is not solved, the failure reflects on the scientist not on the paradigm. As Kuhn puts it, the person who blames the paradigm will be seen as the carpenter who blames his tools. Of course, this is in direct contrast with Popper, who saw experiments as testing theories not people. Kuhn made his claim as a historian; indeed, it was under his influence that philosophers of science became more sensitive to history. The claim that scientists see failure as reflecting adversely on their skill rather than on the underlying basic theory is a claim about actual and historical practice that Donovan et al. (1992) urged should be tested in a range of scientific disciplines: There are not yet the detailed studies to show whether or not difficulties in applying theory are *typically* taken as impugning the scientist or the theory. And whatever one concludes about actual practice, there remains the question of whether that is how it *should* be.

According to Kuhn, scientists do not seek to refute the paradigm; the very fact that a paradigm exists means it has proven itself successful. The time for examining fundamentals is past. The goal now is to assume the paradigm in order to solve puzzles. Seeing how far a paradigm will take you requires commitment to it; and it is that very commitment that will lead scientists unwittingly but inexorably to find its weaknesses. Normal science serves a function; it is useful for scientists to be committed to the paradigm, precisely because their very stubbornness will in time reveal the genuine weaknesses of the paradigm.

Thus, Kuhn suggested that difficult anomalies typically occasion no concern for scientists who readily set them aside for future work. The scientist presumes that the problem will surely succumb to some future line of attack and one cannot deal with all problems at once. Again the claim that scientists have a relatively cavalier attitude to anomalies is not one you should accept uncritically. The fine detail of the motion of Mercury was problematic for Newton's theory; a person working on the problem at the time, Leverrier, maintained that 'no planet has extracted more pain and trouble of astronomers than Mercury, and has awarded them with so much anxiety and so many obstacles' (cited in Andersson, 1994, p. 119). It seems the anomaly was taken very seriously. Dunbar (1997) spent a year in four highly productive molecular biology labs, attending lab meetings, reading research proposals, and in general closely monitoring how the scientists worked. He found that anomalies, especially those that challenged core assumptions in the field, were especially closely attended to and used to generate new hypotheses. Similar work in different domains in psychology would be useful: How are anomalies typically treated? (And is that typical behaviour harmful or beneficial for the field?)

Kuhnian crisis

Although Kuhn suggested that anomalies are often ignored, if sufficient build up that resist repeated attempts at solution, there comes to be a feeling of *crisis* in the field. The crisis creates a growing sense that the paradigm has ceased to function adequately in the exploration of nature. However, crisis in itself does not mean scientists abandon their paradigm. They can only practise science if they have conceptual tools with which to attack problems; it is a paradigm that tells scientists which problems to solve, how to solve them and when they have solved them. A scientist without a paradigm has no means of being a scientist. Thus, one paradigm is declared invalid only if an alternative candidate is available to take its place. According to Kuhn, 'the methodological stereotype of falsification by direct comparison with nature' does not exist in actual science (1962, p. 77). The decision to reject one paradigm is always simultaneously the decision to accept another. Whether scientists reject core theories only if they have an alternative is also an interesting and insufficiently tested conjecture about scientific practice (Donovan et al., 1992).

Crisis finally encourages the development of different paradigms. Choice between paradigms is not easy, however. Kuhn used the term 'incommensurability' to indicate that paradigm comparison is fundamentally difficult. Paradigms tell you what the problems are that need solving; thus different paradigms specify different problems. For example, the questions 'what causes conscious awareness?' or 'how fast can mental images be rotated?' were not legitimate problems for behaviourists. Somewhat less starkly, information processing psychology de-emphasized learning; connectionism brought it back to the fore. If paradigms disagree over what needs solving, then claiming to have solved a non-existent problem by methods that do not count as providing a solution will not impress adherents of a different paradigm.

Paradigms are also incommensurable because of disagreement over how to describe basic observations. Terms refer in different ways in different paradigms: *because* of the change in theory of the solar system, before Copernicus the term 'planet' included the sun and moon; and only afterwards did it include the earth. If terms change meaning, then what counts as a basic description of the data changes too. A hypnotherapist might literally *see* a subject going into trance, while an academic researcher might just see someone relaxing. 'Sam is an extrovert' means different things depending on your theory of extroversion and how the extroversion scale was developed. Thus, according to Kuhn, the actual data are different when seen through the lens of different paradigms. This claim is so radical, it seems to strip science of its objective empirical basis and render paradigm choice irrational. If the paradigm determines the very data, how can there be any empirical basis to paradigm choice? As we will see, Kuhn later denied the charge that his views implied the irrationality of science.

Andersson (1994), re-evaluating the specific historical examples Kuhn used, concluded, 'in all the examples discussed by [Kuhn] it is possible to find test statements common to both theories and unproblematic' (p. 84) for all parties concerned, allowing a rational resolution of which theory the data supported. For example, when Uranus was first discovered, one person *saw* a star and another a planet. But both parties could agree on seeing a disk of light rather than a point and both could agree on the orbit of the heavenly body. This immediately led to a resolution, where all agreed that it was a planet. In general, where there is disagreement on an observation, it would always seem possible to find more basic observation statements that all can agree to and that can form the basis of rational discussion.[1] Observation may depend on theory (as Popper pointed out too), but typically the theory used in generating observations can be neutral with respect to the theory choice under consideration. The same theory of the radio telescope was used for providing data to test big bang and steady-state cosmology paradigms. The same data on children's reading errors can be used for testing connectionist and information processing accounts of reading. The same data on therapeutic outcome can test different therapies for panic attacks.

Nonetheless, one can have some sympathy with Kuhn's observation that proponents of different paradigms often seem to talk past each other in debating their respective positions. Coming to see how the other side thinks can take patience and requires learning to see the problem domain differently, but it is of course possible, and may be common in science. Perrin (1992) found that the chemists on two sides of the conceptual divide of phlogiston and oxygen theory were quite capable of extensive communication and mutual understanding: There did not appear to be impenetrable incommensurability.

But given Kuhn assumed incommensurability, how did he think one can choose between different paradigms? Kuhn argued that when paradigms enter into a debate about paradigm choice, their role is necessarily circular. Each group uses its own paradigm to argue in that paradigm's defence. The rhetoric is to provide a clear exhibit of what scientific practice would be like for those who adopt the new paradigm: Despite its problems, is the new paradigm likely to be more fruitful than the old? Kuhn's emphasis on incommensurability led him to make the claims that elicited the most vitriolic response from philosophers and others, and also inspired post-modernists and social constructionists in ways Kuhn later regretted: He claimed paradigm choice can never be settled by logic and experiment alone. It is an act of faith. In fact, 'in paradigm choice there is no standard higher than the assent of the relevant community' (Kuhn, 1962, p. 94). While not retracting these statements, he later elaborated how they should be interpreted, as discussed below.

To illustrate Kuhn's point, consider two different ways of practising psychology: connectionism and information processing psychology (see Boden, 2006). The connectionist offers one way of living for a scientist. One builds a neural network to solve a learning or constraint satisfaction problem. The questions to resolve in any particular application include: How many layers of neurons to use? How should they be connected? What learning rule should be used? On the other hand, the information processing psychologist offers a different way of life. The aim is to find experimental dissociations to determine how many boxes to draw and how to connect them, and to pinpoint what rules transform representations in each box. In the 1980s, when connectionism was taken up enthusiastically, networks were shown to

---

1. That is not to say that such basic statements are theory-free or infallible; only that if all agree with them there is no current reason to doubt them.

behave somewhat like people in, for example, learning the past tense of verbs. But there were many things they could not do. Indeed, Fodor and Pylyshyn (1988) provided arguments that it was impossible for them to do the things cognitive psychologists were really interested in, like language. But many people started using networks, including to model language. It was a way of practising psychology that had promise. Who knew how the arguments of Fodor and Pylyshyn would stand the test of time. Note that information processing psychology had not solved the problems of language either. As Kuhn said of paradigms in general, there was no compelling logical or empirical argument for why a researcher must have chosen to work in one framework or the other.

Revolution

Kuhn argued that the transfer of allegiance from paradigm to paradigm is a 'conversion experience'. Converting people is difficult. Typically new paradigms are introduced by a person new to the field. Kuhn (1962, p. 151) quoted Max Planck in support of the claim that psychology rather than purely logic is a large determiner of theory choice: 'A new scientific truth does not triumph by convincing its opponents and making them see the light, but rather because its opponents eventually die, and a new generation grows up that is familiar with it.' The claim has become an everyday sentiment now. It is so passé that it is worth considering if there is any general truth in it. In fact, Diamond (1992) found non-significant and tiny correlations between either the chronological or the professional age of chemists who published on the radical theory of polywater and whether they supported the theory or not, on a sample of about 100 chemists. Indeed, as Kuhn himself notes (p. 154), the quantitative success of Planck's own radiation law quickly persuaded many physicists to adopt quantum concepts; quantum theory did not need to wait for a generation of physicists to die out. Similarly, in the 1980s, connectionism was taken up enthusiastically by many cognitive psychologists, both young and old. And for many the experience was not *conversion*, in the sense that many psychologists (though not all) could quite happily work within both new and old paradigms.

Kuhn called the changing of a paradigm a *revolution*. Kuhn initially saw a scientific revolution as a transformation of vision, a gestalt switch. Kuhn himself had personally suddenly *understood* Aristotle's physics with such a gestalt switch – all at once he could see through Aristotlean eyes. It is much like the switch in vision between a duck and a rabbit in Figure 2.1.

Figure 2.1

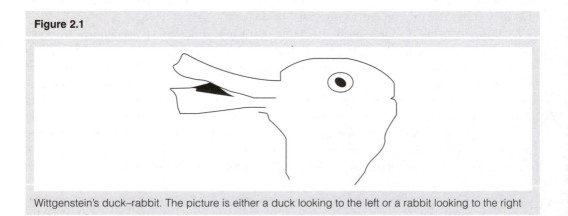

Wittgenstein's duck–rabbit. The picture is either a duck looking to the left or a rabbit looking to the right

Just so, Kuhn said, after a revolution the data themselves change and the sc
a different world. The analogy implies that one way of looking at the data is n
another. Is that how you wish to consider successive scientific theories?

Talk of conversion, of the insufficiency of logic and data, of incommensurability
different worlds seemed to render Kuhn a relativist: One who thinks any belief system
just as good as any other; a winning theory in science is objectively no better than the one
it replaced. We consider relativism more fully below; it became a dominant force in the
social sciences in the 1980s and 1990s under the name of post-modernism and social con-
structionism. Kuhn himself rejected the charge. If there was one thing he respected, it was
the rationality of science, particularly that of the physical sciences. To forestall the common
misunderstandings of his ideas, Kuhn (1977, 2000) refined his notion of incommensurability to mean precisely one thing: the way in which a set of terms can refer differently before
and after a theory change. The example given earlier was 'planet' – the way actual heavenly
bodies were categorized changed after theory had changed. Analogously, different natural
languages can carve up the world in different ways, making direct translation impossible.
There is, apparently, no literal translation of 'the cat sat on the mat' in French, because
English and French classify floor coverings in different ways. This type of incommensurability might make communication difficult between people working with different theories, but
clearly not impossible. They just have to learn each other's language. Clearly, also, incommensurability so defined does not obviously threaten the rationality of theory choice even
in a revolution. Indeed, Thagard (1992) developed an account of conceptual revolutions in
science where conceptual change entailed incommensurability in Kuhn's latter sense, yet
where theory choice was rational. Such incommensurability does mean we have to be careful
in discovering what someone with a different theory is actually talking about.

Kuhn (1970a, b, 1977, 2000) later argued that there was a shared core basis for theory
choice amongst all scientists: namely, the criteria of (at least) accuracy, consistency, scope,
simplicity and fruitfulness. These are all desirable features of any scientific theory. If theory
choice were not made on the basis of these values, it would not constitute science. However,
two scientists committed to this same list of criteria may legitimately end up choosing to
work on different theories. Some criteria might point to one theory and others to the other.
Different scientists may weight the criteria differently. There may also be genuine disagreement about the application of any one criterion (for example, a simple unifying idea may
need to be implemented in a complex way: is the theory simple or complex?). In sum, according to Kuhn, there is no fixed algorithm for theory choice. It is partly a matter of personal
judgment, at least at a stage in history when the two theories are actually competing. (At a
later point in history, when the dust has settled, all criteria may point unambiguously to one
theory and choice is clear. Hence, extreme relativism is avoided by Kuhn's later approach.)

The variability between scientists in how to apply shared standards appropriately and
rationally may seem a weakness in Kuhn's position; he argued that it was a strength. It
enables different people to work on different approaches: How else could the group as a
whole hedge its bets? How could a new idea even get started and its strengths understood
if *everyone* 'rationally' worked on the orthodox theory? Conversely, if everyone gave up on
a theory as soon as a colleague advanced a new one, science would cease. This is (the later)
Kuhn's description of theory choice in revolution. It is also my impression of theory choice
in psychology all the time. There are always different approaches on offer, and one *should
not* reject one approach simply because it has some weaknesses amongst its strengths. This
is a point more referees of journal articles should bear in mind! It *need not* be irrational for
someone to support a different theory than your own! (And it may be positively beneficial for

le working on different approaches.) Variability in theory choice ...science works (in times of revolution, according to Kuhn; more ...hers, such as Lakatos). We consider later, in discussing Lakatos, ...pecific about theory choice and when theories should be rejected.

...ormation

Kuhn's (1962, ...) ...hat people learned science and its conceptual structure on the basis of examples pre-dated a major revolution in cognitive science. Acquiring a concept typically does not involve acquiring an explicit description of what that concept is (as had been believed for most of last century). Rosch (1973) introduced to psychology the idea that learning, for example, what a dog means involves remembering a prototypical dog; subsequent entities can then be classified as a dog according to how similar they are to the prototype. No particular set of features need be necessary and sufficient for being a dog. Brooks (1978) further showed that people could apparently learn the rules of an artificial grammar just by memorizing particular grammatical sequences; subsequent sequences could be classified on the basis of similarity to those memorized. The idea of learning concepts by learning exemplars dominated concept formation research in psychology in the 1980s. Also in the 1980s the notion of case-based reasoning was extensively developed in engineering and artificial intelligence: People might reason not by a list of rules but by considering the best matching prior case. Kuhn's notion that learning the practice of science (and learning concepts generally, Kuhn, 1974) might happen by learning paradigmatic cases and not (just) rules was ahead of its time (see Barker et al., 2003, for further discussion).

Kuhn versus Popper

Kuhn and Popper in fact agreed on many fundamentals. They both agreed that all observations are theory laden; that scientific theories should be falsifiable and testable (Kuhn saw the incompatibility of theory and observation as the ultimate source of every revolution); that difficulties should not in themselves lead to the abandonment of a theory; that in any case conclusive proof of falsification is impossible; that there is also no fixed algorithm determining theory choice; that science does not grow by the addition of truths to a pile but by fundamental conceptual changes and that there exist general metaphysical assumptions that guide research and can be overthrown. In fact, Kuhn commented that on 'almost all occasions' his views and 'Sir Karl's' were 'very nearly identical' (1970a, p. 1). On the other hand, their approaches seemed profoundly different; Popper even described Kuhn's normal science as 'a danger to science and indeed our civilisation' (1970, p. 53). What was the difference between Kuhn and Popper? Worrall (2003) suggested that the main practical disagreement concerned strategy: Kuhn believed that experiments should be designed *assuming* core ideas so that falsification targets auxiliary hypotheses (and hence the ingenuity of the scientist in dreaming them up); Popper apparently thought experiments should be designed to target core rather than auxilliary ideas. I say 'apparently', for Popper did not make this distinction, Kuhn did. However, Popper's examples predominantly reflect the targeting of core rather than auxiliary beliefs and Popper certainly saw core beliefs fit for targeting at any time. In practice, scientists target both on different occasions; perhaps this distinction between Kuhn and Popper is just a matter of the half-full cup.

Related to but not logically following from this disagreement on strategy, Kuhn thought scientists must have faith in the theory they were working on; Popper thought scientists often know they are proposing conjectures. The half-full cup again. In recognizing the other half of the cup, Popper suggested that scientists were rightly resistant to giving up corroborated theories. This brings up the counter-intuitive aspect to Popper's philosophy. On his account a corroborated theory is no more likely to be true than any other theory (remember, he did not accept induction in any form). Thus, Popper's suggestion to prefer a corroborated theory (for practical decisions or as a basis for research) is not justified on any further grounds. According to Popper, it just is constitutive of being rational to prefer such theories (see Box 1.7 where I tried to pump this intuition). We do not need positive justification for all our beliefs to be rational; we just want that they survive continued criticism.

Also related to the disagreement in strategy is the disagreement on demarcation: Popper believed that science consisted of falsifiable theories which the community as a whole seeks to falsify; Kuhn thought science consisted of puzzle solving in a tradition where basic assumptions are sacred and are scarcely challenged by predictive failure. Kuhn regarded the commitment to a theory through thick and thin as paradoxically the only method by which a theory's real weaknesses may eventually be revealed. Conversely, Popper regarded the permanent right to challenge authority (and to challenge fundamentals) as characteristic of science. Both noticed something about the scientific process. But what I have found useful in distinguishing science from the various pseudo-scientific theories I am daily confronted with is surely not uncritical faith but a falsificationist attitude. Nonetheless, we will see that the distinction between a relatively protected core of ideas and other dispensable auxiliary ones is a useful distinction, taken up by Lakatos in his version of falsificationism.

Popper saw theory choice in terms of reasons concerning the objective properties of theories. Kuhn did not always see knowledge as objective knowledge in Popper's sense; the early Kuhn in particular saw theory choice in terms of the psychological states of scientists ('crises', 'conversion', 'gestalt switch') and the behaviour of groups of scientists. Clearly, the psychological state of a scientist is logically independent of the truth of the scientist's theory. Popper was concerned with truth; Kuhn was not. Popper believed that scientists aimed for true theories, truth being the agreement with the facts of what is being asserted. Kuhn did not believe that notion applied to scientific theories.

Popper thought successive theories could be (though were not guaranteed to be) closer and closer approximations to the truth. Kuhn did believe that more recent theories were better than their predecessors in discovering and solving puzzles; but there was no need for an additional notion of truth. Both Kuhn and Popper used evolution as an analogy for science. For Kuhn, the resolution of revolutions is the selection by conflict within the scientific community of the fittest way to practice future science. But science need not to be aiming towards truth, just as, Kuhn points out, evolution is not evolution *towards* anything. Kuhn is right about that very last point. But evolution does produce a close correspondence between organisms and their environment. And is not the analogous correspondence between a theory and the world just how true the theory is?

Relativism and post-modernism

A notion of truth, however fuzzy, is needed for everyday life. To have a belief is to be committed to its truth. To assert a sentence in speech is also to be committed to its truth.

To accept an explanation is to think the explanation is true, otherwise it does not explain anything. To give up on a commitment to truth is to abdicate not only the capacity to have beliefs but also personal morality ('I have not slept with anyone else, honest luv'). Everyday examples also illustrate the intuition that truth is objective. If you think there are some things you do not know, or if you think you could be mistaken, then you are committed to truth being objective, that is, not just dependent on what you think. Similarly, if you think a group of people could be wrong about, say, whether a cave has a hungry lion in it, then you are committed to the truth of that fact being objective in the sense that it does not depend on what the people think. Further, you show that you care about truth when searching for an odd sock in the drawer: Not all answers about the sock's location are equally good, you want a true one. Caring about objective truth is not something to give up lightly (see Lynch, 2005, for elaboration of these arguments). If caring about objective truth is important in everyday life, surely it is important in science too.

Relativism is the belief that different theories or beliefs can be equally true relative to different standards. Some degree of relativism is consistent with caring about truth (you may care about legal truths even though they are relative to culture), but the extreme relativism shown by some commentators on science is not. Kuhn's early rhetoric convinced some people of relativism. Remember Kuhn thought that 'in paradigm choice there is no standard higher than the assent of the relevant community.' Does that mean that the community could not be mistaken? That truth lies in power? That truth changes when the community changes its mind? Was the earth once flat (when people believed that) but now was never flat (as we now believe it was never flat)? You may be surprised to hear some people answer affirmatively to all these questions.

Relativists are often probably motivated by political concerns. Relativism encourages greater toleration of different views, one might be tempted to believe, because if there is no objective truth, there is no reason to impose beliefs on non-believers. For example, if relativism were true, there would be no justification for imposing religious or Imperialist ideology on other cultures. But surely it is the other way round, it is thinking that people are wrong about, for example, Imperialism or sexism, or about the beneficial effects of clitorectomy, that inspires us to engage in action to change it. It is by not being a relativist that there are non-arbitrary reasons for political action (e.g. in promoting tolerance where it is needed). Just so, in science there can be some toleration of different views not because of relativism but because some degree of toleration of different approaches may be best for arriving at objective truths. (And just as we may not wish to tolerate clitorectomy, so some theories in a domain should be rejected too: It is not beneficial, or even possible, to tolerate everything.)

There is a difference between moral relativism (all values are equally good) and epistemic relativism (all beliefs are equally true). We are concerned mainly with the latter. In terms of the latter, some things are constituted by what a group of people believe (like legal systems) so the truth about them is relative to what the group thinks (or what some part of the group has thought when determining the legal system, creating objective knowledge in Popper's sense). The problem comes in generalizing from such examples, where what the group think does matter, to believing that all truth is relative to what people think.[2]

---

2. Even in the case of the legal system, the truth is objective. 'Ignorance of the Law is no excuse' they say. Once the legal system is created (by people's thoughts, Poppers' world 2) it takes on a life of its own: You can be wrong about it. It becomes part of Popper's world 3.

Kuhn emphasized the sociological and subjective elements of theory choice. Various groups were influenced by these ideas, including *science studies* and *social construction-ism* and the already existing *post-modernism* and *sociology of knowledge* movements (see Koertge, 1998 and Sokal and Bricmont, 1998, for illuminating discussion). There are very interesting social questions to be addressed concerning science: for example, the question of how the nature of theories proposed and accepted by scientists is influenced by social, economic, political and cultural factors (see e.g. MacKenzie, 1981, for an interesting account of how the development of statistics depended on the eugenics movement); or the question of what type of research society ought to encourage or discourage (animal research, stem cell treatments for Parkinson's disease, GM crops, racial differences in IQ, the basis of sexual fantasies?). But they are independent questions to the question of how human beings can obtain true knowledge about the world (what is it about science that gets one closer to the truth, when it does?). Confusing these questions leads to extreme views.

Some of the extreme views are the following:

1. 'Scientific knowledge is purely the product of social forces, power struggles, and politics. The natural world has no role in the construction of scientific knowledge'. The basis of the claim is the famous under-determination of theory by data. No matter what the evidence is, there are always a number of possible theories to account for it. Thus, the argument goes, it is the use of rhetoric and power that means one theory is chosen over another. The argument is misguided. First, if evidence underdetermines theory choice, so surely does the social political context. Thus if one does not believe that the natural world influences our theories, why should one believe that the social world does? Second, under-determination of theory by evidence is a logical claim, but its practical implications are often non-existent (Sokal and Bricmont, 1998). The theories that the blood circulates, that genes are composed of DNA, that matter is made of atoms and so on are based on evidence that *could* be accounted for in other ways, but that does not mean there is a single competing theory on or anywhere near the table. Finally, to believe that one's knowledge is based only on social pressure, not on the facts, is to believe you have no good reasons for your beliefs. There would therefore be no good reason for believing that all knowledge is the product of social forces.

2. 'There is no absolute truth; true or false is always relative to someone's perspective, it's just a preference to believe certain things'. Is the claim that truth is relative to each person true for every person or just for the post-modernist who believes it? If the former, the claim is absolutely rather than relatively true and the claim contradicts itself; if the latter, then since the claim is not true for me, I rightly will never be convinced by it. Thus such personal relativism is self-defeating (Lynch, 2005).

3. 'Physical reality is a social and linguistic construct'. This is a confusion of a representation with the fact it refers to. Sokal and Bricmont (1998, pp. 101–102) present the following passage, sadly from training material for teachers: 'For many centuries it was considered to be a fact that the Sun revolves around the Earth each day. The appearance of another theory, such as that of the diurnal rotation of the Earth, entailed the replacement of the fact just cited by another: The Earth rotates on its axis each day'. The quote confuses a fact with the representation of the fact. A fact is a situation in the external world that exists whether we know it or not; beliefs represent those facts. If you think your beliefs could be wrong, then you accept a distinction between your belief (the representation) and the fact it targets (the way the world actually is). In the example in the quote, the facts did not change, just their

representation. In day-to-day life, the distinction between facts and their representations is important to us. If facts are just points of views, why bother with criminal investigations? Do you care whether it is the actual rapist that gets caught? Why not adopt the view one can fly and jump out of an airplane? Blurring the distinction between representations and facts is something few people sincerely wish to do.

Typically people who make such cynical claims about the physical world are naively realist about the social world (see Sokal and Bricmont, 1998, for examples). However, if there are no objective facts about the physical world, there are no objective facts about the social world. If one is sceptical about the physical world, one should be equally so about the social world. Welcome to the world of solipsists, population: you.

4. 'The science of one society is no more valid than that of another'. It is true that medical practices in other cultures may have useful components which we should not arrogantly dismiss. Perhaps some herbs in Chinese, African or South American traditions can genuinely cure specific ailments. But there will be a culture-independent fact as to whether any given herb does have a therapeutic action beyond the placebo effect. The way to find that out is by double-blind trials. Different cultures may have valuable things to teach each other; but that does not mean that greater evidence for one cultural view ('that mountain was caused by tectonic pressure') rather than a competing one ('that mountain was a giant white lion that fell asleep') makes no difference. If you had a major heart attack, would you want your friend to call the witch doctor or the medical doctor?

Lakatos and the research programme

Lakatos saw himself as taking the middle path between Popper and Kuhn, as he saw them. Popper offered a universal methodology for science; Kuhn rejected universal methodologies but illustrated how detailed historical analysis of scientific episodes could inform philosophy. Lakatos searched for a dialectic between 'statute law' (general principles, as per Popper) and 'case law' (the relevance of particular historical cases for judging what is right, as per Kuhn). Lakatos accepted Kuhn's historical analysis as a critique of Popper's specific methodology, but accepted Popper's arguments that the philosopher of science is interested in objective knowledge and its rational basis, not in subjective states or the sociology of scientists. Lakatos firmly rejected the relativistic overtones in Kuhn's thought. Lakatos had grown up in Hungary where he experienced the attempt of the State to impose ideological conformity on scientific theories; thus, he believed passionately in the need for an objective demarcation criterion between science proper and pseudo-science. A relativism in which all 'science' (e.g. State imposed) is just as good as any other is positively dangerous.[3] In a talk on the radio, Lakatos pointed out 'The Catholic Church ex-communicated Copernicans, the Communist Party persecuted Mendelians on the grounds that their doctrines were pseudo-scientific. The demarcation between science and pseudo-science is not merely a problem of armchair philosophy: it is of vital social and political relevance' (Lakatos, 1978, p. 1). It is my sense that with the modern proliferation of ideas on the market commanding attention as practical advice for every area of our life, the need for such a demarcation criterion is as great now as it ever was.

---

3. Of course, Kuhn, would agree – Kuhn was an 'elitist' in believing those in power should decide on which scientific theories are good, but the people in power had to be scientists acting as scientists.

Popper did not believe that his ideas could be *tested* by history. His falsifiability criterion was metaphysics, not science: to the degree in a particular scientific episode scientists did not follow its dictates, so much the worse for the scientists, not his criterion. The criterion, like any metaphysics, could of course be criticized. In fact, Popper (1974, p. 1010) laid down a condition that would lead him to abandon his criterion: he would do so if it were shown that Newton's theory were no more falsifiable than Freud's. Of course, no one has succeeded in doing so. Popper's comment suggested a general strategy Lakatos made explicit: Certain great achievements in the history of science illustrate rational theory choice and genuine science if anything does. Although there has been little agreement over what constitutes a good universal methodology, there has been substantial agreement over single achievements exemplifying best practice. The Copernican, Newtonian, Einsteinian revolutions – amongst others – count amongst the most brilliant achievements of mankind. According to Lakatos, our proposed methodology of science should be answerable to these cases. But Lakatos also thought that a good methodology should also be able to make us change our value judgments in the *odd* historical case, as no methodology worth its salt should be entirely hostage to our pre-theoretical value judgments. Neither *a priori* statute law nor particular cases are ultimate arbiters of what is rational; but both allow us to get a handle on objective rationality and pull ourselves up by our bootstraps. Without wishing to claim the course of history defines what is rational, Lakatos did want to hold *his* theory partially hostage to history.

Lakatos defined himself as coming from the falsificationist tradition of Popper, whom he respected immensely. Thus, Lakatos thought, for example, that 'the hallmark of scientific behaviour is a certain scepticism even towards one's most cherished theories. Blind commitment to a theory is not an intellectual virtue; it is an intellectual crime' (1978, p. 1). But he also incorporated into his methodology two points that Kuhn had highlighted: The constant presence of anomalies and a distinction between core and peripheral beliefs. How can we work these points into a falsificationist methodology?

All theories all through the history of science have been 'born falsified', as Lakatos put it. As we noted in the previous chapter, Popper's claim was not that one uncritically accept every difficulty of a theory as a falsification; in fact, he explicitly claimed the opposite. Popper's claim was that one should carefully consider the conditions under which one would accept a theory as falsified. Theories must be made to stick their neck out. But we can only criticize one thing (e.g. a theory), if we take for true other things. To be critical about anything, we must decide to accept other things. As Popper points out, it may take considerable time in working out what to accept and thus what to reject. At a given point in history different people may have rationally come to different decisions on the same issue, and some may regard a theory as falsified that others do not. But through engaging in critical discussion, normally consensus can eventually be reached, even if over the course of many years. The question is not whether the 'ocean of anomalies' into which theories are historically born, and through which they always struggle, logically threatens Popper's position – they do not. The question is whether the notion of a single direct hit by a piece of falsifying evidence on a core theory captures the rational basis of science as actually practised.[4] Lakatos argued that it does not.

---

4. Note that right from the start Popper (1934/1959) stated that one token observation should not be taken as falsifying a theory. All falsifying evidence must be open to criticism. This is achieved by postulating a low level 'falsifying hypothesis', that is a hypothesis specifying how anyone could recreate the falsifying evidence. The falsifying hypothesis should then be severely tested and corroborated before it is accepted as falsifying the main theory. For example, one person once seeing a black swan is not good enough to falsify 'all swans are white'; but severely testing and corroborating 'There is a black swan at Brisbane zoo' (by various people making a trip to Brisbane zoo and reproducing the observation) would serve to falsify 'all swans are white'.

Lakatos argued that core ideas are protected from such direct hits. He suggested that Newtonians, as much as Freudians, would be similarly non-plussed by the question as to what observations would lead them to give up their theory. For example, Lakatos asks us to consider a hypothetical story. The motion of a planet p deviates from the path it should have given Newton's laws, initial conditions and the influence of other known planets. Does the Newtonian physicist give up Newton's theory? No. He suggests that there must be an unknown planet p′ which perturbs the orbit of p. He works out the required mass and orbit of p′ (this was in fact the stunning fashion in which Neptune was discovered). He asks an astronomer to test his hypothesis. But existing telescopes are not powerful enough. So a new one is built after some years, but it cannot detect the planet. Are Newton's laws abandoned? No. The physicist suggests that maybe the planet is hidden by a cosmic dust cloud. He calculates the location and density of the cloud and asks a satellite be sent up to detect it. And so on. Either the chain of new suggestions peters out, and the whole sorry episode is forgotten, gathering dust in some annals; or the planet is discovered and hailed as a resounding success for Newtonian physics. According to Lakatos, falsifications are not directed towards Newtonian physics as such. The scientist always has a means of generating auxilliary hypotheses to protect the core theory.

The story's point is not as strong as Lakatos would have us believe. It relies on the planet p having motions easily explicable with Newtonian physics. But consider if the planet moved in a circle of constant speed, or worse a rectangular orbit, or in countless other bizarre ways (Popper, 1974, p. 1007). Even pre-Einsteinian scientists historically considered giving up Newton's law of gravitation on the basis of much less. Nonetheless, the story motivates the thought that there is a *hard core* of beliefs which are *relatively* resistant to falsification – in the sense that scientists typically do not try to target it. Further, Lakatos pointed out that postulating a hard core has the advantage of recognizing the continuity over time of scientific research. When there are anomalies, part of the system may be altered to absorb them; but because the hard core persists, the research programme keeps its identity over time *as*, for example, Newtonian physics.

The hard core is the central beliefs of the programme. In connectionism, for example, the hard core includes the belief that psychological states consist of activation flowing between units through adjustable connections. We are 'forbidden' from falsifying the hard core, as Lakatos would have it. Instead one invents auxiliary hypotheses that form a *protective belt* around the core, and direct falsifying conclusions to them; they get adjusted, re-adjusted or replaced to defend the thus hardened core. For example, in a connectionist model of reading, we may use a neural network with written words coded in a certain way in an input layer and spoken sounds coded in a certain way in an output layer. If the model cannot account for some phenomena of reading (e.g. it makes a different pattern of mistakes than children do) the connectionist does not abandon connectionism. She may change the assumption about how the letters should be encoded (perhaps in the process making new predictions about how children perceive letters). Or more layers of units might be added in the network. And so on. A research programme has a *positive heuristic*, which is a unified and coherent set of principles for how to modify and sophisticate the refutable protective belt. In connectionism the heuristic would include: Try coding different features in the input units or try a different learning rule, activation rule or pattern of connections. Boxes 2.1 and 2.2 illustrate hard cores, protective belts and positive heuristics for a couple of research programmes in psychology which we will discuss later.

Box 2.1 Evolutionary psychology (based on Ketolaar and Ellis, 2000)

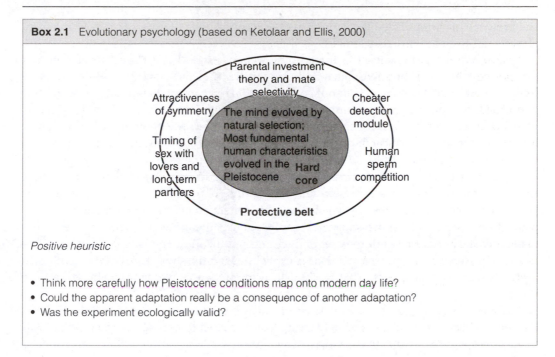

Positive heuristic

- Think more carefully how Pleistocene conditions map onto modern day life?
- Could the apparent adaptation really be a consequence of another adaptation?
- Was the experiment ecologically valid?

Box 2.2 One approach to learning

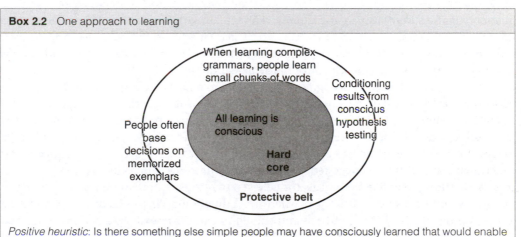

Positive heuristic: Is there something else simple people may have consciously learned that would enable them to perform the task? How could the test of conscious knowledge be made more sensitive?

Progress and degeneration

Lakatos provided criteria for evaluating research programmes. If a modification in a research programme (i.e. in the protective belt) predicts some hitherto unexpected fact, the programme is *theoretically progressive*. Further, if some of these predictions are actually corroborated, the programme is *empirically progressive*. Otherwise the problem-shift is *degenerating*. Note that to be progressive, not all predictions have to be confirmed. Any research programme is allowed a few defeats; a subsequent change may resolve any conflict, turning the defeat into a victory. A few stunning successes carry a programme a long way even in the presence of various failed predictions (whose accounts may, if unresolved as in the story above, simply end up in dusty annals).

Degeneration can show itself in three ways. A change is ad hoc$_1$ if it does not lead to a novel prediction. We considered such ad hocery in the previous chapter. The change is ad hoc$_2$ if a new prediction is made but not corroborated. Finally, a prediction may be made and confirmed, but the change is still unsatisfactory to scientists – ad hoc$_3$ – if it is not generated by the positive heuristic. A succession of ad hoc$_3$ changes shows the programme has no coherence. For example, in a research programme explaining depression, each new anomaly may be dealt with in an arbitrarily different way: first the sampling technique of an experiment is queried; then the weather is raised as a confounding factor in experiments in different countries and so on. (In itself these responses are fine; but if there were a long stream of them and no coherent strategy by which they were generated unique to the programme, the programme would feel unsatisfactory.) In mature science, the protective belt has intellectual coherence, it is not just an arbitrary set of disconnected theories. The hard core and intellectual driving force of the positive heuristic is explicit recognition by Lakatos of the continuity and coherence of real science. That is why 'all swans are white', while falsifiable, is not yet science.

In a progressive programme, theory keeps ahead of the data; in a degenerating programme, theory lags behind the data, desperately trying to adjust itself to keep up. Originally Marxism made novel predictions: that the first socialist revolution would take place in the most economically advanced countries, that socialist societies would be free of revolutions and so on. After the many predictions were falsified, the failures were 'explained' in only ad hoc ways. Lakatos asks what novel predictions has Marxism made since 1917? It is a persistently degenerating research programme, always trying to catch up with data to 'explain' it only retrospectively, and that is why it falls on the pseudo-science side of the demarcation line in Lakatos' book.

Science in general consists of competing research programmes. One programme will eventually be abandoned if it is consistently degenerating while another is progressive. (But Lakatos recommends we do not discard a budding research programme; as long as it is progressive, even if not as successful as its rival, it should be given time to establish its capabilities.) Thus, rejection of a programme is not a two-cornered fight between theory and experiment; as Kuhn also suggested, the failure of one programme involves also the success of another. But unlike Kuhn, Lakatos believed that research programmes have achieved monopoly only rarely; the history of science is and should be the history of competing research programmes. It has not been and should not be a succession of periods of normal science; the sooner competition starts, the better.

Lakatos did not believe that it was irrational to work on a consistently degenerating programme even in the presence of a progressive one. But to be honest, one had to acknowledge the true score and face the consequences: Journal editors and funding agencies should not support such research.

According to Lakatos, Kuhn is right to stress the tenacity of certain theories even with apparent 'falsifications'; but Kuhn is wrong to thereby think he has successfully rejected all types of falsificationism. Lakatos saw himself as providing a means of reconstructing the *objective* rational basis of the history of science, in those episodes where we generally agree that theory choice was rational. Lakatos could provide an account independent of the mental states of scientists (whether scientists felt crisis or curiosity is irrelevant to the objective reasons for theory choice). It is largely the build up of unanswered falsifications of auxiliary theories that slowly drains the blood from a research programme before it is left a

Imre Lakatos

This remark by Lakatos is taken from Berkson (1976), in a collection of essays in memory of Lakatos (Cohen et al., 1976). Lakatos worked at the London School of Economics (LSE) where Karl Popper also worked for most of his life. Lakatos greatly admired Popper, although he was also a staunch critic. Lakatos was known for his quick wit and love of an intellectual punch up. Another influential philosopher of science, Paul Feyerabend, also at the LSE briefly, recollected how Lakatos' office was next to the lecture theatre Feyerbend lectured at: 'when the windows were open Imre could hear every word I said. Feeling outraged, or simulating outrage at the drift of my story – with Imre you were never sure – he [often] came over and tried to set things right' (Lakatos & Feyerabend, 1999, ix).

Imre Lakatos was born Imre Lipsitz in 1922, but changed his name twice – first to the non-Jewish Imre Molnár (he survived the Second World War hidden by a non-Jewish family) and then to Imre Lakatos, a Hungarian working-class name, when Hungary became communist. Nonetheless, he later spent 3 years in a Stalinist jail. Lakatos eventually found his way to Kings College Cambridge, where he completed a ground-breaking PhD on the logic of mathematical discovery. It is written in the form of a dialogue between a set of students and their tutor, who come to successively deeper understandings of a mathematical conjecture, a dialogue which both illustrated and argued for a new approach to the philosophy of mathematics. From 1960, Lakatos worked at the LSE, largely on the philosophy of science, until his death in 1974.

husk. But, according to Lakatos, verifications are also important; it is the corroboration of novel predictions that keeps the programme moving forwards.

For (the early) Kuhn there are no rational standards for comparison between paradigms; each paradigm comes with its own standards. In contrast, Lakatos held, like Popper, that theory change in science can occur on rational grounds, and often does: choice reflects the preference for progressive over degenerating programmes. But there is no one-shot Popperian kill. The battle between programmes is a war of attrition. It may seem there are crucial experiments that finished off one core theory in a single go. But in fact, even if some scientists *believed* at the time the experiment was a crucial one, maybe the defeated programme would eventually absorb the anomaly and convert it into a resounding success. Only when the history books are written many years later is it known whether the defeated programme proved itself exhausted of heuristic power, producing a succession of ad hoc manoeuvres. In hindsight one can then accept the experiment as crucial, not something that could be explained. There is no instant rationality. Thus, for Lakatos, there is no hard and fast distinction between anomaly and falsification for core theories, except in how the history books like to reconstruct the gradual downfall of a programme as a single event. The distinction between anomaly and falsification is crucial for Popper; virtually irrelevant for Lakatos. Thus in Lakatosian eyes the ocean of anomalies is a refutation of Popper; but in Popperian eyes, it is not. For Popper, falsification of a core theory occurs when critical discussion has led people to agree on background knowledge such that the evidence actually targets the core theory rather than a peripheral hypothesis. It is simply a logical fact that accepting some statements means other statements are false. Popper urged people to strive for consistency; Lakatos regarded it as rational to work on inconsistent foundations if the outcome was progressive.[5]

An example

Lakatos (1978) applied his *methodology of scientific research programmes* to many episodes in physics. It was Lakatos' style to develop his ideas and argument by a detailed exchange between his principles and historical data.[6] Later others applied the methodology to episodes in economics and other social sciences. Box 2.1 indicates an application by Ketelaar and Ellis (2000) to evolutionary psychology. The hard core consists of assuming natural selection and that crucial selection of human psychological characteristics happened in the Pleistocene epoch (from about a million to 10,000 years ago). These assumptions are not directly fal-sifiable. Indeed, the non-falsifiability of natural selection led Popper to characterize it as metaphysics. For Popper, natural selection was a metaphysical framework that proved its worth by the specific scientific theories it generated (and thus was properly part of the scientific enterprise, unlike, say, creationism). Lakatos articulated that same idea by distinguishing core from protective belt. In the Pleistocene it would have been important to detect when someone was liable to cheat on an agreement. Thus, maybe a 'cheater detection module' evolved. If this is falsified the core remains unscathed. But to the extent thinking about natural selection for cognitive abilities (in especially Pleistocene conditions) generates cor-roborated novel predictions of current human behaviour then the programme is progressive (as Ketalaar and Ellis argue it is). For example, people do seem especially able to reason about conditionals when the task involves detecting someone cheating rather than dealing with simply abstract content. Another hypothesis, based on the notion that people seek genetic diversity, is that women in a pair bond but going to a nightclub alone will present them-selves as more sexually available when they are in the fertile phase of their cycle rather than other phases (so that they can be fertilized by an illicit lover). This novel and non-trivial prediction has been confirmed (Baker and Oram, 1998). On a Lakatosian account, it is the fact that evolutionary psychology has been progressive that accounts for it acquiring some popularity. Conversely, those opposed to evolutionary psychology focus on the frequently ad hoc nature of evolutionary stories – stories not used to derive novel predictions.

5. For example, the early Bohr atom was built on known inconsistent foundations; but using it as a model produced novel corroborated predictions for some time, so it was a progressive research programme.
6. Lakatos was not concerned with all aspects of the data; details irrelevant to the unfolding of the episode as a rational episode were not his interest. Similarly, if you were to write up a debate to capture its logical structure, much repetition, dead-ends and sequencing details may be worked over to capture the spirit of the debate rather than the irrelevancies (Larvor, 1998). Thus, Lakatos saw himself as *rationally reconstructing* history with true details sometimes relegated to footnotes. Relegating true history to footnotes horrified Kuhn; Lakatos saw it as enabling him to get nearer to the underlying truth than Kuhn did.

Novelty

Both Popper and Lakatos valued *novel* predictions. It is only through making novel predictions that a programme can become progressive. Popper and originally Lakatos took a prediction to be novel if it concerned a fact that was not yet known. Making predictions in advance of seeing the data is generally valued by scientists. It is an integral feature of Neyman–Pearson philosophy considered in the next chapter, the philosophy forming the foundation of inference in the social and behavioural sciences. By contrast, in Chapters 4 and 5 we consider alternative philosophies of statistical inference, the Bayesian and likelihood approaches, in which the timing of an explanation is regarded as utterly irrelevant to the evidential force of the relevant data. Donovan and colleagues (1992) present three historical studies arguing that the ability to make surprising predictions was not relevant to the acceptance of core theory in those cases. Lakatos himself revised his concept of novelty when studying the Copernican revolution, taking up a suggestion of Elie Zahar. What made a prediction novel in the relevant way was not temporal factors (whether the prediction literally came before discovering the fact). A prediction is novel for a theory if it was not used in constructing the theory (*use novelty*) (see Lakatos and Feyerabend, 1999, p. 109–112). Indeed, Einstein constructed the general theory of relativity without considering the orbit of Mercury at all; having constructed the theory on other grounds, he realized he could resolve a very old problem concerning Mercury's orbit. On discovering this, Einstein reported himself as being in 'a state of delirious joy' for days (Lanczos, 1974, p. 214). It was one of the two key results that won scientists over to the theory (the other corroborated prediction did involve temporal novelty). Of course, temporal novelty implies use novelty, so the value of use novelty can indicate why people find temporal novelty impressive. The conceptual stretching in the definition of novelty illustrates Lakatos' sensitivity to history and the dialectic between specific cases and general principles.

Why are novel predictions important? Lakatos took them to be conjectural signs of truth. Consider a crime investigation where you hypothesize that the butler stole the college wine. Based on the hypothesis, you infer he must have taken a train between two distant towns on a certain date. The tickets are later found in his jacket pocket. No one thought of checking for these items before. The corroboration of our prediction could be taken as a *conjectural* sign of the truth of the hypothesis. (Only conjectural because there may be some other explanation; Lakatos, following Popper, did not think one could reliably induce certain or even probable truth.) But Lakatos did not base his methodology on such thought experiments or a priori considerations (by contrast, you could derive Popper's methodology from first principles). He regarded it as arising from an interplay between such principles and the consideration of exemplary cases in actual history. Thus, he considered progressiveness as a conjectural sign of truth *in our universe*.

How to choose a methodology of science

A key difference between Kuhn and Popper that we pointed out is that Kuhn believed falsifications are always targeted at peripheral rather than core theories whereas Popper regarded all theories as open to such targeting. Lakatos clearly sided with Kuhn on this issue, both as a matter of historical fact and in terms of what constitutes rational behaviour. However, despite the powerful rhetoric of Kuhn and Lakatos, and their virtually uncritical acceptance by some scientists, you should not accept their claims at face value. Box 2 illustrates one research programme concerning how people learn. The core claim is that all learning is con-scious. Specific hypotheses in the protective belt include the claim that conditioning is based on conscious hypothesis testing. For example, when people are conditioned to, for example, blink to a tone because the tone has in the past signalled a puff of air into their eyes, it is because during the trials pairing the tone and puff of air, people consciously worked out a hypothesis that the tone predicts the air puff. Then when there is a tone, they consciously expect an air puff. Another theory in the protective belt is that when people have seemed to have learnt a complex rule system of, say, an artificial grammar, it may be because they have consciously memorized some grammatical examples and can classify new examples as similar to the old ones. Such subjects cannot tell you the rules of the grammar; but that does not mean they know the rules unconsciously. Rather, they have not learnt the rules either consciously or unconsciously. And so on. The positive heuristic urges such researchers to investigate any claim of unconscious learning and look to see if people have consciously learnt something not previously detected by the experimenter. Falsifying one such hypoth-esis in the protective belt does not lead to abandoning the programme but to using the heuristic to generate other hypotheses. One can readily analyse this research programme in Lakatosian terms and it is reasonably progressive. However, some people, such as myself, belong to a rival programme that holds unconscious learning does exist. I (amongst many others) conduct experiments which are meant to show learning can be unconscious, that is that directly target the core theory of the programme in Box 2.2 for falsification. Similar examples are rife in psychology. As a community, people target each other's core ideas for falsification all the time. But what implications, if any, does this have for the methodology of scientific research programmes? How are we to evaluate Lakatos' methodology?

If we accept the targeting of the core ideas of one person by another person in the same research area as contradicting Lakatos, one response is to say such practice *falsifies* Lakatos' theory. But that would be to apply 'Popperian' standards to Lakatos' theory. It would be more consistent to apply Lakatosian standards to Lakatos' theory. Just so, Lakatos is happy for his theory to exist in an ocean of anomalies; they do not in themselves refute him. If the theory can make novel predictions about the history of science which are confirmed by historical analysis, it will be a progressive methodology. Such an evaluation is not simple. For a start, Lakatos meant the theory to be tested against those episodes universally rec-ognized as brilliant achievements. Its failure to work exactly in the case of psychology, or parts of psychology, may merely reflect badly on psychology (Lakatos thought psychology was very ad hoc). But who is to be the jury to decide on what counts as brilliant achieve-ments? Lakatos would not expect an algorithmic answer to this question; the aim is to get a handle on rationality, not pin it down and formalize it (Lakatos did not believe that even the rationality of mathematics could be captured by formalism). Perhaps for psychologists there would be a rough consensus about the best achievements which could be used as test cases for a methodology for psychology. (Does this lead to relativism?) But then there is the need for the methodology to make novel predictions[7] (and not *just* be used by high-minded people to legitimate or disgrace certain lines of enquiry, useful as it is for this latter pur-pose). Remember here Lakatos' theory is a budding methodology and should, by its own standards, be given a chance. Finally there are some interesting questions for it to get to

7. Lakatos (1978, p. 133) offers two specific examples : On Popper's account, as Lakatos sees it, it was irrational to work on Newtonian physics after Mercury's orbit was found to be anomalous, and it was irrational to work on Bohr's old quantum theory on inconsistent foundations. Lakatos' theory *reverses* these judgments, thus post-dicting novel value judgments in line with those of scientists.

grips with. Why are some theories raised to the status of hard core and protected and others not? And surely hard cores can sometimes change over time? How? And, further stretching the concepts of Lakatos' theory, under what conditions are core theories targeted? (cf. Thagard, 1992, who developed a computational model of scientific theory revision showing how certain beliefs could become more entrenched than others yet not become immune to criticism.)

There are further questions Feyerabend (1975) asked of Lakatos that may or may not have useful answers. When a research programme has, as is typical, both successes and failures, when does it become progressive or degenerating? After how long should one persist in a degenerating programme before it is irrational to continue or the programme becomes pseudo-science? Rationality is perhaps just fuzzy in many cases; and why should not it be? Most things are. But that does not mean there are not also clear cases.

Using Kuhn and Lakatos' ideas to evaluate research

As the early Kuhn recommended the abandonment of critical discourse, it is unclear what general advice he would give in judging research other than to look down on those who stray from the dominant paradigm, especially if it is not in a state of crisis. The latter Kuhn made clear that research should be judged on the basis of a number of criteria, including accuracy, consistency, scope, simplicity and fruitfulness. Both Kuhn and Lakatos urge judging a core theory over a long period and not on the basis of a single paper.

In reading a research article, see if you can identify the hard core and protective belt of the author's research programme. Remember the hard core will not be directly tested by the author; it will be used to set up an auxiliary hypothesis which will take the blame if anything goes wrong. Together the hard core and auxiliary hypotheses should produce a novel prediction, according to Lakatos. That is, the result predicted should not have been used in constructing the hypotheses. Is the prediction novel in this sense? (It will appear so by being in the introduction section of the paper, but do you think the authors would have predicted the opposite from their core theory if the results had been different?) Also, is the prediction novel in the sense that it was made first by this research programme? Could the prediction be derived from any competing research programme you can think of?

According to Lakatos, take with a pinch of salt any claim by the author that their research is a crucial test of different core theories. Even if it seems that a research programme can fail to explain one or more results, it is perfectly rational to remain committed to it so long as it has some successes. The point is to judge the programme over a period of time: Has it made some successful novel predictions in that time? Take with a pinch of salt any results presented as problematic for a research programme when no other programme can explain them either. They can be dealt with in time.

If predictions failed, how were hypotheses modified? Did the modifications lead to new predictions? Were the modifications created by a coherent set of principles distinctive to that programme (the positive heuristic) or just cobbled together for this particular problem?

In evaluating the worth of a theory do not worry if it does not seem to be directly testable in practice. If it is used to generate other hypotheses that are tested, and sometimes successfully so, the theory has proved its scientific status by being the hard core of a progressive research programme.

Concluding note

In discussing Lakatos' approach, I finished with questions not to undermine Lakatos' philosophy but the converse: To show there is, just as Lakatos wanted, room for it to be explored (and hence improved). Similarly, I have indicated how the textbook account of the overthrow of Popper is far too simple. Never presume that because a writer came later (or earlier) they said something better. And never take textbooks seriously. But I do want you to take philosophy seriously: If you decide to ignore it, it only means you will have a half-baked and half-thought-out philosophy. You cannot escape philosophical issues. The works of Popper, Kuhn and Lakatos should stimulate your own thinking on how to carry out and evaluate research. They will help you bake your ideas some more.

In the subsequent chapters we will deal with an issue we have skirted over thus far: What is to be our practical philosophy of inference when dealing with probabilistic theories and data? Theories in psychology do not state '*All* x are y'. The theories state tendencies, or describe mechanisms that produce only tendencies, not deterministic relationships. You have probably been taught rock-solid final answers to how to go about the business of statistical inference. We will see that all is not as it seems.

Review and discussion questions

1. Define the key words of: paradigm, normal science, crisis, revolution and incommensurability.
2. Define the key words of: research programme, hard core, protective belt, positive heuristic, progressive and degenerating.
3. How did the relativistic implications of Kuhn's views change over time?
4. Do you value the novelty of a prediction in assessing a theory? Why or why not?
5. Is Darwin's theory of evolution scientific?
6. How did Lakatos believe we should choose between his, Popper's and Kuhn's views of how science works?

Further reading

Kuhn was a master of word craft. Kuhn's 1962 and the 1969 edition with the added postscript is an excellent place to start. His 1977 and 2000 collections of papers contain some very readable chapters showing the development of his thought. The exchange between Kuhn and others in Lakatos and Musgrave (1970) is entertaining. Lakatos also had a wonderful way with words – but a more complex style, and if you have not studied physics you may find him difficult. The best start is the introduction to his 1978 collection of papers, and then his lectures in Part I of Lakatos and Feyerabend (1999). I found Larvor's (1998) introduction to Lakatos illuminating. After that, to go deeper, try the 1978 collected papers. A similar but different approach to understanding science is given in Laudan's very readable 1977 edition, also providing commentary on Popper, Kuhn and Lakatos.

3 Neyman, Pearson and hypothesis testing

In this chapter we will consider the standard logic of statistical inference. That is the logic underlying all the statistics you see in the professional journals of psychology and most other disciplines that regularly use statistics. It is also the logic underlying the statistics taught in almost all introductory statistics courses for social or natural scientists. This logic is called the Neyman–Pearson approach, though few users of it would recognize the name.

Statistics are often taught to scientists in a peculiarly uninspiring cook-book style. Thus, many users of statistics would be surprised to learn that the underlying (Neyman–Pearson) logic is both highly controversial, frequently attacked (and defended) by statisticians and philosophers, and even more frequently misunderstood by experienced researchers (and many writers of statistics textbooks). The result of these misunderstandings makes a real practical difference to what research is conducted and how it is interpreted. It makes a real practical difference not just to researchers but to anybody who is a consumer of research. It makes a difference, therefore, to just about everybody.

The material of this chapter illustrates the relevance of understanding core philosophical issues. Fisher (1935, p. 2) said, 'The statistician cannot excuse himself from the duty of getting his head clear on the principles of scientific inference, but equally no other thinking person can avoid a like obligation.'

A common retort to the use of statistics is 'there are lies – damned lies – and statistics' (a phrase apparently coined by Leonard Courtney in 1895[1]). The latter category certainly includes untruths based on the misuse of statistics *but also* valuable knowledge that could only be gained by statistical inference. The misuse of statistics does not make statistics bad; it makes it important for people to understand how to use statistics. But what is the appropriate way of making statistical inferences?

In this chapter we will clarify the common confusions concerning the Neyman–Pearson logic and discuss common objections. The issues will be especially highlighted by showing alternative ways statistics could be done – the Bayesian and likelihood approaches – described in the next two chapters. We will go through key arguments motivating each approach.

This chapter presumes that you have had some exposure to significance testing. You should understand the following concepts before reading the chapter: standard deviation, standard error, null hypothesis, distribution, normal distribution, population, sample and significance. The issues we will talk about apply to any significance test; we will use the *t*-test as an example and I will presume you understand what a *t*-test is and have used one before. If you have not come across these concepts before, consult an elementary statistics book; for example, Wright (2002). If you have come across these concepts before, you might like to revise the logic of a *t*-test, from whichever book you have, before continuing.

To limber up with, consider the example in Box 3.1 and answer the questions. We will return to the answers later in the chapter.

---

1. See http://www.york.ac.uk/depts/maths/histstat/lies.htm. In 1924 the phrase was mistakenly attributed to Disraeli by Mark Twain.

Box 3.1 Limbering up

You compare the means of your control and experimental groups (20 subjects in each sample). Your result is $t(38) = 2.7$, $p = 0.01$. Please decide for each of the statements below whether it is 'true' or 'false'. Keep a record of your decisions.

(i) You have absolutely disproved the null hypothesis (that there is no difference between the population means).

(ii) You have found the probability of the null hypothesis being true.

(iii) You have absolutely proved your experimental hypothesis (that there is a difference between the population means).

(iv) You can deduce the probability of the experimental hypothesis being true.

(v) You know that if you decided to reject the null hypothesis, the probability that you are making the wrong decision.

(vi) You have a reliable experimental finding in the sense that if, hypothetically, the experiment were repeated a great number of times, you would obtain a significant result on 99 % of occasions.

From Oakes (1986)

Fisher, Neyman and Pearson

Many of the techniques and concepts we use in statistics come from the British genius, Sir Ronald Fisher (1890–1962). At the beginning of last century he coined the terms 'null hypothesis' and 'significance', urged the systematic distinction between sample and population, introduced degrees of freedom into statistics, suggested a p of 0.05 as an arbitrary but convenient level to judge a result significant (a convention that has since become sacrosanct), urged random assignment to conditions, and proposed many techniques, including the analysis of variance. These are just some of his achievements you may recognize; the true extent of his accomplishments runs even deeper. Fisher created much of what we users of statistics now recognize as statistical practice.

In 1947, Fisher gave this advice to young scientists on BBC radio:

A scientific career is peculiar in some ways. Its raison d'être is the increase of natural knowledge. Occasionally, therefore, an increase in natural knowledge occurs. But this is tactless, and feelings are hurt. For in some degree it is inevitable that views previously expounded are shown to be either obsolete or false. Most people, I think, can recognise this and take it in good part if what they have been teaching for 10 years or so comes to need a little revision; but some undoubtedly take it hard, as a blow to their amour proper, or even as an invasion of the territory they have come to think of exclusively their own, and they must react with the same ferocity as we can see in the robins and chaffinches these spring days when they resent an intrusion into their little territories. I do not think anything can be done about it. It is inherent in the nature of the profession; but a young scientist must be warned and advised that when he has a jewel to offer for the enrichment of mankind some certainly will wish to turn and rend him

(quoted in Salsburg, 2002, p. 51)

Despite Fisher's enormous contributions, it was the Polish mathematician Jerzy Neyman (1894–1981) and the British statistician Egon Pearson (1895–1980) who provided a firm consistent logical basis to hypothesis testing and statistical inference, starting with a series of papers in the 1920s and 1930s. It was not a jewel that Fisher appreciated, and nor did he revise any of his lectures in the light of it. Nonetheless, the work of Neyman and Pearson transformed the field of mathematical statistics and defined the logic that journal editors in psychology, medicine, biology and other disciplines came to demand of the papers they publish.

Egon's father, Karl Pearson (as in the Pearson correlation coefficient), held the Galton Chair of Statistics at University College London. When Karl retired, his department split into two, with Egon Pearson becoming Head of the Department of Applied Statistics, and Fisher, for some years, Head of the Department of Eugenics. Despite being in the same building, Fisher avoided any contact with Egon Pearson. Neyman, briefly a lecturer at University College London after leaving Poland, left to set up a statistical laboratory at University of California at Berkeley in 1938, a lab that would become under Neyman's leadership one of the most prestigious in the world. Fisher made repeated attempts in print to rend Neyman, but it was Neyman's philosophy of statistical inference that largely prevailed.

Probability

We start by considering what probability means. The meaning of probability we choose determines what we can do with statistics, as will become clear over the course of this chapter and next. The proper way of interpreting probability remains controversial, so there is still debate over what can be achieved with statistics. The Neyman–Pearson approach follows from one particular interpretation of probability; the Bayesian approach considered in the next chapter follows from another.

Interpretations often start with a set of axioms that probabilities must follow. The first axioms were formulated by Christiaan Huygens in 1657, though these considered probability in only one narrow application, gambling. The Russian polymath Andrei Kolmogorov (1903–1887) put the mathematical field of probability into respectable order in 1933 by showing that the key mathematical results concerning probability follow from a simple set of axioms. Box 3.2 lists a standard set of probability axioms.

Box 3.2 *The axioms of probability*

For a set of events A, B, …

1. $P(A) \geq 0$
   All probabilities must be greater than or equal to zero.
2. If S refers to one or other of the events happening then $P(S)=1$
   The probability of at least one event happening is 1.
3. $P(A \text{ or } B)=P(A) + P(B)$ if A and B are mutually exclusive.
   A and B are mutually exclusive if they cannot both happen.
4. $P(A \text{ and } B)=P(A) * P(B|A)$

where $P(B|A)$ is 'the probability of B given A'. Axiom (4) is often presented as a definition of $P(B|A)$ rather than an axiom as such. The next chapter will explain and make use of axiom (4).

Probabilities are things that follow the axioms of probability. But what sorts of things? How could the abstract mathematical entity picked out by the axioms make contact with the real world? We will broadly distinguish two interpretations of probability: the subjective and the objective. According to the subjective interpretation, a probability is a degree of conviction in a belief. For example, if I say it will probably snow tomorrow, it means I have a certain conviction in my belief that it will snow. (The "events" in Box 3.2 are statements I believe in to various degrees. For example, $P(A)$ is the extent to which I believe in statement A.) By contrast, objective interpretations locate probability not in the mind but in the world.

Sometimes people say we only need to use probabilities in situations where we are ignorant; if we could know enough to make exact predictions, we would not need to talk in terms of probabilities. That is, probabilities just reflect our subjective states, our states of knowledge or ignorance. If I knew the exact state of nature today in nanoscopic detail, I would not need to talk about the probability of it snowing tomorrow. I would just talk about whether it would snow or not. If I knew the precise velocity and position of every gas molecule in a box, I would not need to calculate the probability of a molecule hitting a wall to work out the gas pressure: I would just work it out from summing all the molecules actually hitting it. Popper (1982) argued that such subjective interpretations of probability did not apply in science. The statistical laws producing gas pressure, or governing why gas will escape the box when opened but not spontaneously return to it, are nothing to do with our knowledge or ignorance of the locations of particular molecules. It is irrelevant whether or not we know what every molecule is doing; the statistical laws apply regardless. According to the objective interpretation of probability, probabilities are not in the mind but in the world. It is an objective fact of the world that gas molecules have a certain probability of hitting a wall, or escaping through an opening. Such objective probabilities exist independently of our states of knowledge. Probabilities are to be *discovered* by examining the world, not by reflecting on what we know or on how much we believe. If I want to know whether a coin has a probability of $\frac{1}{2}$ of producing heads, I need to examine the coin and how it is tossed, and hopefully discover the relevant probability.

The most influential objective interpretation of probability is the long-run relative frequency interpretation of von Mises (1928/1957). A probability is a relative frequency. For example, if I toss a coin, the probability of heads coming up is the proportion of times it produces heads. But it cannot be the proportion of times it produces heads in any finite number of tosses. If I toss the coin 10 times and it lands heads 7 times, the probability of a head is not therefore 0.7. A fair coin could easily produce 7 heads in 10 tosses. The relative frequency must refer therefore to a hypothetical infinite number of tosses. The hypothetical infinite set of tosses (or events, more generally) is called the *reference class* or *collective*. The collective might be, for example, the set of all potential tosses of this coin using a certain tossing mechanism – for example, my right arm, given the command sent to it to throw the coin. Because the long-run relative frequency is a property of all the events in the collective, it follows that a probability applies to a collective, not to any single event. That is, I cannot talk about the probability of the next toss being a head. The next toss, as a singular event, does not have a probability; only the collective of tosses has a probability. The next toss is just heads or tails.

One way to see clearly that probabilities do not apply to singular events is to note that a single event could be a member of different collectives. Take a particular coin toss. It lands heads. On the one hand, that event is part of a collective defined by my right arm repeatedly given the instruction 'toss the coin!'. For this collective, the precise way my arm moves on each trial is variable, and the probability of heads is $\frac{1}{2}$. On the one hand, that same toss is part of another collective involving events with a more precise description: My right arm moving in a very precise way, with wind conditions being very precisely so, such that every toss results in heads. For this collective, the long-run relative frequency of heads is 1. The event, part of both collectives, does not have a long-run relative frequency. A singular event does not have a probability, only collectives do.

Consider another example. What is the probability I will get cancer? If the reference class or collective is the set of all men, we can look at the proportion of men with cancer. If the collective is men who do not smoke, we can look at the proportion of non-smoking males who get cancer. I am part of both collectives, but each has a different probability associated with it. Objective probabilities do not apply to single cases. They also do not apply to the truth of hypotheses. A hypothesis is simply true or false, just as a single event either occurs or does not. A hypothesis is not a collective, it therefore does not have an objective probability.

Data and hypotheses

Let us symbolize some data by D and a hypothesis by H. We can talk about $P(D|H)$, the probability of obtaining some data given a hypothesis; for example $P($'getting 5 threes in 25 rolls of a die'$|$'I have a fair die'$)$. We can set up a relevant collective. Each event is 'throwing a fair die 25 times and observing the number of threes'. That is one event. Consider a hypothetical collective of an infinite number of such events. We can then determine the proportion of such events in which the number of threes is 5. That is a meaningful probability we can calculate. However, we *cannot* talk about $P(H|D)$, for example $P($'I have a fair die'$|$'I obtained 5 threes in 25 rolls'$)$, the probability that the hypothesis that I have a fair die is true, given I obtained 5 threes in 25 rolls. What is the collective? There is none. The hypothesis is simply true or false.

$P(H|D)$ is the inverse[2] of the conditional probability $p(D|H)$. Inverting conditional probabilities makes a big difference. For example, consider

$P($'dying within two years'$|$'head bitten off by shark'$) = 1$

If you take all the people who have had their head bitten off, clean off, by a shark, and then see if they are dead 2 years later, you will find that they all are. The probability is 1.

$P($'head was bitten off by shark'$|$'died in the last two years'$) \sim 0$

By contrast, if you went to all the places where the dead are kept, the morgue, the graveyard, bottom of the sea and so on, dug up all the bodies of people who had died in the last 2 years, and found how many were missing heads because of a shark bite, you would find practically none were. The probability is very close to zero.

In general, $P(A|B)$ can have a very different value from $P(B|A)$. If ever you feel doubtful about that, consider the shark example.

If you know $P(D|H)$, it does not mean you know what $P(H|D)$ is. There are two reasons for this. One is that inverse conditional probabilities can have very different values. The other is that, in any case, it is meaningless to assign an objective probability to a hypothesis.

---

2. Really it is just one sort of inverse; taking the reciprocal of $p(D|H)$ would be another, for example.

Hypothesis testing: α

Neyman and Pearson subscribed to an objective relative frequency interpretation of probability. Thus, statistics cannot tell us how much to believe a certain hypothesis. What we can do, according to Neyman and Pearson, is set up decision rules for certain behaviours – accepting or rejecting hypotheses – such that in following those rules in the long run we will not often be wrong. We can work out what the error rates are for certain decision procedures and we can choose procedures that control the long-run error rates at acceptable levels.

The decision rules work by setting up two contrasting hypotheses. One, H_0, is called the null hypothesis. For example, H_0 could be μ_1 (population mean blood pressure given drug) $= \mu_2$ (population mean blood pressure given placebo). The alternative hypothesis is symbolized as H_1 and could be $\mu_1 < (\mu_2 - 10)$ (i.e. that the drug reduces blood pressure by at least 10 units).[3] The null hypothesis need not be the hypothesis of no difference (e.g. $\mu_1 = \mu_2$ or in other words that $\mu_1 - \mu_2 = 0$), it could be a hypothesis concerning a specific difference (e.g. $\mu_1 - \mu_2 = 5$) or a band of differences (e.g. $\mu_1 > \mu_2$). The alternative could also be a hypothesis of some specific difference as well as being a band. The only difference between the null and the alternative is that the null is the one most costly to reject falsely. For example, a drug company may find it more costly to bring a drug forward for further testing (for toxicity, etc.) if the drug is actually useless than to fail to detect that the drug is useful.[4] In that case, the null would be the hypothesis of no difference.

There is a convention in statistics that 'parameters', which are properties of *populations*, are symbolized with Greek letters, like μ (mu). 'Statistics', which are summaries of *sample* measurements, are symbolized by Roman letters, like M. M could be, for example, the mean of your sample. The null and alternative hypotheses are about population values (parameters); they are not about particular samples. We wish to use our samples to make inferences about the population. Make sure in formulating your null and alternative hypotheses you do not refer to sample properties, just population properties.

We collect data on the blood pressure of people given either a drug or a placebo. Let us call the sample mean blood pressure with drug M_d and the sample mean blood pressure with placebo M_p. Call the standard error of difference SE. Thus, we have $t = (M_d - M_p)/SE$.

In order to calculate any probabilities, we need a collective or reference class. A collective can be constructed by assuming H_0, and imagining an infinite number of experiments, calculating t each time. Each t is an event in the collective. The distribution of the infinite number of ts in the collective can be plotted, as in figure 3.1.

Next we work out a 'rejection region'; that is, values of t so extreme (as extreme or more extreme than a critical value, t_c) that the probability of obtaining a t in that region is equal to some specified value, α (alpha). If our obtained t is as extreme or more extreme than the critical value, we reject H_0. Figure 3.1 illustrates the probability distribution of t. The shaded area is the rejection region. The area under the whole curve is 1 and the area of the rejection region is α; this just means the probability of obtaining a t in the rejection region is α if the null hypothesis is true. You may know α by another name; it is just the level of significance

---

3. '<' means 'less than'. That should be easy to remember: The more narrow end is always on the side of the smaller element.
4. This cost–benefit analysis is unlikely; normally a drug company would regard as more important that they did not miss a new effective drug rather than they brought a useless one forward to the next stage of testing. In this case, the hypothesis of 'no difference' should NOT be H_0 by the strict logic of the Neyman–Pearson approach. But which way round one names the hypotheses does not really matter in the end, so long as the relative error rates are controlled appropriately. So if H_0 is the hypothesis of no difference, in what follows β should actually be kept below α if the drug company regards Type II errors as worse than Type I errors. Type I, Type II and α and β are explained in the text that follows.

Figure 3.1

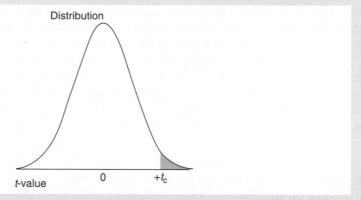

Distribution

t-value   0 $+t_c$

The probability distribution of t. The shaded area is a predetermined rejection region.

we set in advance. 'Significance' is Fisher's term; Neyman preferred the term 'size of the test' (the bigger the shaded area, the bigger the 'size' of the test). The term 'size' never caught on, so we will use the name 'significance', which is now universally used (though maybe Neyman and Pearson introduced the term 'size' to escape the Fisherian connotations of the term 'significance'. We will return to the difference between Fisher and Neyman–Pearson later). By convention α is typically set at 0.05. Assuming the null hypothesis is true, if we run an indefinite number of experiments following this decision procedure, in the long run we will reject the null hypothesis in 5 % (i.e. α) of the experiments.

Put another way, for a given experiment we can calculate $p = P$('getting t as extreme or more extreme than obtained'$|H_0$), which is a form of $P(D|H)$. This p is the 'p-value' or simply 'p' in statistical computer output. If p is less than α, the level of significance we have decided in advance (say 0.05), we reject H_0. By following this rule, we know in the long run that when H_0 is actually true, we will conclude it false only 5 % of the time. In this procedure, the p-value has no meaning in itself; it is just a convenient mechanical procedure for accepting or rejecting a hypothesis, given the current widespread use of computer output. Such output produces p-values as a matter of course.

α is an objective probability, a relative long-run frequency. It is the proportion of errors of a certain type we will make in the long run, if we follow the above procedure and the null hypothesis is in fact true. Conversely, neither α nor our calculated p tells us how probable the null hypothesis is; they are not $P(H|D)$, as we will now illustrate in a concrete example.

I have a coin I know is biased such that P(heads) $= 0.6$. Imagine I have some very reliable way of knowing it is biased. Maybe the metallurgist who made it is an expert in making coins biased to a specified amount and he has tested it on a million trials to be sure. He gives it to me. I throw it six times and it lands heads three times. We test a null hypothesis H_0 that P(head) $= 0.5$. We will set α as 0.05 as per convention. Our p-value is P('getting data as extreme or more extreme as three heads'$|H_0$). Any possible outcome is more extreme than the one we obtained; getting four heads out of six is more extreme than getting three out of six. Getting four tails is more extreme than getting three tails out of six. In fact, all possible outcomes are as extreme or more extreme than the one we obtained. Thus, $p = 1$, greater than 0.05. Non-significant! But that does not change our conviction that the coin is biased – we know it is biased. Indeed, getting three heads out of six tosses is pretty likely, given a coin with a P(heads) of 0.6. The probability of the null hypothesis (i.e. that the coin is fair) is not 1. Our p-value, a form of $P(D|H_0)$ (and equal to 1 in this case), does not tell us $P(H_0|D)$ (we know H_0 to be false; that is, our subjective probability $P(H_0|D)$ is 0). The p-value does not tell us the probability of the null being true. (If your statistics textbook tells you otherwise – and many do – I suggest you get a new statistics textbook.)

Maybe when the metallurgist gave me the coin, and I threw it six times, it landed heads four times. That is a sample proportion of 4/6 or 0.67, closer to P(heads) of 0.6, the true value, than 0.5, the value we happen to be treating as the null. Our p-value, that is the probability of obtaining a sample proportion as extreme or more extreme than 0.67, given the null hypothesis is true, can be calculated to be 0.69. p is greater than 0.05, so the result is once again non-significant! The null is not rejected by our decision procedure. But clearly, the probability of the null hypothesis is not 0.69. We know the null is false. We just did not throw the coin enough times to have a powerful test.

Our procedure tells us our long-term error rates BUT it does not tell us which particular hypotheses are true or false or assign any of the hypotheses a probability. Remember objective probabilities are properties of a collective, not an individual event. We cannot assign an objective probability to THIS experiment, and we especially cannot assign one to any hypothesis tested in the experiment. All we know are our long-run error rates.

Hypothesis testing: α and β

α is the long-term error rate for one type of error: Saying the null is false when it is true. But there are two ways of making an error with the decision procedure. Table 3.1 shows the situation. We divide the world into two: Either the null hypothesis is true or it is false. We make a binary decision: Accept the null (and reject the alternative) hypothesis or reject the null (and accept the alternative). We are right when the null is true and we accept it and when the null is false and we reject it. A Type I error is when the null is true and we reject it. In the long run, when the null is true, we will make a Type I error in α proportion of our decisions. We can also make an error by accepting the null when it is false. This is called a Type II error and is illustrated by the coin tossing example just given. In that example, the coin was biased, but the results were non-significant. In the long run, when the null is false, the proportion of times we nonetheless accept it is labelled β (beta). That is, $\alpha = P(\text{rejecting } H_0|H_0)$ and $\beta = P(\text{accepting } H_0|H_0 \text{ false})$. Both α and β should be controlled at acceptable levels.

Table 3.2 illustrates an imaginary case in which 4000 true null hypotheses and 1000 false null hypotheses are tested. In practice, of course, we never know how many of the null hypotheses we test are true and how many are false. What α rate and what β rate does the table illustrate?

Table 3.1 Two ways of making an error

	State of world	
Decision	**H_0 true**	**H_0 false**
Accept H_0		Type II error
Reject H_0	Type I error	

Table 3.2 A world in which 80 % of the nulls tested are in fact true		
	State of world	
Decision	H_0 **true**	H_0 **false**
Accept H_0	3800	500
Reject H_0	200	500
Totals	4000	1000

Sometimes significance or α is defined simply as 'the probability of a Type I error', but this is wrong. α is specifically the probability (long-run relative frequency) of a Type I error *when the null hypothesis is true*. So to work out α from Table 3.2, we must consider only the cases when the null hypothesis was true. The proportion of Type I errors shown when the null hypothesis is true is $200/4000 = 0.05$. That is, the researchers used the conventional 5 % level for all their tests. Another meaning of 'the probability of a Type I error' could be the probability of a Type I error *when we have rejected the null*. This probability is determined by considering only the cases where we have rejected the null (i.e. the $200 + 500 = 700$ cases shown in the "*Reject H_0*" row). The proportion of Type I errors that occur when we have rejected the null is $200/700 = 29$ %. This illustrates that strictly using a significance level of 5 % does not guarantee that only 5 % of all published significant results are in error (Oakes, 1986)!

The β illustrated in Table 3.2 is $500/1000 = 0.5$. Notice how β can be very different from α. Controlling one does not mean you have controlled the other. *Power* is defined as $1 - \beta$. That is, power is $P(\text{reject } H_0 | H_0 \text{ false})$, the probability of detecting an effect, given an effect really exists in the population.

In the Neyman–Pearson approach, one decides on acceptable α and β levels before an experiment is run. By convention, α is generally set at 0.05. If one thinks Type II errors are as important as Type I, one would also set β at 0.05 as well (i.e. power $= 0.95$). If one thought Type II errors were not quite as important, one could set β at, for example, 0.10. How does one control β at the level you wish?

In order to control β, you need to:

(1) Estimate the size of effect (e.g. mean difference) you think is interesting, given your theory is true. For example, if a drug company is testing different drugs for their ability to reduce blood pressure, they may not be interested in a drug (/dose) that reduced blood pressure by only 1 mmHg (millimeter of mercury). They need to detect drug doses that reduce blood pressure by at least 5 mmHg. The drug example is a practical one; we can say we want to detect an effect of at least 5 mmHg because we know what use we want to put the drug to. If you are testing a psychological theory, the theory may not seem to say what size effect is minimally interesting. The theory might just seem to say one condition will be faster than another. One way of getting a fix on what size difference would be meaningful is to see what size difference has in the past been explained by this theory in other contexts or by similar theories. What would you think if you found one condition differed from the other by only 1 ms? If previous applications of this or similar theories were for effects of 10–15 ms, then other things being equal, the theory should predict an effect of about 10 ms in this new context. You may decide a difference a little less than 10 ms would be acceptable. If a 5 ms effect would be *just* acceptable to you as the size of difference you would expect on the theory, then that is your minimal meaningful difference needed for a power analysis. Our

alternative hypothesis becomes $\mu_1 - \mu_2 > 5\,\text{ms}$ (the null is $\mu_1 - \mu_2 = 0\,\text{ms}$). In general, the bigger the minimal effect you are interested in detecting, then the more power you have for detecting it, other things being equal.

(2) Estimate the amount of noise your data will have. The probability of detecting an effect depends not just on how big the effect is, but how much noise there is through which you are trying to detect the effect. In a between-participants design, for example, the noise is provided by the within-group variance. The greater the population variance, the less the power you have. You can use the variances from past similar studies to estimate the population variance in your case. Or you can run a pilot study with your procedures to get an estimate.

Having determined (1) and (2) above, you can use standard statistics textbooks to tell you how many participants you need to run to keep β at 0.05 (equivalently, to keep power at 0.95) (e.g. Howell, 2001, contains a chapter on how to calculate power and determine sample sizes for t-tests; see Murphy and Myors, 2004, for power analysis for many different types of design). The more participants you run, the greater your power. Typically people are astonished at how many participants they need to achieve decent power, say 0.95. A typical reaction is to reduce the power of the study first to maybe 0.90, then finding the number of participants still too much, reducing further to 0.80, and settling for that.

Power in practice

Most studies do not systematically use power calculations to determine the number of participants. But they should. Strict application of the Neyman–Pearson logic means setting the risks of both Type I and II errors (α and β) in advance. Many researchers are extremely worried about Type I errors but allow Type II errors to go uncontrolled. Ignoring the systematic control of Type II errors leads to inappropriate judgments about what results mean and what research should be done next, as we will discuss next. First have a go at the exercise in Box 3.3; then the exercise in Box 3.4 (both based on Oakes, 1986).

Box 3.3 Picking a sample size

Smith and Jones, working in New York, USA, publish an experiment on a new method for reducing prejudice, with 20 participants in each of two groups, experimental and control. They obtain a significant difference in prejudice scores between the two groups, significant by t-test, $p = 0.02$.

You are based in Sussex, UK, and decide to follow up their work. Before adding modifications to their procedure, you initially attempt as exact a replication as you can in Sussex.

How many subjects should you run?

Box 3.4 Interpreting null results

Presume that like Smith and Jones you ran 20 participants in each group. You obtain an insignificant result in the same direction, $t = 1.24$ ($p = 0.22$)

Box 3.4 *continued*

Should you

(a) try to find an explanation for the difference between the two studies?
(b) regard the Smith and Jones result as now thrown into doubt; you should reduce your confidence in the effectiveness of their method for overcoming prejudice?
(c) run more participants? (how many?)

Many researchers in this sort of situation instinctively respond with both reactions (a) and (b). But assuming the population effect was estimated exactly by the American study and the within-group variance was exactly as estimated by the American study, the power of replicating with the same number of subjects as the original study was only 0.67. That is, even if the same effect was there in the Sussex as American population, the decision procedure would fail to detect it fully a 1/3 of the time. With such a large probability, failing to replicate is uninformative. There is no justification for either trying to invent explanations for the difference in outcomes of the two studies or for thinking that the original findings have been thrown into doubt. (On the second point, note that if the data from the two studies were combined, and analysed together, we have $t(78) = 2.59$, $p = 0.011$.)

For this example, the power provided by different sample sizes are as follows:

Power	N per group
0.67	20
0.8	26
0.9	37
0.95	44

A sensible number of participants to use in a replication of this particular study would be around 40. That is, given the estimates of the original study, if you used 40 participants and accepted the null whenever your t-value was less than the critical value, you would only falsely accept the null about 5% of the time.

You are now in a position to consider what would happen if an original study obtained a significant result, with $p = 0.05$ (or 0.0499 if you like). They used an N of 20, and you replicate the experiment with a sample also of 20. Assuming *there really is* an effect of exactly the size found in the original experiment and the population variance had been exactly estimated by the original study, what is the probability that you will also obtain a significant result?

If in your sample you also happen – miraculously – to obtain a mean sample difference exactly equal to the population one and a sample variance exactly equal to the population one, your obtained t-value would be exactly equal to the critical value, just as the original team obtained. You have exactly even odds that your mean difference will be a little bit more rather than a little bit less than the population mean difference. If your mean difference is a little bit more, your t-value will be slightly higher than the critical value; but if your mean difference is a little bit less, your obtained t-value will be a little bit less than the critical value. Similarly, you have about even odds that your variance will be a little bit more or a little bit less than the population value. If your variance is a little bit more than the population value, your t-value will be a little bit less than the critical value; but if your variance is a little bit less than the population value, your t-value will be a little bit more than the critical value.

Box 3.5   Reviewing a set of studies

You read a review of studies looking at whether meditation reduces depression. One hundred studies have been run and 50 are significant in the right direction and the remainder are non-significant.

What should you conclude?

If the null hypothesis were true, how many studies would be significant? How many significant in the right direction?

You are sitting on a knife edge. You have a 50% probability of obtaining a significant result. That is, you have a power of 50%.

In reviewing the 100 studies mentioned in Box 3.5, some reviewers will be tempted to think that the result is thrown in doubt by all the non-significant studies. How often have you seen an author disputing an effect because she can count as many null findings as significant findings? But if the null hypothesis were true one would expect 5% of studies to be significant. That is what a significance of 5% means. There can be a 'file drawer problem'; that is, not all non-significant results may become generally known about, because the experimenter thinks, 'I cannot publish this; I will just file it in my cabinet'. Even so, if the null hypothesis were true, one would expect an equal number of studies showing a significant effect in one direction as the other. Finding 50 studies significant in the right direction (and none in the wrong direction) is highly unlikely to happen by chance alone. The pattern shown in Box 3.5 is just what you would expect if an effect really existed and the average power of the studies was 50% – a power sadly typical of much research.

The process of combining groups of studies together to obtain overall tests of significance (or to estimate values or calculate confidence intervals) is called *meta-analysis* (see Rosenthal, 1993, for an introduction, and Hunter and Schmidt, 2004, for a thorough overview). A convenient and easy technique you can use when you have run a series of studies addressing the same question with the same dependent variable is create a data file with all the experiments in; then test for the effect using all the data.[5] You might have six studies all non-significant but when combined together they are significant! (On reflection that should not be very surprising. You can put it the other way round. Imagine you had a study that was *just* significant at the 0.05 level. If you split it into six equal parts, would you expect any part to be significant on its own?) A set of null results does not mean you should accept the null; they may indicate that you should reject the null. To take a simple example, let us say for each of these six non-significant studies the effect was in the right direction. The probability of obtaining six effects in the right direction assuming either direction is equally likely is $1/2^6 = 1/64$ on a one-tailed test, or $1/32$ on a two-tailed test, $p < 0.05$ in both cases. That is, those six non-significant studies allow one to reject the null!

The situations we have just considered should convince you of the importance of power. To summarize, if your study has low power, getting a null result tells you nothing in itself. You would expect a null result whether or not the null hypothesis was true. In the Neyman–Pearson approach, you set power at a high level in designing the experiment, before you run it. *Then you are entitled to accept the null hypothesis when you obtain a null result*. In following

---

5. You should also put in 'experiment' as a factor and test if the effect interacts with experiment.

this procedure you will make errors at a small controlled rate, a rate you have decided in advance is acceptable to you.

Once you understand power, the need for considering it is self-evident; it may seem strange that so many researchers seem so willful in disregarding it. Why do people ignore power, when it has been part of the orthodox logic for over 70 years? Oakes (1986) suggests that it is because many people interpret the p-value as telling them about the probability of the null (and logically hence the alternative) hypothesis. Bayesian statisticians have developed techniques for actually assigning probabilities to hypotheses in coherent ways. Many people interpret significance levels in a Bayesian way, and a Bayesian has no need for the concept of power. Once I know the probability of my hypothesis being true, what else do I need to know? But Neyman–Pearson methods are not Bayesian, and confusing the two leads to mistakes in conducting research. In the next chapter we will discuss the Bayesian approach.

Now we will return to the questions in Box 3.1, here repeated as Box 3.6. Have a go at the questions again and compare your new answers with your original answers.

Box 3.6   Revisiting Box 1

You compare the means of your control and experimental groups (20 subjects in each sample).

Your result is $t(38) = 2.7$, $p = 0.01$. Please decide for each of the statements below whether it is 'true' or 'false'. Keep a record of your decisions.

 (i) You have absolutely disproved the null hypothesis (that there is no difference between the population means).
 (ii) You have found the probability of the null hypothesis being true.
 (iii) You have absolutely proved your experimental hypothesis (that there is a difference between the population means).
 (iv) You can deduce the probability of the experimental hypothesis being true.
 (v) You know that if you decided to reject the null hypothesis, the probability that you are making the wrong decision.
 (vi) You have a reliable experimental finding in the sense that if, hypothetically, the experiment were repeated a great number of times, you would obtain a significant result on 99 % of occasions.

From Oakes (1986)

Statistics never allows absolute proof or disproof, so most people are happy to reject – correctly – options (i) and (iii). Options (ii) and (iv) may have been initially tempting, but hopefully you see now that as they refer to the probability of hypotheses they cannot be correct (an objective probability refers to a collective of events, not the truth of a hypothesis). Option (v) is a sneaky one and often catches people out; but notice it refers to the probability of a single decision being correct; thus, option (v) cannot be correct (an objective probability does not refer to a single event). Many people, initially, think option (vi) is right. But option (vi) is a description of power, not significance. As Oakes (1986) comments, no wonder people ignore power if they think they already have it in the notion of significance! In fact, none of the options are correct. Oakes put these questions to 70 researchers with at least 2 years of research experience, and including full professors. Only two researchers showed they had a sound understanding of the concept of statistical significance. I dare say not too much has changed in the two decades since Oakes conducted his research.

Sensitivity

Fisher talked loosely about the sensitivity of an experiment; Neyman and Pearson gave precision to one way of specifying sensitivity, namely power. Also both Fisher and Neyman introduced a notion of confidence intervals (which is Neyman's term; his term – and logic for them – stuck), discussed later. Sensitivity can be determined in three ways: power, confidence intervals and finding an effect significantly different from another reference one. We will discuss confidence intervals later. Here is an important methodological maxim which is often ignored: *Whenever you find a null result and it is interesting to you that the result is null, you should always indicate the sensitivity of your analysis*. If in getting a null result you fail to replicate someone's study, you must provide some indication of the sensitivity of your study. For example, you could calculate the power of your procedure for detecting the size of effect the original authors found.[6] Let us say, you find a significant effect of ginseng on the reaction time of men, and in a subsequent study using only women you find a null result. From this pattern of result you cannot conclude that ginseng affects men and women differently. Maybe you had a power of 50% for detecting the effect of ginseng and so found an effect in one study but not another, a success rate which is just to be expected. If, however, you showed that the effect of ginseng on men was significantly different from the effect on women, you have demonstrated a differential effect of ginseng. Similarly, if you found a correlation between two variables was significant in one condition but not another that does not mean the two correlations can be regarded as different. Perhaps you had low power. If, however, a test of the difference between the correlations was significant, you can conclude that the correlations differed. Further, before you could accept the null result in the condition that was null, you would need to show you had appropriate power to pick a minimally interesting effect.

Stopping rules

The conditions under which you will stop collecting data for a study define the *stopping rule* you use. A common stopping rule is to run as many participants as is traditional in that area. The trouble with this rule is that it does not guarantee that power is controlled at any particular value. Another stopping rule one might follow is to continue running until the test is significant. The problem with this rule is that even assuming the null hypothesis is true, you are guaranteed to obtain a 'significant' result eventually if you are prepared to continue collecting data long enough! That may sound astonishing, but it is true. So this procedure, although having a power of 1, also has an α of 1! You are guaranteed to obtain a 'significant' result eventually, whether or not the null hypothesis is true. Running until you have a significant result is not a good stopping rule. You may decide to test for 'significance' with a t-test after every participant, stopping if $p < 0.05$ or until 100 participants had been reached. Then the α would actually be 0.39, not 0.05 at all.

The standard Neyman–Pearson stopping rule is to use power calculations in advance of running the study to determine how many participants should be run to control power at a

6. Some statistical packages report power for effects along with their significance. If the power is calculated assuming the population effect size and noise level that is estimated in that very sample, such power calculations are not informative. If the *p*-value is less than 0.05, the power will be less than 0.5. You want to calculate power based on the minimal effect size *you are interested in detecting* or maybe the effect size found by prior researchers.

predetermined level. Then run that number of subjects. Both α and β can then be controlled at known acceptable levels. Another legitimate stopping rule involves the use of confidence intervals, which we will describe later.

A development of the standard Neyman–Pearson approach is to consider sequential stopping rules. These are particularly important in clinical trials but can be used in any domain. In clinical trials it may be unethical to continue a study when there is strong evidence that one treatment is more effective than another. In sequential testing you can look at your data several times and decide to stop collecting data at any of those times and still control α at 0.05. If each time you looked you tested nominally at the 0.05 level, α would actually be greater than 0.05 because you have given yourself several chances to reject H_0 and stop. So to control α at 0.05, single tests need to be conducted at less than the 0.05 level. For example, if you decide in advance you will check five times at equal intervals, each test can be conducted at a nominal significance level of 0.016 and overall α is controlled at 0.05. Armitage, et al. (2002, pp. 615–623) provide an introduction and further references, discussing various sequential schemes that also control power.

Multiple testing

In the Neyman–Pearson approach it is essential to know the collective or reference class for which we are calculating our objective probabilities α and β. The relevant collective is defined by a testing procedure applied an indefinite number of times. For example, 'Collect data and calculate the t-value at five points in time; reject H_0 whenever any of the ts individually is greater than 2.41' is a test procedure defining a collective and we can make sure this procedure has definite values of α and β. Another collective is defined by the procedure, 'Calculate the difference between the control group and each of the three experimental groups; reject any of the three corresponding null hypotheses whenever the t is greater than 2'. If this procedure were applied an indefinite number of times where all three H_0s were true, how often would we reject one or more of the H_0? In other words, when we perform a set or 'family' of tests, how often would we make a Type I error? If we conduct one t-test, the probability that it is significant by chance alone is 0.05 if we test at the 0.05 level. If we conduct two t-tests, the probability that at least 1 is significant by chance alone is slightly less than 0.10. If we conduct three t-tests, the probability that at least one is significant by chance alone is slightly less than 0.15. In the Neyman–Pearson approach, in order to control overall Type I error ('familywise error-rate'), if we perform a number of tests we need to test each one at a stricter level of significance in order to keep overall α at 0.05. There are numerous corrections, but the easiest one to remember is Bonferroni. If you perform k tests, then conduct each individual test at the $0.05/k$ level of significance and overall α will be no higher than 0.05. So with the three tests mentioned, each would have to have a p-value less than $0.05/3 = 0.017$ to be accepted as significant.

A researcher might mainly want to look at one particular comparison, but threw in some other conditions out of curiosity while going to the effort of recruiting, running and paying participants. She may feel it unfair if the main comparison has to be tested at the 0.017 level just because she collected data on other conditions but need not have. The solution is that if you *planned* one particular comparison in advance then you can test at the 0.05 level, because that one was picked out in advance of seeing the data. But the other tests must involve a correction, like Bonferroni. A collective defined by 'Calculate three t-tests; if any one of them are significant at the 5 % level, reject H_0 for that one' will involve an α of about 0.15. That is because you can pick and choose which test to accept AFTER the data have been collected; such tests are called *post hoc* ('after the fact'). Thus, post hoc tests require a correction of the nominal significance level; single planned tests do not. Even in the post hoc case, the family of tests is decided in advance of looking at the data; that is, you cannot just look and see which three tests are most significant and choose these for your family. That would defeat the object. The family is chosen in advance.

Fisherian inference

Despite Fisher's contribution to statistics, it was the Neyman–Pearson approach that dominated statistical theory. Neyman provided an internally coherent logic for developing mathematical statistics based on objective probability as a long-run relative frequency. Fisher had a notion of probability neither clearly objective nor subjective, 'fiducial probability'; but few people could understand it. The consensus seems to be that the notion was flawed. Fisher regarded the *p*-value calculated as a property of the particular sample it was calculated from; in the Neyman–Pearson approach, significance level or α is a property of the testing procedure not of the sample. α is an objective probability and hence a property of a collective and not any individual event, not a particular sample. Fisher wanted significance testing to provide evidence concerning the truth of the null hypothesis; and, according to Fisher, the smaller the *p*-value, the stronger the evidence provided by the sample against the null hypothesis. According to Fisher, 'From a test of significance . . . we have a genuine measure of the confidence with which any particular opinion may be held, in view of our particular data' (Fisher, 1955, quoted in Gigerenzer, 1993, p. 318). It was Fisher who motivated the belief that, for example, a *p*-value less than 1 % is very strong evidence against the null hypothesis, between 1 and 5 % is moderate evidence, and between 5 and 10 % is suggestive or marginal evidence.

On a frequentist notion of probability, this use of the *p*-value does not follow at all. In the Neyman–Pearson approach, the relevant probabilities α and β are the long-run error rates you decide are acceptable and so must be set in advance. If α is set at 0.05, the only meaningful claim to make about the *p*-value of a particular experiment is either it is less than 0.05 or it is not. If you obtain a *p* of 0.009 and report it as $p < 0.01$, that is misleading. You are implying that your test procedure has a long-term error rate of 1 %, but in fact if the *p* had been 0.04, you would still reject the null; in fact, your test procedure has an error rate of 5 %.

The Neyman–Pearson approach urges you to engage in a certain behaviour: Whatever your beliefs or degree of confidence, act as if you accept the null when the test statistic is outside the rejection region, and act as if you reject it if it is in the rejection region. Amazingly, the statistics tell you nothing about how confident you should be in a hypothesis nor what strength of evidence there is for different hypotheses.

Fisher found this philosophy irrelevant to the true concern of scientists, if not offensive. But it has an unassailable logical purity. If you want statistics to tell you what confidence you should have, you need to develop statistics based on the subjective notion of probability; that is what the Bayesians did, discussed in the next chapter. The procedures are quite different. Fisher tried to mix the logic of the two.

But, you may object, surely the smaller the *p*-value the stronger the evidence IS against the null? Perhaps Fisher's muddling the two is actually taking the sensible middle path?

An argument for *p*-values can at first blush be based on the logic Popper used for non-probabilistic theory (though this is not an argument put forward by either Fisher or Popper in the probabilistic case):

If H then NOT R

R

_____

Not H

If a hypothesis says R will not occur, but it does occur, it follows the hypothesis has been falsified. On first blush, one may be tempted to extend the logic to the probabilistic case:

If H then probably NOT R

R

_____

Probably not H

That is, if given the hypothesis is true it is unlikely for data to occur in the rejection region, it follows (according to the schema above) the hypothesis is unlikely to be true when data does in fact fall in the rejection region.

On second blush, as Pollard and Richardson (1987) point out, the logic in the probabilistic case is flawed. For example, consider the obvious fallacious reasoning, 'If a person is American then they are probably not a member of Congress; this person is a member of Congress; therefore this person is probably not American'.

In fact, it is hard to construct an argument for why *p*-values should be taken as strength of evidence per se (see Royall, 1997, Chapter 3). Conceptually, the *strength* of evidence for or against a hypothesis is distinct from the *probability* of obtaining such evidence; *p*-values confuse the two (we will disentangle them in Chapter 5). Part of Fisher's lasting legacy, and a tribute to his genius, is that in 1922 he *did* devise a way of measuring strength of evidence (using 'likelihoods', to be discussed in the next two chapters), an inferential logic in general inconsistent with using *p*-values, but which is the basis of both Bayesian inference and a school of inference of its own, likelihood inference (Edwards, 1972; Royall, 1997). There is no need to force *p*-values into taking the role of measuring strength of evidence, a role for which they may often give a reasonable answer, but not always. Fisher frequently used *p*-values in his examples and that is what many scientists took on board from reading Fisher.

Gigerenzer et al. (1989, Chapter 3) pointed to an analogy between Popper's ideas, in his classic *Logic der Forschung* officially published in 1935 (see Chapter One), and Fisher's *Design of Experiments*, also published in the same year. In coining the phrase 'null hypothesis', Fisher said,

> In relation to any experiment we may speak of this hypothesis as the "null hypothesis", and it should be noted that the null hypothesis is never proved or established, but is possibly disproved, in the course of experimentation. Every experiment may be said to exist only in order to give the facts a chance of disproving the null hypothesis
>
> (p. 18).

Fisher vacillated somewhat about what to conclude when the null hypothesis is not rejected. Because he rejected the notion of power, there remain no clear grounds for accepting the null when the null fails to be rejected. Perhaps one is just left unable to conclude anything. But just as Popper developed the idea of corroboration for a hypothesis that had withstood attempts at falsification, Fisher later said (in 1955) that while the null is not established it may be said to be 'strengthened'. Popper insisted that theories were corroborated only to the extent that tests were severe; in the statistical case, a null has been tested severely only when the test is powerful. By rejecting power, Fisher opened the way to all the problems of low power experiments discussed above.

Further points concerning significance tests that are often misunderstood

Significance is not a property of populations. Hypotheses are about population properties, such as means, for example that two means are equal or unequal. Significance is not a property of population means or differences. Consider the meaningless statement (often made by undergraduates but not seasoned researchers): 'The null hypothesis states that there will be no significant difference in mean reaction time between the conditions'. Hypothesis testing is then circular: a non-significant difference leads to the retention of the null hypothesis that there will be no significant difference! Type I errors are therefore impossible (Dracup, 1995)! The null hypothesis in this case should be simply that in the population mean reaction time is the same in the two conditions.

  Decision rules are laid down before data are collected; we simply make black and white decisions with known risks of error. Since significance level is decided in advance, one cannot say one result is more significant than another. Even the terms 'highly significant' versus 'just significant' versus 'marginally significant' make no sense in the Neyman–Pearson approach. A result is significant or not, full stop. Having decided on a significance level of 0.05, you cannot then use 0.01 if the obtained p is, for example, 0.009. Sample size is also decided in advance. Having decided to run, say, 20 subjects, and seeing you have a not quite significant result, you cannot decide to 'top up' with 10 more and then test as if you had set out to run that amount from the start.

  A more significant result does not mean a more important result, or a larger effect size. Maybe 'significant' is a bad name; but so is the alternative sometimes used, 'reliable', which implies the concept of power. Wright (2003) suggests a good term 'detected': 'A difference between the two conditions was not detected, $p > 0.05$'. If you have a sensitive enough test, an effect as small as you like can be significant to as low a level as you like. For example, if you run enough participants, a difference of 0.001 ms could be detected between two conditions. Getting a 'marginally significant' result does not mean the effect was smallish, despite what papers sometimes say. 'Women were somewhat ($p < 0.10$) faster than men in the gossip condition': The speed being 'somewhat faster' is an incorrect inference from the p-value. A large mean difference can be insignificant and a small difference significant – depending on, for example, sample size.

Confidence intervals

The Neyman–Pearson approach is not just about null hypothesis testing. Neyman also developed the concept of a confidence interval, a set of possible population values the data are consistent with. Instead of saying merely we reject one value ('I reject zero'), one reports the set of values rejected, and the set of possible values remaining. To calculate the 95 % confidence interval, find the set of all values of the dependent variable that are non-significantly different from your sample value at the 5 % level. For example, I measure blood pressure difference before and after taking a drug. Sample mean difference is 4 units. That may be just significantly different (at the 5 % level) from −1 units and also from +9 units. So the '95 % confidence interval' runs from −1 to +9 units. All these points are non-significantly different from the sample mean. Outside this interval, out to infinity either way, all the values are significantly different (at the 5 % level) from the sample mean, so can be rejected as possible population values. The points within the interval cannot be ruled out as population values. My data are consistent with a population value somewhere between −1 and +9 units. This tells me that the data are consistent both with the drug having no effect AND with the drug having an effect as large as almost 9 units. I know if my study is sensitive enough to detect the sort of effect I would be interested in. Say I am interested in whether the drug has an effect of 5 units or more. The fact that zero is in the confidence interval means the sample is non-significantly different from zero; but since it is also non-significantly different from +5 the data do not distinguish the interesting states of affairs. The drug may be effective. I would need to collect more data to find out.

Use of the confidence interval overcomes some of the problems people otherwise have with Neyman–Pearson statistics:

First, it tells you the sensitivity of your experiment directly; if the confidence interval includes the value of both the null hypothesis and the interesting values of the alternative hypothesis, the experiment was not sensitive enough to draw definitive conclusions. It tells you sensitivity in a way that is more intuitive than power. It directly tells you about effect sizes. Conversely, if the interval includes an interesting effect size and excludes zero, but also includes uninterestingly small values (e.g. in an interval going from +2 to +7, +2 units might be too small an effect to be interesting), you may wish to collect more data as well. If the lower limit of your interval is +3 units, you can act as if the population value is not lower than 3 units, and conclude that you are dealing with effects of a size that interest you. Confidence intervals allow you to act in a more fine-grained way than just rejecting zero.

Second, it turns out you can use the confidence interval to determine a useful stopping rule (see Armitage et al., 2002, p. 615): Stop collecting data when the interval is of a certain predetermined width (a width that is chosen so as to make sure you exclude, for example, either zero or the minimal interesting difference). Such a stopping rule would ensure that people do not get into situations where illegitimate stopping rules are tempting. For example, I decide an interesting drug effect would be +5 units. So I decide to collect data until the width of the interval is +4 units. Then if the interval includes zero it will exclude +5; and if it includes +5 it will exclude zero. There is no need to 'top up' with some more participants because p = 0.06.[7] This stopping rule is very sensible but virtually no one knows about it.

If people thought in terms of confidence intervals, rather than just significance tests, they would be more likely to draw appropriate conclusions. For example, they would immediately see if the failure to replicate a previous study was because of a lack of sensitivity. They could tell if an already published null study had sufficient sensitivity. There is a quick interval estimate one can do if a study reports a null effect but does not give a confidence interval. If the mean was 4 units and non-significantly different from zero with a t-test, then it was also

---

7. One could set oneself more demanding tasks. For example, if you wanted to either exclude drugs with an effect of +2 units or lower but accept drugs with an effect of +5 units or higher, you could run until the confidence interval had a width of 2.9 units.

non-significantly different from 8 units. The 95 % confidence interval spans at least 0–8 (or, in general, if the mean is m, it spans at least 0–$2m$; Rosenthal, 1993). If that interval includes interesting effect sizes, the study was not sensitive enough.

Confidence intervals are a very useful way of summarizing what a set of studies as a whole are telling us. You can calculate the confidence interval on the parameter of interest (mean difference, slope, correlation, proportions, etc.) by combining the information provided in all the studies (a type of meta-analysis): 'This manipulation could change preferred meal size by between −5 and 30 %'. How much more informative is that than saying 'there were six null results'? It is a tragic waste of data simply to count the number of null results. Maybe a change in meal size of, say, 20 % or more is theoretically or practically important. Imagine the unjustified decision to stop pursuing the theory tested that might have followed from just counting null results.

Like all statistics in the Neyman–Pearson approach, the 95 % confidence interval is interpreted in terms of an objective probability. The procedure for calculating 95 % confidence intervals will produce intervals that include the true population value 95 % of the time. There is no probability attached to any one calculated interval; that interval either includes the population value or it does not. There is not a 95 % probability that the 95 % confidence limits for a particular sample includes the true population mean. But if you acted as if the true population value is included in your interval each time you calculate a 95 % confidence interval, you would be right 95 % of the time (Box 3.7).

Box 3.7 Using confidence intervals

Confidence intervals can be used in many situations. Anytime your statistical software reports a standard error you can calculate a confidence interval; for example for a regression slope. Confidence intervals can also be used in standard analysis of variance (ANOVA) designs by using *contrasts*. Imagine you test the comprehension of males or females on either a romance or a science fiction story. Based on pilot data you expect the men to understand the science fiction better than the women but the women to understand the romance better than the men (who got lost after the bit where she said, 'Do you love me?'). This design is as illustrated in the table below, where the m_is are the sample means for comprehension scores. Each group also has a standard deviation, SD_i.

	Romance	Science fiction
Males	m_1	m_2
Females	m_3	m_4

A contrast is a difference between the average (or equivalently sum) of some conditions and the average (or sum) of others, which we can represent as a set of numbers, a_i. For example, the difference between m_1 and m_2, which is the effect of text type for men, is a contrast, $C = (1) \times m_1 + (-1) \times m_2 + (0) \times m_3 + (0) \times m_4 = m_1 - m_2$. In this case, $a_1 = 1$, $a_2 = -1$, $a_3 = 0$ and $a_4 = 0$.

The effect of text type for females is another contrast ($m_3 - m_4$). The main effect of gender is the difference between all the men's scores and all the female's scores, $C = (1) \times m_1 + (1) \times m_2 + (-1) \times m_3 + (-1) \times m_4 = (m_1 + m_2) - (m_3 + m_4)$. If you want to test a theory that the genders are socialized differently to understand different topics you would need to show that the difference in understanding between the text types is different for the genders. Thus the *interaction* between gender and text type, $C = (1) \times m_1 + (-1) \times m_2 + (-1) \times m_3 + (1) \times m_4 = (m_1 - m_2) - (m_3 - m_4)$.

Box 3.7 *Continued*

For example, consider the imaginary data below (with standard deviations shown in parentheses), with 20 subjects in each cell:

	Romance	Science fiction
Males	5 (1.5)	8 (2.1)
Females	9 (1.7)	7 (1.9)

The obtained size of interaction is $C = (5-8) - (9-7) = -5$. That is, female's ability to comprehend the romance rather than the science fiction was 5 comprehension points better than the male's ability to comprehend the romance rather than the science fiction. For roughly normally distributed data and equal variances within each group, C has a standard error $\sqrt{(\sum a_i^2)} \times SD_p/\sqrt{n}$, where n is the number of subjects in each group and $SD_p = \sqrt{(1/4 \times (SD_1^2 + SD_2^2 + SD_3^2 + SD_4^2))}$. For our example data, $SD_p = 1.81$, and $SE = \sqrt{(1+1+1+1)} \times 1.81/\sqrt{20} = 0.81$.

For any contrast, you can calculate a confidence interval:

$$C \pm t_{crit} \times SE$$

where t_{crit} is the critical value of t with $4(n-1)$ degrees of freedom.

For our example, there are 76 degrees of freedom and (consulting tables of the t-distribution in Howell, 1987) the critical value of t at the 5 % level is 1.99. So the confidence interval for the contrast is $(-5) \pm 1.99 \times 0.81$, which gives an interval of $(-6.6, -3.4)$. The interval excludes zero, so the interaction is significant at the 5 % level. More informatively, we reject any value less than -6.6 or more than -3.4 as population values of the advantage of females over males in understanding the romance over the science fiction text. The substantial meaning of the result depends on the comprehension scale used. If it were number of key terms recalled out of 15, the interaction strikes me as substantial and the theoretical basis of the interaction well worth pursuing further. Conversely, one could imagine an interaction, though significant, spanning such a small range of effects, it was of no further interest; or an interaction, though non-significant, spanning such an interesting range of effects, more data were required to draw any practical conclusion. Whenever you have an important effect that is non-significant, calculate the confidence interval on the relevant contrast to see what range of effect sizes your data are consistent with.

In a within-subjects design, you can calculate a contrast for each subject separately. Now you end up with a single number for each subject – the contrast – and you can find the mean, C, of these numbers and their standard error $(= SD/\sqrt{n})$, and calculate the confidence interval:

$$C \pm t_{crit} \times SE$$

where t_{crit} is the critical value of t with $n-1$ degrees of freedom.

The skill is in working out how to translate your research questions into contrasts. Once you have achieved this, you can have all the benefits of confidence intervals over null hypothesis testing in 'ANOVA designs'.

You can also calculate confidence intervals on correlations. Pearson correlations can be transformed to be roughly normal using Fisher's transform

$$r' = (0.5) \ln |(1+r)/(1-r)|$$

where r is the correlation, $|x|$ means take the absolute value of x ignoring its sign, and ln is the natural logarithm, a function you can find on your calculator. r' is roughly normally distributed with standard error $SE = 1/\sqrt{(n-3)}$. The 95 % confidence interval is

$$r' \pm 1.96 \times SE$$

r' can be converted back to r, $r' = (e^{2r'} - 1)/(e^{2r'} + 1)$ where $e = 2.71828$.

For example, if on 50 people you obtained a correlation of 0.30, $r' = 0.31$. $SE = 0.15$. The 95 % confidence interval for r' runs from 0.02 to 0.60. These limits correspond to correlations of 0.02 and 0.54, respectively.

Criticism of the Neyman–Pearson approach

(1) *Inference consists of simple acceptance or rejection.* According to Neyman, deciding to accept a hypothesis does not mean knowing it or even just believing it to some extent. By strictly following the demands of a frequentist objective probability, statistical inference becomes 'inductive behaviour', as Neyman puts it, rather than the process of strengthening certain beliefs. It is statistical inference that is scarcely inference at all (Oakes, 1986). Do not the data indicate more than just a black and white behavioural decision? Data seem to provide *continuous* support for or against different hypotheses. Fisher tried to capture this intuition with *p*-values. He found it arbitrary that Neyman–Pearson required us to simply behave one way if $p = 0.048$ and the opposite if $p = 0.052$; and identically when $p = 0.048$ as when $p = 0.0001$. The Fisherian urge to use what appears to be useful information carried in the continuous *p*-value, as strength of evidence has been irresistible to researchers (we will consider measuring strength of evidence in Chapter 5).

Arguably, what a scientist wants to know is either how likely certain hypotheses are in the light of data (in which case Bayesian statistics should be used) or, more simply, how strong the evidence supports one hypothesis rather than another (in which case likelihood inference should be used). It is meaningless to use the tools and concepts developed in the Neyman–Pearson framework to draw inferences about the probability of hypotheses or the strength of evidence. We will discuss the alternative frameworks in the next two chapters, which allow graded conclusions, conclusions which can be expressed in terms of intervals similar to confidence intervals.

(2) *Null hypothesis testing encourages weak theorizing.* This is one of the most important criticisms of significance testing as it is generally used. Meehl (1967) contrasted how 'soft' psychology and hard sciences test their theories. In psychology the scientist typically sets up a null hypothesis of no difference between conditions, or of zero correlation between variables. When this point hypothesis is rejected, the scientist regards his own substantive theory as confirmed, or at least as having survived the test. But notice how little content the alternative hypothesis actually has; it rules out virtually nothing, just one point. The hypothesis that '$m_1 <> m_2$' has virtually zero content; the directional hypothesis ('$m_1 - m_2 > 0$') is still weak. The hard scientist, by contrast, often predicts a certain value (not just ruling out one point, 'the force will be different from zero'; not just directional, 'gravity pulls things down rather than up'; but a specific value, e.g. 'the force will be 13 units down'); when the point hypothesis lies within the margin of error of the data her substantive hypothesis has survived the test. Instead of trying to reject the null (to corroborate a theory of virtually no content), she wants to accept the null (to corroborate a highly falsifiable theory). The difference is symptomatic of the relative state of theory development in psychology and hard sciences. Psychologists are often wary of predicting the null and then accepting it; but this is precisely what they should be aiming for.

Most point null hypotheses – of no difference, no correlation and so on (so-called 'nill hypotheses') – are virtually certain to be false; it is just a matter of to what decimal place. A good theory should specify the size of effect not just that it is different from zero.

Of course, as Meehl pointed out, there are difficulties with the subject matter of psychology that make such precise theories very hard to construct. But such theories do exist even within psychology. Why are they so few? The problem may be that by training and requiring psychologists to get excited by rejecting null hypotheses, there is no incentive to think more carefully about effect sizes. If our statistical tools required at least the reporting of the range of effects the data were consistent with, it would encourage more careful theorizing, motivate more precise theories where they were possible. The habitual use of confidence intervals instead of simple null hypothesis testing would overcome this objection. The objection can be taken as one against how the Neyman–Pearson approach is typically used (or mis-used) rather than against the approach per se. Nonetheless, after reading the next two chapters you may agree that the other approaches invite this misuse less than does the Neyman–Pearson approach.

(3) *In the Neyman–Pearson approach it is important to know the reference class – we must know what endless series of trials might have happened but never did.* This is important when considering both multiple testing and stopping rules. A particular event can be a member of various reference classes. Probabilities, including α and β, belong to reference classes, not singular events like particular experiments. Thus, a particular experiment must be assigned to a reference class. The choice of reference class can be determined by what else the experimenter did even if it was unrelated to the hypothesis under consideration (we will discuss this under multiple testing). Other than the actual experiment, the remainder of the chosen reference class includes an infinite number of experiments that never happened. Which set of experiments that never happened are included defines the reference class and hence the probabilities. It strikes some as unreasonable that what never happened should determine what is concluded about what did happen.

In the Neyman–Pearson approach, as explained above, when conducting a number of tests, there should be a correction for repeated testing. (By contrast, a Bayesian does not have to.) The data relevant to judging one hypothesis will legitimate different judgments depending on how many other hypotheses were tested. If I test one correlation by itself, I can test at the 0.05 level; if I test five correlations, each concerning a different null hypothesis, I should test at the 0.01 level (with Bonferroni correction). When do we correct for repeated testing? We do not correct for all the tests we do in a journal, a paper, or for an experiment, or even in one analysis of variance. Why not? Why should we correct in some cases and not others? The decision is basically arbitrary and tacit conventions determine practice.

Further, in multiple testing one must distinguish planned from post hoc comparisons: Was the difference strongly predicted in advance of collecting the data? In Bayesian and likelihood inference, by contrast, the evidential import of the data is independent of the timing of the explanation, a point we will return to in the next chapter. In Bayesian and likelihood inference there is no distinction between planned and post hoc comparisons. Whether this is a strength or weakness of Neyman–Pearson is controversial, depending on whether it is thought the timing of data relative to explanation should be important.

The reference class of possible outcomes by which to judge an obtained statistic is also determined by the stopping rule. In testing the efficacy of a drug for reducing blood pressure, Mary tests 30 patients and performs a t-test. It is not quite significant at the 0.05 level and so she tests 10 more patients. She cannot now perform a t-test in the normal way at the 0.05 level. Jane decides to test 40 patients and collects exactly the same data. She CAN perform a t-test at the 0.05 level. If $p = 0.049$, Jane can reject the null hypothesis at the 0.05 level; Mary cannot (and, interestingly, could not no matter how much additional data she collects[8]). *Should* the same data lead to different conclusions because of the intentions of the experimenter? Whether this is a strength or weakness of Neyman–Pearson is controversial.

---

8. Having tested once at the 0.05 level, the testing procedure can never have an α value of less than 0.05: The probability of one or other of two events happening is never less than the probability of one of them. So even if the calculated p-value at the second test is $p = 0.0000003$, the 'actual' p-value is greater than 0.05.

Consider another often discussed type of example. Mary and Jane wish to estimate the proportion of women in a population that report having had a G spot orgasm. Mary decides in advance to sample 30 women and count the number which report G spot orgasms. She finds six which do. The best estimate of the population proportion is 6/30.

Jane decides to count women until her sixth woman reporting a G spot orgasm. That happens to be the 30th woman. In the Neyman–pearson approach, the best estimate of population proportion is now 5/29! To explain why the same data lead to different conclusions, we need to consider the respective reference classes.

For the stopping rule 'Stop after 30 observations', the reference class is the set of all samples with $n = 30$. This set defines what else the researcher might have done (e.g. counted 5/30

"Two scientists, Peter and Paul, are collecting data and happen to agree on stopping at the same time despite having different stopping rules. Peter decided to stop after 30 subjects. Paul decided we would also have stopped at 15 subjects if the result had been significant then. They have the same data, but on the Neyman Pearson approach, whether or not to reject the null depends on which stopping rule was used – that is, on what would have happened if their stopping rules had disagreed."

or 10/30 or 22/30, etc.). If we take an infinite number of samples, we might get 5/30, 6/30, 10/30 and so on. If we average all those proportions, the expected mean is the population proportion. So in this case, unbiased estimate of population proportion is 6/30.

Now consider the stopping rule: 'Stop when have six positive outcomes'. The reference class is the set of all samples with six positives. Some will be $n = 30$, some $n = 6$, some $n = 1000$ and so on. This set defines what else the researcher might have done. In infinite number of samples we might get 6/30, 6/50, 6/243 and so on. If we averaged all of these proportions, the mean would be higher than population proportion! The final observation is known to be a positive in advance, so it is unfair to count that trial; it is not free to vary but is fixed. So one should ignore the final trial. And in fact if you averaged the proportions of all the possible samples generated by a given population proportion *ignoring the final trial*, 5/29, 5/49, 5/242 and so on, the expected mean is the population mean. In this case the unbiased estimate is 5/29!

The point about what way of averaging in the reference class is unbiased is just a mathematical fact; but why should we be concerned with which other sort of events that never happened we should average over? Why should it matter what else the experimenter might have done (but did not)? Should not what actually happened be the only thing that matters? Philosophers and statisticians have not agreed what the correct answer to this question is. What if the experimenter was not sure of her intentions of when to stop? What if two experimenters are collecting data together and they have different stopping rules in mind – do we need to know who would win if there were an argument? What if the experimenter unconsciously held one stopping rule while believing she held another? Why should what is locked in someone's head affect the objective statistics we compute?

For Bayesian and likelihood inference both sets of data lead to an estimate of the population proportion of 6/30; what matters is only what the data were. In the Neyman–Pearson approach, the same data can lead to different conclusions. Whether this is a strength or weakness of Neyman–Pearson is controversial. (These issues are discussed again in the next two chapters; hopefully at the end of those chapters you will have your own opinion.)

The limits of confidence intervals are sensitive to the stopping rule and multiple testing issues as well. In the next two chapters we consider interval estimates like a confidence interval but insensitive to stopping rule and multiple testing.

Using the Neyman–Pearson approach to critically evaluate a research article

If the article uses significance or hypothesis tests, then two hypotheses need to be specified for each test. Most papers fall down at the first hurdle because the alternative is not well specified. One hypothesis is the null which often states that there will be no effect. How big an effect would just be interesting on the theory in question? The size of a just interesting effect determines the alternative hypothesis (e.g. 'The difference is bigger than five units'). Does the paper specify how big an effect would be just interesting or instead does it just indicate vaguely that there will be some difference (or some difference in a certain direction)?

Note from the introduction section of the paper whether any specific comparisons were highlighted as the main point of the experiment. These comparisons, if few in number, can be treated as planned comparisons later. If a direction is strongly predicted at this point, one-tailed tests could be considered later.

The stopping rule should be specified. Do the authors state their stopping rule? Usually they do not, but the default assumption is that the number of subjects was planned in advance at a fixed number and significance testing took place once at the end of data collection. Was a power calculation performed to determine the appropriate number of subjects? Are the chosen levels of α and β stated in advance? If very different numbers of subjects are used in different experiments in the paper for no apparent reason, it may be a sign that multiple significance tests were conducted, as each experiment progressed and stopping occurred when the required results were obtained. (Other genuine reasons for differing subject numbers in different experiments include whether the subjects were run in large groups, for example teaching groups, and the researchers made sure they had a minimum number of subjects but if the groups were larger than that they still tested everyone.)

When families of tests were conducted (e.g. a table of t-tests addressing a common issue, a table of correlations, a set of post hoc tests following a significant overall test) is a correction to significance levels made to control family-wise error rate? No correction is needed for planned comparisons, identified by specifically being mentioned in the introduction.

Now we come to one of the most important points. Even if minimally interesting effect sizes were not stated in advance and if power were not stated in advance, a crucial point is how the authors dealt with interesting null results. *Given a null result was obtained, did the authors give some measure of sensitivity of the test?* For example, were confidence intervals provided together with an indication of what effects would be interesting based on the theory? If there were a set of results over experiments bearing on one question, perhaps all or some of them null, was a meta-analysis conducted to determine what decision is allowed by the data as a whole? (The more data that goes into an analysis, the more sensitive it is.) In the case of a meta-analysis, did the authors also give some measure of the sensitivity of null results (e.g. confidence intervals)?

In the discussion section of the paper, were only effects treated as real that had been specifically tested and found significant? Was serious consideration given to null results as null results only when the test had been shown to have adequate sensitivity? Or did the authors mistakenly treat a very non-significant p-value as in itself a measure of their high confidence in the null under the conditions of their experiment?

Summary

The Neyman–Pearson approach defines the dominant framework within which mathematical statistics is developed and the often tacit orthodox philosophy in journals of researchers who use statistics, including psychology journals. Many if not the vast majority of published papers deviate from the orthodoxy; but in the case of dispute about correct interpretation or use of statistics in standard journal articles in psychology, appeal to the Neyman–Pearson philosophy will normally trump appeal to any other. It has its own coherent logic which all researchers and consumers of research should understand. The persistent failure to understand it has led to many mistakes in the interpretation of results and in faulty research decisions generally. A large part of the confusion probably comes from people unwittingly having a Bayesian understanding of statistics and unthinkingly believing Neyman–Pearson statistics give them Bayesian answers (Oakes, 1986). The confusions are so wide spread that there have been regular calls over many decades for psychologists to give up significance testing altogether (see e.g. Harlow et al., 1997, for an overview). Indeed, Fisher regarded significance testing as the tool one uses in only the most impoverished stages of theory development. Neyman rarely used hypothesis testing as such in his own numerous statistical applications – instead, he often gave confidence limits around estimates of model parameters. Relatedly, there have been many calls over the decades for researchers to rely more habitually on confidence intervals. For example, the 2001 version of the Publication Manual of the American Psychological Association tells us that confidence intervals constitute 'the best reporting strategy' (p. 22). Change has been slow. But you, dear reader, can help make a start.

Review and discussion questions

1. Define the key terms of: population, null and alternative hypotheses, α, β, power, significance, p-value, stopping rule, family-wise error rate, probability.
2. What is the difference between p-value and alpha?
3. When is a null result meaningful?
4. Describe two legitimate stopping rules and two illegitimate ones.
5. Why should one correct for multiple testing?
6. What would be the advantages and disadvantages of reporting confidence intervals rather than p-values in psychology papers?

Further reading

Hacking (2001) provides an excellent clear introduction to different theories of probability and how they motivate different approaches to statistical inference, including the Neyman–Pearson approach. It assumes no previous knowledge of mathematics nor statistics. The focus is on theories of probability rather than the details of the Neyman–Pearson approach.

The material in this chapter is discussed in more detail in Oakes (1986). The latter is now out of print, but anyone in research or thinking of going into research should try to get hold of a copy. The material in the book formed Oakes' PhD thesis at University College London; his examiner was so impressed that he told Oakes to publish it. While many of the ideas in the Oakes book are around generally in the literature, Oakes (1986) is one of the best single sources available. Most of it will be accessible once you have read and understood this chapter and the next two.

The following sources are also useful for theoretical discussion: Chow (1998), Cohen (1994), Gigerenzer (e.g. 2000, 2004, Chapter 13) , Howson and Urbach (1989, Chapters five and seven), Mayo (1996, Chapter nine), and Meehl (1967).

Many stats books will have information on power and confidence intervals. See, for example, Howell, D. *Fundamental Statistics for the Behavioural Sciences*, or *Statistical Methods for Psychology*. Duxbury, any of the editions.

A collection of anecdotes concerning statistics is provided by Salsburg (2002). Finally, a highly informative and engaging account of ways of thinking about data (analysed by orthodox methods) is Abelson (1995), which also should be read by anyone engaged in research.

4 Bayes and the probability of hypotheses

We saw in Chapter 3 that interpreting probability as *objective* probability, namely a long-run relative frequency, meant developing statistical tools that only allow inferences consistent with that meaning, namely inferences about long-run relative frequencies. Classic (Neyman–Pearson) statistics can tell you the long-run relative frequency of different types of errors. Classic statistics do not tell you the probability of any hypothesis being true. We also saw that, in contrast, many people mistakenly believe that significance values do tell them the probability of hypotheses. This common belief leads in practice to erroneous decisions in reviewing studies and conducting research (Oakes, 1986).

An alternative approach to statistics is to start with what *Bayesians* say are people's natural intuitions: People apparently want statistics to tell them the probability of their hypothesis being right. In this chapter, we will define *subjective* probability (subjective degree of conviction in a hypothesis) and then see how we can develop statistical tools to inform us how we should change our conviction in a hypothesis in the light of experimental data. Many aspects of classic statistical inference are simplified in this Bayesian approach. We shall review some surprising consequences of such an approach. We will finish by considering how well the classic and Bayesian approaches really are consistent with or conflict with our intuitions about appropriate research decisions.

Amongst users of statistics, like psychologists, Neyman–Pearson statistics is the unchallenged establishment view. But few users of statistics are even aware of the names of the approaches to statistical inference, let alone the conceptual issues, and thus have scarcely made an informed choice. Amongst statisticians and philosophers, there is a raging debate concerning what we are even trying to do with statistics (let alone how we do it), and as yet no clear intellectual victor (despite protests to the contrary). In this chapter and the next, we consider the main rivals to the orthodoxy. Maybe you personally will find that, after considering the arguments, you favour one side of the dispute more than the others.

Subjective probability

In everyday life, we often say things like 'It will probably snow tomorrow', 'There are even odds that the next colour will be red', 'Uzbekistan is most likely to win the match', and 'Baker's theory of sperm competition is probably true'. As you now know, none of these statements are legitimate statements about objective probability (long-run relative frequency). But the everyday use of 'probable' does not respect the strict demands of objective probability. In the everyday use, we are quite willing to talk about how probable single events or hypotheses are. *Subjective* or *personal* probability is the degree of conviction we have in a hypothesis. Given this meaning, probabilities are in the mind, not in the world. If you say 'It is highly probable it will snow tomorrow', you are making a statement about how strongly you believe that it will snow tomorrow. No expert on the weather can tell you that you are wrong in assigning a high personal probability to snow tomorrow. Although the weather expert knows about weather patterns, she does not know better than you yourself about what state your mind is in. She might change your mind by giving you more information, but your statement about how strongly you believed (at that point in time) that it will snow tomorrow still stands as a true statement.

The initial problem to address in making use of subjective probabilities is how to assign a precise number to how probable you think a proposition is. Let's use a number between 0 and 1, where 0 means zero probability, there is no chance that the statement is true; and 1 means you are certain that the statement is true. But if you are neither certain that the statement is false (probability = 0) nor certain that it is true (probability = 1), what number between 0 and 1 should you choose? A solution is to see how much money you would be willing to bet on the statement.

To determine your personal conviction in the statement 'it will rain here tomorrow', statement (1) below, choose either that statement or statement (2) below. For whichever statement you have chosen, if it turns out to be true, I will pay you £10:

1. It will rain here tomorrow.
   I have a bag with one red chip and one blue chip in it. I shake it up, close my eyes and draw a chip:
2. I draw the red one.
   If you chose the first statement, then your probability that it will rain tomorrow is greater than 0.5; otherwise it is less. We can narrow down your probability more precisely by choosing a bag with different proportions of red chips in it. For example, let us say you chose option 1 above. Then, we could ask you to choose between 1 again and:
   I have a bag with three red chips and one blue. I shake it up, close my eyes and draw a chip:
3. I draw the red one.
   You can choose 1 or 3. If your chosen scenario turns out to be true, I will pay you £10. Which do you choose?

If you choose 1 again, then your personal probability is greater than 0.75; otherwise it is between 0.5 and 0.75. You can specify your probability as precisely as you think it is worth by giving yourself repeated choices between the proposition in question 1 and a bag with different proportion of red chips in. (The Appendix provides a procedure for honing in one's subjective convictions in a single gamble.) The initial personal probability that you assign to any theory is just up to you. Reach deep inside your soul and see what you are willing to bet.

Sometimes it is useful to express your personal convictions in terms of *odds* rather than probabilities:

$$\text{odds(theory is true)} = \text{probability(theory is true)}/\text{probability(theory is false)}.[1]$$

For example, if your personal probability that the theory is true is 0.5, your odds in favour of the theory are $0.5/(1-0.5) = 1$, or as we say 1:1 (1 to 1), or even odds. If your personal probability is 0.75, your odds in favour of the theory is $0.75/(1-0.75) = 3:1$ (3 to 1). Conversely, if your personal probability is 0.25, your odds are 1:3.

Now let us stipulate something that does not come naturally to people: These numbers we get from deep inside us must obey the axioms of probability. This is the stipulation that ensures the way we change our personal probability in a theory is coherent and rational.

1. Hence probability(theory is true) = odds/(odds + 1).

People's intuitions about how to change probabilities in the light of new information are notoriously bad (see e.g. Sutherland, 1994). This is where the statistician comes in and forces us to be disciplined.

At first sight, making our personal probabilities obey the axioms of probability seems just like common sense. There are only a few axioms, each more-or-less self-evidently reasonable. Two axioms effectively set limits on what values probabilities can take; namely, all probabilities will lie between 0 and 1, inclusive. The next asserts $P(A \text{ or } B) = P(A) + P(B)$, if A and B are mutually exclusive. For example, imagine rolling a die; it can come up as '1' or '2' or '3' and so on up to '6'. Each of these possibilities is mutually exclusive: if '1' comes up then a '2' does not. Let my personal probability for a '1' coming up be a 1/6 and my personal probability for a '2' coming up also be 1/6. The axiom asserts that my personal probability P(getting '1' OR getting a '2'), the probability of getting either a '1' or a '2' on a roll of the die, should be $P(\text{getting '1'}) + P(\text{getting '2'}) = 1/6 + 1/6 = 1/3$. Finally, there is an axiom that says, $P(A \text{ and } B) = P(A) \times P(B|A)$. $P(B|A)$ is the probability of B given A, which just means assuming A is the case, then what is the probability of B? Box 4.1 illustrates this final axiom.

It is surely not too much to ask of our personal probabilities that in updating, they do no more and no less than obey these axioms.

Box 4.1 $P(L \text{ and } C) = P(L) \times P(C|L)$

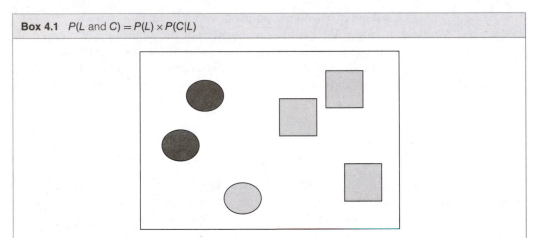

Imagine you have a box with the above objects in, circles and squares which are light or dark. You shake it and repeatedly put your hand in, to draw out an object. You regard each object as equally likely to be drawn. What is the probability that you will draw something that is both light and a circle, $P(L \text{ AND } C)$?

The probability of drawing a circle is a half ($P(C) = 1/2$). That is, you expect that half of the draws will be circles. Given that you have drawn a circle, the probability that it is light is a third ($P(L|C) = 1/3$). That is, a third of those half of draws that are circles are expected to be light circles: $P(L \text{ and } C) = P(C) \times P(L|C) = 1/2 \times 1/3 = 1/6$.

One can think of this the other way round as well. The probability of drawing a light object is 4/6 ($P(L) = 4/6$). Given that you have drawn a light object, the probability that it is a circle is a quarter ($P(C|L) = 1/4$). That is, a quarter of those 4/6 of draws that are light will be light circles: $P(L \text{ and } C) = P(L) \times P(C|L) = 4/6 \times 1/4 = 1/6$.

Bayes' theorem

Thomas Bayes (1702–1761), a nonconformist minister, was a fellow of the Royal Society, despite the fact that he had no published papers in his lifetime, at least none under his name. (The good old days.) After the reverend Bayes' death, a friend of his, Richard Price, found a manuscript among Bayes' papers, and considered it of such importance that he presented it to the Royal Society on behalf of his friend in 1764. Bayes had worked on the problem of how one may obtain the probability of a hypothesis given some data, that is $P(H|D)$.

Bayes' theorem is easy to derive from first principles using the axiom in Box 4.1. If you ever forget Bayes' theorem, you can always derive it for yourself. Consider hypothesis H and data D. We have

$$P(H \text{ and } D) = P(D) \times P(H|D) \tag{4.1}$$

and

$$P(H \text{ and } D) = P(H) \times P(D|H) \tag{4.2}$$

Equations (4.1) and (4.2) are just statements of the axiom in Box 4.1.

We see the right hand sides of (1) and (2) are equal, so

$$P(D) \times P(H|D) = P(H) \times P(D|H)$$

Moving $P(D)$ to the other side

$$P(H|D) = P(D|H) \times P(H)/P(D) \tag{4.3}$$

Equation (4.3) is one version of Bayes' theorem. It tells you how to go from one conditional probability to its inverse. We can simplify Equation (4.3) if we are interested in comparing the probability of different hypotheses given the *same* data D. Then $P(D)$ is just a constant for all these comparisons. So we have

$$P(H|D) \text{ is proportional to } P(D|H) \times P(H) \tag{4.4}$$

Equation (4.4) is another version of Bayes' theorem.

$P(H)$ is called the *prior*. It is how probable you thought the hypothesis was prior to collecting data. This is your personal subjective probability and its value is completely up to you. $P(H|D)$, the probability of the hypothesis given the data, is called the *posterior*. 'Posterior' means literally 'coming after'. The posterior is how probable your hypothesis is to you, after you have collected data. $P(D|H)$ is the probability of obtaining the data, given your hypothesis; this is called the *likelihood* of the hypothesis. (Strictly, because the posterior is merely *proportional* to the likelihood times the prior, the likelihood is defined as anything proportional to $P(D|H)$). In words, Equation (4.4) says that

your posterior is proportional to the likelihood times the prior.

This is the mantra of Bayesian statistics. It tells us how we can update our prior probability in a hypothesis given some data. Your prior can be up to you; but having settled on it, the posterior is determined by the axioms of probability. From the Bayesian perspective, scientific inference consists precisely in updating one's personal conviction in a hypothesis in the light of data.[2]

2. Thus, if you think back to Chapter 1, you see Bayesians apparently are *inductivists*, engaging in what Hume and Popper argued does not exist: inductive logic, using specific observations to progressively confirm general statements. Bayesians do not see the Bayesian part of what they do as violating Hume's arguments though; Bayes is just a piece of valid mathematics, so it only makes explicit what was already implicit in your existing beliefs. In order to calculate probabilities, you need a model of the world. If you already believe the world is described by a certain type of model, Bayes will tell you how to update probabilities for different variants of that model.

The likelihood

According to Bayes' theorem, if you want to update your personal probability in a hypothesis, the likelihood tells you *everything* you need to know about the data (Edwards, 1972). All support for a hypothesis provided by the data is captured by the likelihood. Posterior is proportional to *likelihood* times prior. The notion that all the information relevant to inference contained in data is provided by the likelihood is called the *likelihood principle*. At first sight, the likelihood principle may seem like a truism, something that just follows from the axioms of probability. In fact, it is controversial. While Bayesian inference respects it (as does likelihood inference, considered the next chapter), Neyman–Pearson inference violates it, as we will see later (and discuss further in the next chapter). So what does a likelihood look like exactly?

Imagine we are interested in how men respond to people telling them about their problems. Let us say a man can respond in one of two ways: He can offer a solution to the friend or he can offer no solutions, but provide empathy. We call the first type of man a solver and the second type an empathizer. Gray (2002) suggested that men habitually offer solutions when women describe problems, and this gets the man in deep trouble because women are looking for empathy! Our research question is: What proportion of men in a population are solvers? We tell five men our problems. All five men suggest solutions to our problems; they are solvers. Our *data* are the fact that five out of the five men in the sample were solvers.

The likelihood is the probability of obtaining these data given a hypothesis. One hypothesis is that the proportion of men who are solvers in our population is 0.1. The likelihood, $P(D|H) = P$(obtaining 5 solvers | proportion of solvers = 0.1), is $0.1^5 = 0.000001$. Another hypothesis is that the proportion of men who are solvers is 0.5. Likelihood = P(obtaining 5 solvers | proportion of solvers is 0.5) $= 0.5^5 = 0.03125$. Figure 4.1 plots the likelihood against different hypotheses. The data could be obtained given many different population proportions, but the data are more probable for some population proportions than others. The data are most probable for a population proportion of 1. The hypothesis that 'the population proportion is 1' has the highest likelihood.

Notice a possible misinterpretation. In everyday speech, saying that a hypothesis has the highest likelihood is the same as saying it has the highest probability. But for statisticians, the two are not the same. The probability of the hypothesis in the light of our data is $P(H|D)$, which is our posterior. The likelihood of the hypothesis is the probability of the data given the hypothesis, $P(D|H)$. We can use the likelihood to obtain our posterior, but they are not the same. Just because a hypothesis has the highest likelihood, it does not mean you will assign it the highest posterior probability. The fact that a hypothesis has the highest likelihood means the data support that hypothesis most. If the prior probabilities for each hypothesis were the same, then the hypothesis with the highest likelihood will have the highest posterior probability. But the prior probabilities may mean that the hypothesis with the greatest support from the data, that is with the highest likelihood, does not have the highest posterior probability.

In the previous chapter, we talked about testing whether a new drug changes blood pressure. We have a group of people treated with the drug, and they have a mean blood pressure of M_d; and we have a placebo group treated only with saline, and they have a mean blood pressure of M_p. The difference in blood pressure between the groups is thus $M_d - M_p$.

The observed sample (drug–placebo) mean could be obtained if the actual population (drug–placebo) mean was of exactly the same value as the sample mean. But the observed sample mean could also be obtained from a population with a mean slightly different from the sample, or indeed from a population with a mean greatly different from the sample. However,

Figure 4.1

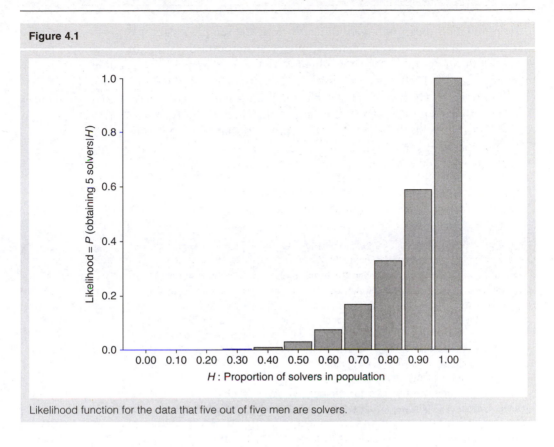

Likelihood function for the data that five out of five men are solvers.

Figure 4.2

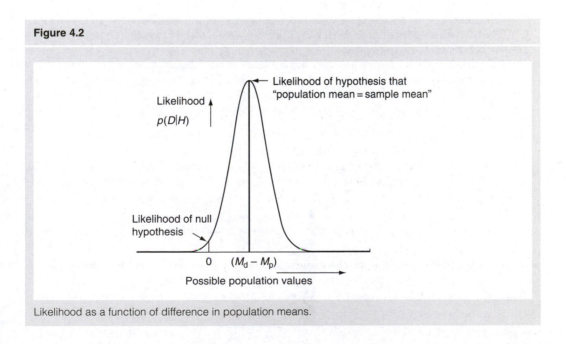

Likelihood as a function of difference in population means.

if the population mean were very different from the sample mean, it is not very probable that the population would generate sample means around the value of our sample mean. Figure 4.2 illustrates how likely it would be to obtain the sample mean for different possible population means. Each different possible population mean on the horizontal axis is a different hypothesis, H. The height of the curve is highest when the hypothetical population mean is the sample mean, $(M_d - M_p)$. The height of the curve when the hypothetical population mean is zero is the likelihood of the null hypothesis that the population mean is zero.

If the dependent variable can be assumed to vary continuously (as blood pressure does) – that is, the values do not come in steps – then its distribution is properly called a *probability*

Box 4.2 Probability density versus probability

In general, if a variable varies continuously, the probability distribution of that variable is properly called a probability density distribution function. Blood pressure varies continuously and so its distribution is a probability density distribution. Why invent a special name – probability density – for continuous variables? If the variable really varies continuously, then it can take an infinite number of values. If all values had some positive probability, then the probability of one value or another being true would be

$p(\text{value} = 1 \text{ OR value} = 2.3 \text{ OR value} = 5 \text{ OR} \dots) = p(\text{value} = 1) + p(\text{value} = 2.3) + p(\text{value} = 5) + \dots$ for all the uncountable infinite number of values

which would be infinite!

But we know from the axioms of probability that probability cannot be greater than one. Thus, for these infinite number of values, we cannot assign a positive probability to each precise value! But we CAN assign a probability to an interval: that is, we can say there is some probability that the true value of blood pressure change lies in the interval 3–4 units of blood pressure. The required probability is the area under the curve between 3 and 4 units, as shown in the figure. A probability density distribution tells you how probable it is that the variable takes a value in any interval.

The probability that the variable has a value in one or other of the intervals is the sum of the areas for each interval. The sum is just the area under the whole curve. Thus, so long as the area under the curve is 1, our probabilities will behave properly!

Note the area under the curve for just one value of blood pressure change, for example for a value of precisely 2 units of blood pressure, is zero. So the probability of the change being *exactly* 2 units is zero. Similarly, the probability of there being exactly no change is also zero.

By convention, $P(A)$ is the probability of A and $p(A)$ is the probability density of A.

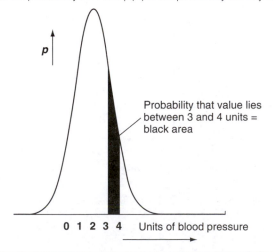

Probability that value lies between 3 and 4 units = black area

0 1 2 3 4   Units of blood pressure

density distribution. See Box 4.2 for an explanation of probability density. A likelihood could be (or be proportional to) a probability density as well as a probability.

In significance testing, we calculate a form of $P(D|H)$. But the $P(D|H)$ used in significance testing is conceptually very different from the likelihood, the $p(D|H)$ we are dealing with here. The 'p-value' in significance testing is the probability of rejecting the null, given the null is really true: $P(\text{reject null }|H_0)$. Another way of saying the same thing is that the p-value is the probability of obtaining data as extreme or more extreme as we obtained, given the null hypothesis is true: $P(\text{obtaining data as extreme or more extreme than }D|H_0)$. In calculating a significance value, we hold fixed the hypothesis under consideration – namely H_0 – and we vary the data we might have obtained (we ask, what is the probability – or probability density – of obtaining this sample mean or this sample mean or this sample mean ... given H_0). The likelihood is $p(\text{obtaining exactly this }D|H)$, where H is free to vary; but the D considered is always exactly the data obtained.

Figure 4.3 illustrates the differences. For the curve on the left, what varies along the horizontal axis is different possible population values. Each value corresponds to a different H; it is a hypothesis about what the true population value might be. For the curve on the right, what varies along the horizontal axis is different possible sample values, that is different possible data. On the left, the likelihood of the null is the height of the curve corresponding to the null hypothesis. On the right, we take a corresponding part of the curve (the height of the curve above $M_d - M_p$ is the same value as the likelihood); however, we are not interested in the height of the curve at this point but the area under the curve beyond this point. The area represents the probability of obtaining data as large as the obtained mean or larger given the null hypothesis.

Likelihood analysis regards the data as fixed but the hypothesis can vary. Significance testing regards the hypothesis as fixed but the data can vary. In calculating the likelihood, we are interested in the height of the curve for each hypothesis. In significance testing, we are interested in the 'tail area', the area under the curve beyond the obtained data. This area is the probability

Figure 4.3

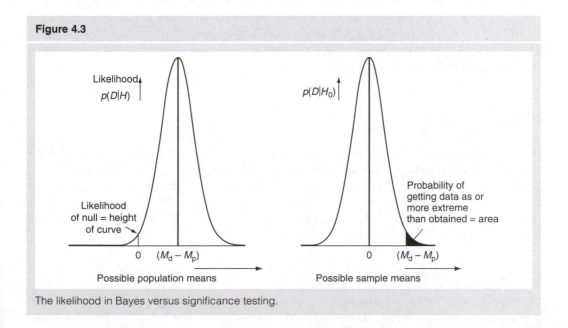

The likelihood in Bayes versus significance testing.

of obtaining our data OR data more extreme – data that we did not observe but might have. Likelihood reflects just what the data were (the curve is plotted only for the actually obtained data); significance tests, using tail areas, reflect what might have happened but did not (the data might have been more extreme, but were not). In significance testing, we make a black and white decision: Is the tail area smaller than our preset alpha value (e.g. 5%) or not? In contrast, likelihoods give a continuous graded measure of support for different hypotheses.

In significance testing, tail areas are calculated in order to determine long-run error rates. The aim of classic statistics is to come up with a procedure for making decisions that is reliable, which is to say that the procedure has known controlled long-run error rates. To decide the long-run error rates, we need to define a collective (see Chapter 3). What exactly is it that defines the procedure that constitutes an element of the collective? A procedure could be performing one t-test. The elements of the collective are individual acts of performing a t-test, and the error probabilities can be controlled by rejecting the null when the tail area is less than the preset alpha, as discussed above. But if the procedure is conducting a set of five t-tests, the elements of the collective are sets of five t-tests performed at once (often called a 'family' of t-tests), and we want to control the error of rejecting any one of the five possible null hypotheses when they are true (we want to control 'family-wise error rate'). Now we need to adjust the tail area. For example, if we used the Bonferroni adjustment, we would multiply the tail area of each test by five, and only reject the null for that test if this adjusted area was less than our preset alpha. (See Chapter 3 for discussion.) The tail error needs to be adjusted also according to the stopping rule. If we had a different stopping rule, we might have stopped at a different time. In classic statistics, we need to take into account what else we might have done: performed one test or five? When else might we have stopped? Further we need to know whether the test is post hoc or planned (what came first – the explanation or the data)? The likelihood – the probability (or probability density) of obtaining exactly these data given a hypothesis – is clearly the same whatever other tests you might have done, whether you decide to stop now or carry on collecting data, and whatever the timing of your explanation (before or after the data). The insensitivity of the likelihood to what other tests you might have done, to stopping rules, and to the timing of the explanation is a profound philosophical and practical difference between Bayesian and classical statistics which we will discuss in detail later. The sensitivity of classical statistics to multiple testing, stopping rules, and timing of explanation is how classical statistics violates the likelihood principle: In these ways, classical statistics regards more aspects of the data than just the likelihood as relevant to inference.

Bayesian Analysis

Bayes' theorem says that posterior is proportional to likelihood times prior. We can use this in two ways when dealing with real psychological data. First, we can calculate a credibility interval, which is the Bayesian equivalent of a confidence interval. Second, we can calculate how to adjust our odds in favour of a theory we are testing over the null hypothesis in the light of our experimental data (the 'Bayes factor'), which is the Bayesian equivalent of null hypothesis testing. We discuss each in turn.

Credibility intervals

We wish to test the extent to which 1 g of a new drug can change blood pressure. Each possible value of population change in blood pressure is a hypothesis. You need to decide what your prior probability density is for each of these hypotheses. Before we have collected data, presumably you have some, albeit vague, idea of what sort of changes in blood pressure are relatively more probable than others. Let us say a normal distribution would not violate the shape of your prior too much, that is you think certain values are reasonably probable and more extreme values less probable in a symmetric way. The value you think is most probable defines the centre (or mean) of your prior distribution. The spread in your values – the standard deviation – can be assigned by remembering: You should think that plus or minus one standard deviation from the mean has a 68% probability of including the actual population value; and you should think that plus or minus two standard deviations has a 95% probability of including the actual population value. You should be virtually certain that plus or minus three standard deviations includes the true population value. If the standard deviation is infinite (or just very large compared to what is practically possible), you think all population values are equally likely. This is called a 'flat prior' or 'uniform prior'. You have NO idea what the population value is likely to be. That is OK, if that is how you feel. Remember there are no 'right' answers: This is YOUR prior! In sum, in choosing a prior decide (a) whether your prior can be approximated by a normal distribution and if so (b) what the mean of this distribution is (call it M_0) and (c) its standard deviation (call it S_0).

Conduct the following exercise before you continue reading. Consider a research question you are interested in. The research will probably involve estimating the value of a population parameter; for example, the difference in means between one condition and another. Construct your prior probability distribution for the parameter in question. See Box 4.3 to help you.

Box 4.3   An example in constructing a prior

Often as a psychologist you will be interested in the mean difference between two conditions. For example, you may be interested in people's self-esteem on a 0–6 scale after seeing an advert with a skinny model compared with after seeing an advert with a model of average body shape. You may believe that on average, self-esteem will be lower after the advert with a skinny model than the average model. Label changes in that direction as positive. What size change do you consider most likely? One thing to bear in mind is that a 0–6 scale does not allow much room for change. If people normally have a self-esteem in the middle of the scale (say a 3), and assuming that seeing the average model does not change the viewer's self-esteem, then the most self-esteem can be lowered by on average is 3 points. That is the very most, and *everyone* would have to reduce maximally for the population change to be 3. So even average changes of 1 or 2 points would be reasonably large. To determine quite what change is most likely, you might like to consider previous similar studies. In any case, your final guess is your personal guess and completely up to you.

You feel optimistic about the strength of your manipulation and you pick 1 as the mean of your prior. Next consider how uncertain you are about the population mean, that is the standard deviation of your prior. Ask yourself what is the probability that the population mean could be less than zero, that is that the average change goes in the opposite direction. You might think that the probability of the change being negative is only a few percent. If we can call it 2.5% without doing your intuitions an injustice, then the difference between the mean and zero is two standard deviations (the normal curve has 2.5% of its area less than two standard deviations below the mean). With a mean of 1, it follows the standard deviation for the prior is 0.5. *It is not that you think 2.5% of people will score in the negative direction.* It is that you think the probability of the population mean being less than zero is 2.5%. You may think that the probability the population mean being less than zero is zero, but also think that a good proportion of people in the population would score below zero.

Box 4.3 *continued*

You need to check if you are really happy with that standard deviation. If we go two standard deviations above the mean $(1 + 2 \times 0.5 = 2)$, you should believe there is a 2.5% probability that the true population mean is above 2. If that does not seem reasonable, you might consider revising either the mean or the standard deviation of your prior. Or you might consider revising the idea that your prior can be represented by a normal distribution (e.g. your prior may not drop off symmetrically about the mean). But see if you can produce a reasonable fit with a normal before giving it up; the exact details of your prior will not be important if you have a decent amount of data, so the aim is only to see if you can capture your prior intuitions without doing them gross violation.

You might think that the probability of the population mean being less than zero is more like 10%. Normal tables show that 10% of the area of a normal curve lies below 1.28 standard deviations below the mean. With a mean of 1 for your prior, it follows that 1.28 SDs = 1, so one SD = 1/1.28 = 0.78 units. Using that figure as a working value, see if you are happy with its consequences. For reference, 20% of the area of a normal lies below 0.84 standard deviations below the mean, and 30% of the area below 0.52 standard deviations below the mean. So if you thought there was a 30% probability of the population mean being below zero, you know there are 0.52 standard deviations between 0 and your mean. Hence, one standard deviation = mean/0.52.

If you settle on a mean of 1 and an SD of 0.78, there is 10% probability of the population mean being below zero. Conversely, there is a 90% probability of the population mean being above zero. *Thus, there is a zero probability of the population mean being exactly zero.* Of course, the probability of the mean being exactly zero is always zero, no matter what your mean and standard deviations are. (There is a finite probability of the mean being a small interval around zero. For example, for the mean and SD chosen, the prior probability of the population mean being within 0.1 scale points around zero is 0.09. Can you work this out yourself using normal tables?)

Sketching a prior for your experiment is an excellent exercise to carry out before you run your experiment, whether or not you accept Bayesian statistics. Thinking hard about effect sizes is important for any school of statistical inference, but sadly a process often neglected.

Figure 4.4 shows a possible prior for the effectiveness of a new drug. The units are whatever you measure effectiveness of the drug in; for example, it could be millimetres of mercury (mmHG) as a measure of blood pressure change. This prior shows that you think a mean of zero effect is most plausible $(M_0 = 0)$ and you are virtually certain that the true effect, whatever it is, lies between -9 and $+9$ units (here $S_0 = 3$).

Figure 4.4

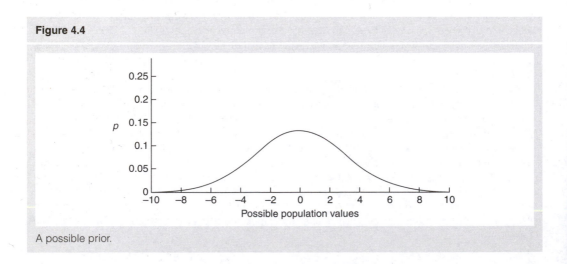

A possible prior.

Figure 4.5

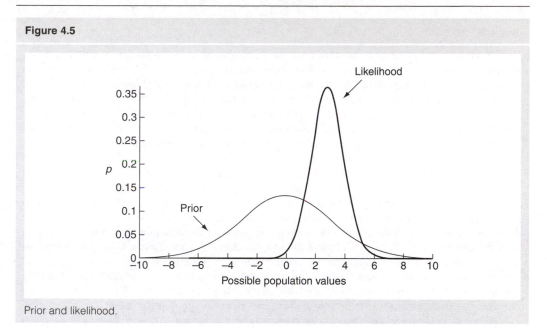

Prior and likelihood.

Figure 4.4 shows what you felt before you collected data. You collect data from a normally distributed population. Your sample has a mean of 2.8 and a standard error of 1.09. Assuming your data are based on 30 or more observations, you can represent your likelihood as a normal distribution with a mean of 2.8 and a standard deviation of 1.09, as shown in Figure 4.5. See Box 4.4 for calculating your likelihood distribution.

Box 4.4   Determining the likelihood

Imagine each subject took part in two conditions; your dependent variable is continuous and roughly normally distributed. For each subject, calculate the difference between the two conditions. The mean for your likelihood function is the mean of these difference scores. The standard deviation of the likelihood function is the standard *error* of the difference scores. If the difference scores have a standard deviation S, then the standard error is $S/\sqrt{n}$, where n is the number of subjects. S is the standard deviation of the *difference* scores, not of the scores in any one condition. You might wish to perform a Bayesian analysis on data reported in a paper comparing two conditions using a within-subjects design (i.e. each subject participated in each condition). The tables in a paper typically report the standard deviation of the scores in each condition but do not give you what you want: the standard error of the difference scores. There is a trick you can use to get the information though. The paper may report a t-test for the difference. $t =$ (mean difference)/(standard error of difference). Thus, standard error of difference = (mean difference)/t.

If each subject took part in just one of two conditions, the standard deviation of the likelihood function is still the standard error of the difference. But now we cannot take a difference score for each subject because each subject participated in just one condition. Let the conditions have standard deviations S_1 and S_2, and also have n_1 and n_2 subjects.

The standard error of the difference is now given by $\sqrt{(S_1^2/n_1 + S_2^2/n_2)}$. Alternatively, the paper may have reported a t-test for the difference. $t =$ (mean difference)/(standard error of difference), as before. Thus, standard error of difference = (mean difference)/t, as before.

Box 4.4 *continued*

We are considering examples of mean differences where the means can be considered (roughly) normally distributed because the equations turn out to be simple for Bayesian analyses in this case. But bear in mind Bayesian procedures can be used for all the common situations for which researchers need statistics, from the simple to the complex, with new solutions coming out all the time. The introductory textbook by Berry (1996) explains how to construct priors, likelihoods and posteriors for data involving proportions (as well as for means from roughly normal distributions). McCarthy (2007) illustrates the use of free software (winBUGS) for the Bayesian analysis of many designs, from the simple to the very complex.

We have considered your prior uncertainty in the mean of the population distribution, but we have not mentioned your uncertainty in its standard deviation. Technically, the equations we will use in Box 4.5 assume the population standard deviation is known, which is rather unlikely. When the standard deviation is unknown (only estimated by your sample), Berry recommends a correction when $n < 30$. Transform the standard deviation, S, of scores in each group by an amount $S' = S(1 + 20/n^2)$ and use S' in the above equations for calculating likelihood. The WINbugs software described by McCarthy allows a more principled Bayesian solution: One can construct priors for both mean and standard deviation, and these are jointly used in determining the posteriors for both mean and standard deviation.

The equations given in this chapter will cover you in many cases though; namely, wherever a roughly normal distribution is involved or a t-test would be used using orthodox statistics. For example, Pearson correlations can be transformed to be normal using Fisher's transform, r', given in Box 3.7. In that case, the likelihood function has a mean equal to the observed r' and a standard deviation given by the SE given in the box.

Box 4.5   Formulae for normal posterior

Mean of prior $= M_0$

Mean of sample $= M_d$

Standard deviation of prior $= S_0$

Standard error of sample $= SE$

Precision of prior $= c_0 = 1/S_0{}^2$

Precision of sample $= c_d = 1/SE^2$

Posterior precision $c_1 = c_0 + c_d$

Posterior mean $M_1 = (c_0/c_1)M_0 + (c_d/c_1)M_d$

Posterior standard deviation, $S_1 = $ square root$(1/c_1)$

Bayes tells us that $p(H|D)$ is proportional to $p(D|H) \times p(H)$; that is that the posterior is given by the likelihood times the prior. Each value on the horizontal axis of Figure 4.5 is an H, a hypothesis about the population value of the drug's effectiveness. For each H, we need to multiply the likelihood by the prior to get the posterior for that H, as shown in Figures 4.6 and 4.7. (You might worry about what the constant of proportionality should be. In fact, we need not worry about it. We just make sure the area under the posterior distribution is equal to one.)

Notice how similar the posterior is to the likelihood. For a reasonably diffuse prior (i.e. one representing fairly vague prior opinions), the posterior is dominated by the likelihood, i.e. by the data. If you started with a flat or uniform prior (you have no opinion concerning which values are most likely), the posterior would be identical to the likelihood. Further, even if people started with very different priors, if you collect enough data, as long as the priors were smooth and allowed *some* non-negligible probability in the region of the

Figure 4.6

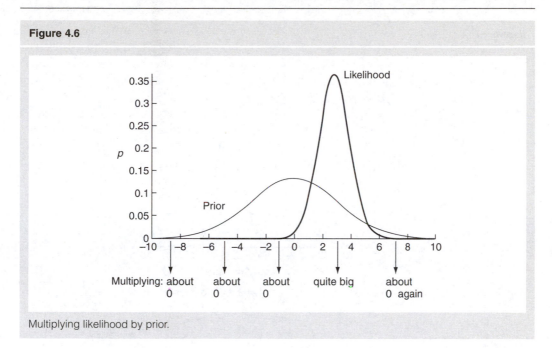

Multiplying likelihood by prior.

true population value, the posteriors, being dominated by the likelihood, would come to be very similar (Edwards et al., 1963, discuss the conditions more precisely). In this sense, Bayesian statistics emphasizes the objective nature of science: Different starting opinions will be brought together by sufficient data. The likelihood, representing the data, comes to dominate conclusions.

It turns out that if the prior and likelihood are normal, the posterior is also normal. There also turn out to be simple formulae for determining the mean and standard deviation of the posterior given the mean and standard deviation of the prior and likelihood. One doesn't have to literally go through and multiply prior and likelihood values for every population value. Box 4.5 gives the formulae.

Having found the posterior distribution, you have really found out all you need to know. It can be convenient to summarize the distribution in terms of a *credibility interval* (also called a probability interval or a highest density region, or HDR). For example, we could find the range of drug effects which have a 95% probability of including the true drug effect. We generally stipulate that this is centred on the mean of the posterior distribution. You will remember that in a normal distribution, the mean plus or minus 1.96 standard deviations includes 95% of the area. Thus, if the standard deviation of the posterior is S_1, and the mean is M_1, then going from $(M_1 - 1.96 \times S_1)$ to $(M_1 + 1.96 \times S_1)$ defines the 95% credibility interval. The posterior in Figures 4.7 and 4.8 has a mean of 2.47 and a standard deviation of 1.10 (confirm these values using the formulae in Box 4.5). The 95% credibility interval thus runs from 0.5 to 4.5 units. That is, there is a 95% probability that the true effect of the drug lies in the interval from 0.5 to 4.5. Our prior had a mean of 0 and a standard deviation of 3. A 95% credibility interval based only on the prior runs from $(0 - 1.96 \times 3)$ to $(0 + 1.96 \times 3)$, that is, from −5.9 to +5.9. Because we have collected data, we have gained in precision: as we have just noted, with the posterior the interval runs from 0.5 to 4.5.

Figure 4.7

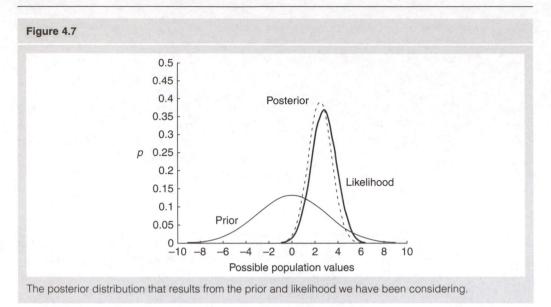

The posterior distribution that results from the prior and likelihood we have been considering.

Figure 4.8

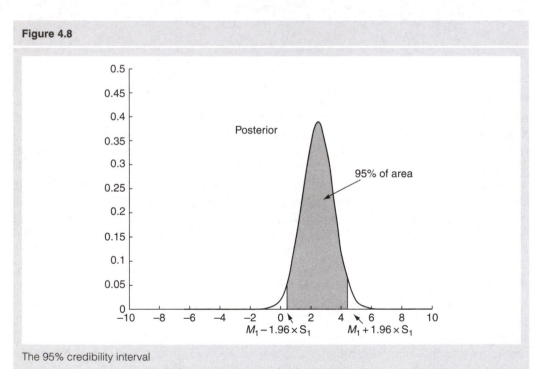

The 95% credibility interval

If you needed information more precise than this, you could simply collect more data until the credibility interval had shrunk to a sufficiently small precision. How precise you want the answer to be is just up to you; you can collect data until you are satisfied, and there is no need to define in advance how precise that has to be. Just stop when you know enough for your purposes at that point in time. For example, if after some more participants had been run your 95% credibility interval went from 2.9 to 3.2, you might decide to stop: A drug that changes blood pressure by around +3 units on average will do the job you want.

If the priors were flat, the 95% credibility interval would be numerically the same interval as the 95% confidence interval of Neyman–Pearson. But the meanings of the intervals are very different. The confidence interval is associated with an objective probability: If you repeated your experiment an indefinite number of times, the interval calculated each time would include the true population value 95% of the time. But you cannot make any claim about how likely THIS confidence interval is to enclose the true population mean. You cannot really be 95% confident that the population value lies in the 95% confidence interval. But as Savage (1962, p. 98) said in criticism of the Neyman–Pearson approach 'The only use I know of for a confidence interval is to have confidence in it!' The Bayesian credibility interval allows you to be confident in it.

Further, there is a profound practical difference between confidence and credibility intervals. The confidence interval will have to be adjusted according to how many other tests you conducted, under what conditions you planned to stop collecting data, and whether the test was planned or post hoc. The credibility interval is unaffected by all these things. On the other hand, the credibility interval IS affected by any prior information you had (because such information will change your prior distribution) whereas the confidence interval is not. All these respective differences are seen as strengths by each side; we will discuss the contrasting intuitions later.

The Bayes factor

There is no such thing as significance testing in Bayesian statistics. All one often has to do as a Bayesian statistician is determine posterior distributions. However, sometimes people like to compare the probability of their experimental theory to the probability of the null hypothesis. We can do this with the 'Bayes factor', the logic of which is now described. It is the Bayesian equivalent of null hypothesis or significance testing. Notice in the example used for calculating a credibility interval, the prior and posterior were both probability *density* distributions. Because the dependent variable plotted horizontally was continuous, the distributions only allow probabilities to be assigned to intervals. Any single point, such as a blood pressure change of exactly 2.3331564 units, had a probability of zero. Thus, the hypothesis that the population blood pressure change was exactly zero also has a probability of zero. That is, the null hypothesis both before and after data collection had a probability of zero. In such a context, it does not make much sense to talk about accepting or rejecting the null hypothesis. And typically in real research contexts, it indeed makes no sense to think of an independent variable having absolutely no effect on a dependent variable, or a correlation between two psychological variables being exactly zero, whatever the truth of one's favourite theory. Even given your theory is false, there are bound to be other reasons for why there is some at least tiny relation between the variables. But sometimes we might want to assign some finite non-zero probability to a particular hypothesis, like the null hypothesis, and see how that probability changes as we collect data. This is what the Bayes factor allows us to do.

Bayes says that $P(H|D)$ is proportional to $P(D|H) \times P(H)$. Thus to consider two particular hypotheses, your experimental hypothesis H_1 and the null H_0, we have

$$P(H_1|D) \text{ is proportional to } P(D|H_1) \times P(H_1) \qquad (4.5)$$

$$P(H_0|D) \text{ is proportional to } P(D|H_0) \times P(H_0) \qquad (4.6)$$

Dividing (4.5) by (4.6),

$$P(H_1|D)/P(H_0|D) = P(D|H_1)/P(D|H_0) \times P(H_1)/P(H_0)$$

Posterior odds = likelihood ratio × prior odds

The likelihood ratio is (in this case) called the Bayes factor B in favour of the experimental hypothesis. Whatever your prior odds were in favour of the experimental hypothesis over the null, after data collection multiply those odds by B to get your posterior odds. If B is greater than 1, your data support the experimental hypothesis over the null; if B is less than 1, your data support the null over the experimental hypothesis. If B was about 1, then your experiment was not sensitive.[3] You did not run enough participants, so the data do not distinguish your experimental hypothesis from the null. (Notice how you automatically get a notion of how sensitive your experiment was. Contrast just relying on p-values in significance testing.) The Bayes factor gives the means of adjusting your odds in a continuous way; you are not being asked to make a black and white decision. Arguably, in reality we typically do not make black and white decisions accepting or rejecting hypotheses; we let the data more or less strongly nudge our strength of belief one way or the other. If we really made black and white decisions, there would be little need to replicate experiments exactly.

Example of calculating the Bayes factor

We will now consider an example with real data. Some years ago, I ran a series of experiments to test the theory of morphic resonance postulated by English biologist Rupert Sheldrake. Morphic resonance will be a useful example to contrast Bayesian with classical analyses because people start with wildly different prior odds in favour of Sheldrake's theory. Morphic resonance is an idea so radically in conflict with existing scientific paradigms, some scientists are like Kuhnian Normal scientists and react in abject horror to Sheldrake's theory; on the other hand, a few, acting in a more Popperian manner, note with interest it is a bold conjecture that could be tested.

According to the theory of morphic resonance, any system by assuming a particular shape becomes associated with a 'morphic field'. The morphic field then plays a causal role in the development and maintenance of future systems. 'Morphic' means shape; the effect of the field is to guide future systems to take similar shapes.

The subsequent systems 'resonate' with previous systems through the fields. The effect is stronger the more similar the future system is to the system that generated the field; and the effect is stronger the more times a form has been assumed by previous similar systems. The effect occurs at all levels of organization, for example from crystallization of chemical substances to brain patterns. In terms of brains, for example, if a group of rats have solved a certain maze, future rats should find the same maze easier because they can resonate with the brains of the previous successful rats, a type of rodent ESP (Sheldrake, 1981; 1988).

Repetition priming is a phenomenon well known to experimental psychologists: People identify a stimulus more quickly or more accurately with repeated presentation of the stimulus. This can be shown in, for example, the lexical decision task, in which people

---

3. This statement is typically true but not always. If your theory predicts just one possible population value, and the true population value lies *exactly* in between the null and the value predicted by theory, the Bayes factor tends to 1 as you collect more and more observations!

have to decide whether a presented letter string makes a meaningful English word or not, with the letters in the presented order. People are faster to make a lexical decision when a letter string is repeated. The theory of morphic resonance predicts that repetition priming should occur: The person will resonate with themselves in the past facilitating future performance. Of course, other theories also predict repetition priming should occur. But there is a unique prediction of morphic resonance not made by other theories favoured by psychologists; namely, that there should be repetition priming between separate people (i.e. a form of ESP) (see box 4.6).

I ran the following experiment in 1989. One set of words and non-words was called the shared set; another set was called the unique set. The first, 10th, 20th, 30th, … and 100th participant performed a lexical decision task on both the unique and shared sets. These participants were called 'resonators'. The intervening participants, the 'boosters', were just exposed to the shared set. Thus, over successive participants, the shared stimuli were receiving morphic resonance at 10 times the rate as the unique stimuli. Thus, resonators should get progressively faster on the shared rather than unique stimuli. (At the end of the experiment, some extra resonators were run, just to stabilize the measurement of the morphic field at that point in time.)

Figure 4.9 shows the non-word data. The slope of the line is −2.8 ms per resonator, with a standard error of 1.09. With Neyman–Pearson statistics, this gives a p of 0.018, significant at the conventional 5% level.

On a classic analysis, we have a significant result, and we reject the null hypothesis. We categorically accept that resonators get faster on the shared rather than unique stimuli as the experiment progresses. (Of course, this does not mean we categorically accept *morphic resonance*. That depends on whether we can come up with other mechanisms for the effect.)

Figure 4.9

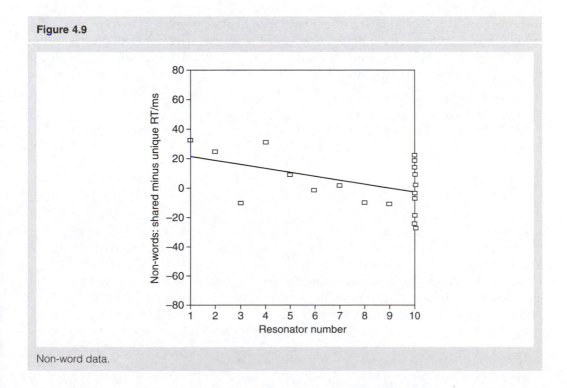

Non-word data.

Now consider the Bayesian analysis. If 'MR' stands for the theory that morphic resonance is true:

$$P(MR|D)/P(H_0|D) = p(D|MR)/p(D|H_0) \times P(MR)/P(H_0)$$

Posterior odds = Bayes factor, $B \times$ Prior odds

Before we continue, remind yourself of your personal prior odds in favour of morphic resonance you determined previously.

To calculate the Bayes factor, we need to determine $p(D|H_0)$ and $p(D|MR)$. H_0 is that the population slope is zero. $p(D|H_0)$ can be obtained by plotting the probability density of getting different slopes in a sample given the null hypothesis is true, as illustrated in Figure 4.10. For these data, we will assume a normal distribution. Naturally, the sample mean with the highest probability density is zero, the hypothetical population mean. The standard deviation is the standard error (the standard error in the study was 1.09). $p(D|H_0)$ is just the height of this normal curve for a slope of -2.8 (see Figure 4.13). The height here is 0.014. That is, $p(D|H_0) = 0.014$. In sum, to determine $p(D|H_0)$ decide if a normal distribution is adequate for the shape of $p(D|H_0)$. Next you need to know your sample mean and its standard error. If you use the program called 'Bayes factor' given at the end of the chapter, enter the sample mean and standard error, it will tell you $p(D|H_0)$.

The difficult part is to determine $p(D|MR)$. Morphic resonance is consistent with a number of population slopes; in fact, at first blush, any slope < 0. The theory says that resonators will get faster on shared relative to unique words, but the theory does not predict a precise value (in this respect, its quantitative vagueness, it is like almost all theories in psychology). But in fact, morphic resonance does not allow any slope < 0. The between-subject priming (shown in Figure 4.9) must be less than the priming shown by a person resonating with themselves (because people are more similar to themselves than to other people). In fact, boosters in the study saw each stimulus three times, so we know what the effect of repetition was within a person. People sped up by 20 ms with a repetition. So the speed up in reaction time from one resonator to the next certainly could not be more than 10 people × three repetitions per

Figure 4.10

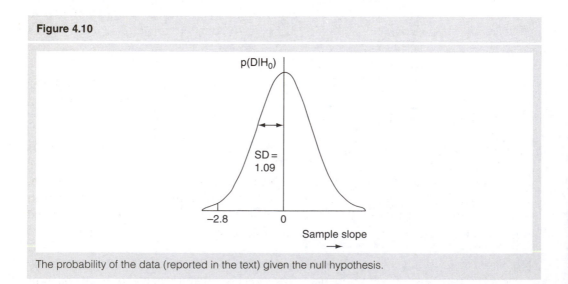

The probability of the data (reported in the text) given the null hypothesis.

Figure 4.11

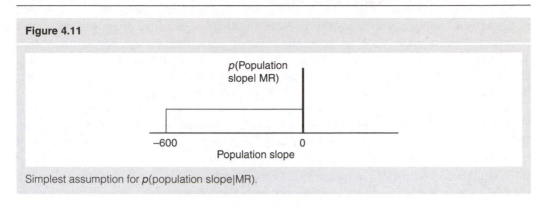

Simplest assumption for p(population slope|MR).

person $\times$ 20 ms per repetition = 600 ms. The slope predicted by morphic resonance cannot be steeper than -600 ms per resonator.

Now assume that given we accept morphic resonance is true, we have no preference whatsoever for thinking any of the slopes in the range from 0 to -600 ms (exclusive) are more likely than any others (see Figure 4.11). This is an implausible assumption, but we will assume it now to see the consequences. Shortly, we will make a more plausible assumption about how likely different slopes are, assuming morphic resonance is true.

To go from p(population slope|MR) to p(observing a slope|MR), i.e. $p(D|MR)$, we need to smear each point on the graph in Figure 4.13 by the standard error of the sample. Figure 4.10 illustrates p(observing a slope| null hypothesis) where the null only allows one population value, namely a slope of zero. The data are distributed around this point. Just so, assuming morphic resonance, each population slope can produce a sample slope somewhat lower or higher than the population value. Thus, a population slope of -599 ms could produce a sample slope of -601 ms. A population slope of -599 ms is unlikely to produce a sample slope more than about two standard errors away. Because the standard error of the sample is about 1 ms, this smearing is tiny; we are unlikely to see sample slopes lower than about -601 ms. In this case, $p(D|MR)$ looks pretty much like p(population slope|MR).

Assume the distribution in Figure 4.11, and smearing with a standard error of 1.09 to obtain $p(D|MR)$. Do not worry about how exactly this is done, the provided program will do it for you; we will come to what you enter in the program for your own data later. Since the distribution is very long (600 ms long), that is, so many values are possible, the probability of observing a slope in any one 1 ms interval, e.g. 2–3 ms, is actually very small. The actual sample value was 2.8 ms. p(observing slope = 2.8 ms| this model of morphic resonance) = 0.0017. We determined above that $p(D|H_0)$ was 0.014. So Bayes factor = $p(D|M)/p(D|H_0)$ = 0.0017/0.014 = 0.12.

Remember posterior odds = Bayes factor $\times$ prior odds. Our Bayes factor is 0.12. This Bayes factor means data should REDUCE your confidence in morphic resonance and INCREASE your confidence in the null hypothesis! Contrast Neyman–Pearson in this case: $p = 0.018$, so we reject the null hypothesis! This is one of the counter-intuitive findings of Bayesian analysis. Sometimes a significant result on a Neyman–Pearson analysis, meaning one should categorically reject the null hypothesis on that approach, actually means one should be more confident in the null hypothesis because of the data! (Not all the time, just sometimes.) Remember (no matter what anyone tells you) Neyman–Pearson analyses do not directly license assigning any degree of confidence to one conclusion rather than another. If you want to know how confident you should be in different statistical conclusions, you need to deal with statistics designed to address what your confidence should be, namely Bayesian statistics. The differences between the approaches are not just a matter of philosophical quibbles; they can produce radically different research decisions. Neyman–Pearson may license a certain behaviour, but Bayesian analyses can tell you how confident you can be in your hypothesis.

Why does the Bayesian analysis indicate we should have more confidence in the null hypothesis? Because the theory we tested allowed a large range of outcomes; it was vague. The moral is that on a Bayesian analysis, a significant result may lead one to prefer the null hypothesis even more rather than a poorly specified theory. To see the logic of this, contrast the distributions p(slope|MR) in Figure 4.12. One of the distributions is the one considered so far, 600 ms long. But let us say for some reason we decide morphic resonance would not allow slopes greater than 150 ms (the filled-in distribution). This account of morphic resonance is more precise; it rules out more. The distribution is a quarter as long. Now remember that the area under a probability density distribution has to be one. The filled-in distribution therefore has to be higher. Each slope for the filled-in distribution has a higher probability density than the other distribution because the theory is more precise.

Evidence most supports the theory that most strongly predicted it. A vague theory might allow some obtained data but the data hardly supports that theory if the theory would have allowed virtually any data. That is the intuition that our Bayes factor of 0.12 illustrated: For a very vague theory, evidence supports it less than the null, even when the probability density of the data assuming the null is low. The probability density of the data is even lower assuming the vague theory (see Figure 4.13, which puts Figures 4.10 and 4.11 on the same scale). By embedding this intuition in the heart of its techniques, Bayesian analyses punish those with vague theories, whereas significance testing does not.

Our example thus far has done an injustice to morphic resonance. The theory is not so poorly specified as in this example. The assumption that morphic resonance allows all slope values between 0 and 600 ms per resonator equally is implausible. Sheldrake (1988) discusses the application of morphic resonance to data on learning and memory. The most striking example taken to be a case of morphic resonance is McDougal (1938), in which successive generations of rats learn a choice task with progressively fewer errors, despite the

Figure 4.12

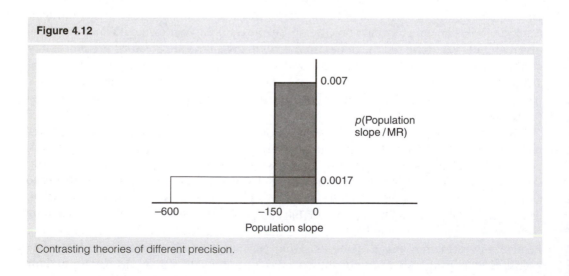

Contrasting theories of different precision.

Figure 4.13

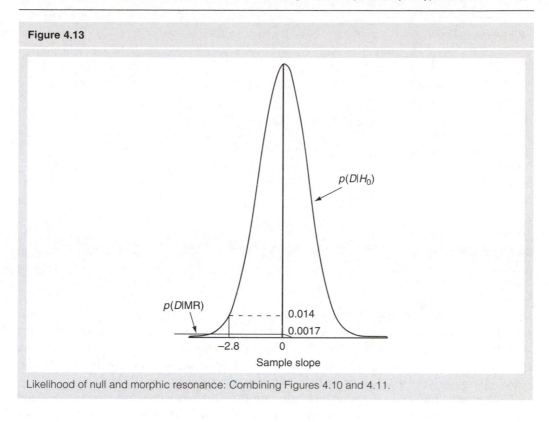

Likelihood of null and morphic resonance: Combining Figures 4.10 and 4.11.

fact McDougal selected the worse performers in each generation to sire the next. After a mere 500 rats have learned the task, average errors dropped from 215 to 27 per rat (McDougal, 1938, p. 331). That is, it took about 500 rats for between-rat resonance to produce almost the learning achieved by each rat in its lifetime (resonating with itself). The theory of morphic resonance, by linking disparate domains, can gain precision by using the data in one domain to constrain expectations in the other. Thus, it seems rather unlikely in our study that the between-participant effect would be much more than 1/500th of the within-participant effect, i.e. our population slope is not very likely to be much greater than 600 ms/500 = about 1 ms per resonator. Even then, a rectangular distribution does not capture our intuitions very well; presumably, the probability of large effects is smaller than small effects. On balance, effects smaller than 1 ms per resonator seem more likely than effects greater than 1 ms per resonator. One way of representing p(population slope|MR) is as a normal distribution centred on zero, and with half of it removed, as shown in Figure 4.14. If we are 95% sure that the true population slope allowed by morphic resonance is not more (in absolute terms) than 4 ms per resonator, then we can assign a standard deviation to the normal curve we are using of 2 ms.

Now morphic resonance, by allowing itself to be reasonably constrained in the domain of human repetition priming by knowledge we have about the application of the theory to other domains, is a more precise theory. A theory in having generality can gain in precision. The gain in precision is reflected in the Bayes factor. With the new assumptions concerning the theory, the Bayes factor is 12. Whatever your odds were in favour of morphic resonance before the data were collected, you should multiply them by 12 in the light of these data (given the assumptions we have made). This seems a reasonable type of conclusion to draw

Figure 4.14

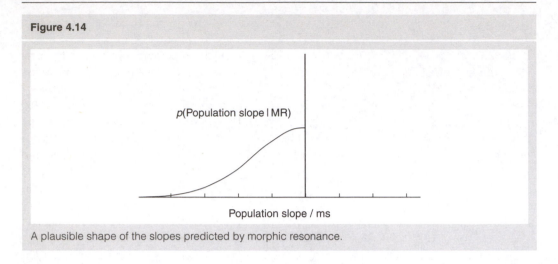

p(Population slope I MR)

Population slope / ms

A plausible shape of the slopes predicted by morphic resonance.

from the data. We are not making a black and white decision. If you thought morphic resonance was wildly implausible before the data, you will still think it implausible in the light of these data; it's just that your odds have been nudged up. If you had even odds in favour of the theory before hand, now you will think on balance it is more likely than not. It will take a lot more data before everyone agrees; and that is just as it should be.

The morphic resonance example highlights another difference between Neyman–Pearson and Bayesian analysis. Given a theory of morphic resonance which allows effects arbitrarily close to zero (as illustrated in Figure 4.14), then assuming the null hypothesis to be true, significance testing would not allow the conclusion that morphic resonance does not exist, no matter how big our sample. We can only accept the null given we have enough power to detect a minimally interesting effect size, and in this case, any effect above zero is possible. In contrast, notice how the Bayesian analysis can allow us to either increase or decrease our confidence in the null, depending on how the data turn out. A Bayesian analysis can allow us to draw inferences from data where significance testing is mute.

I ran two further studies with a similar design. One study (experiment 2) varied from the first in that there were 20 instead of 9 boosters between each resonator (so 200 boosters were run in total) and two rather than one resonators were run after each set of boosters. The other study (experiment 3) involved resonators being run not only in Sussex but also in Goetingen by Professor Suitbert Ertel; his job was to tell me which set of stimuli I had been boosting in Sussex. All results were flat as a pancake. For the same assumptions we used above to get a Bayes factor of 12 for the first experiment, the Bayes factors for the new data for non-words were 0.49 (experiment 2), 0.14 (experiment 3 Goetingen data), and 1.58 (experiment 3 , Sussex data). For these extra experiments, the overall Bayes factor for non-words is therefore: $0.49 \times 0.14 \times 1.58 = 0.11$. These new data do not rule out morphic resonance, no black and white decision need be made; the data just change our odds. For these data taken together including the first experiment, our odds in favour of morphic resonance should remain roughly unchanged (12×0.11 is about 1). If we take into account the data for the words as well as the non-words, and assume the effect for words is half that for non-words (i.e. the standard deviation is 1 ms), then the overall Bayes factor is 0.5. With further data, the Bayes factor will be driven either up or down, and at some point, the data will change which side of the decision bound in Figure 4.17 the theory falls for different people.

This discussion should have provided you with the concepts needed to consider a Bayesian analysis of your own data, if you can assume your data are roughly normally distributed. To use the provided program to calculate a Bayes factor for your data, you need to enter your sample mean and standard error. You also need to decide: Does my theory predict a rectangular distribution for the population effect (as in Figure 4.11) or a normal distribution? If rectangular, what are the limits? If a normal, what is its mean and standard deviation? If a normal, does the theory allow both positive and negative effects or only effects in one direction? Answers to these questions will enable the program to calculate a Bayes factor for you. You do not need to know how to do the calculations, just the concepts behind them.

Finally, a comment on what the Bayes factor means about your personal probability in a theory, say morphic resonance. A Bayes factor tells you how much to multiply your prior odds in favour of morphic resonance *relative to the null hypothesis* in the light of data. If those were the only two theories that could be conceived of, then your personal probability of morphic resonance is given by (posterior odds)/(posterior odds + 1) where the posterior odds are obtained from the prior odds by multiplication with the Bayes factor. However, in practice other theories will exist that compete in explaining the data. Morphic resonance may have increased odds relative to the null but decreased odds relative to other theories that predict the data more strongly. The final effect of the data on the probability of morphic resonance depends on spelling out all the other relevant theories. But this is not possible; there are bound to be theories one has not yet conceived of. So it is best to treat your posterior probability as a probability conditional on the theories you have actually considered. You should reserve some of your personal probability for theories as yet undreamt of.

Summary

A Bayes factor tells you how much to multiply your prior odds in favour of your experimental theory (over the null hypothesis) in the light of data. An advantage of using a Bayes factor to analyse your experiments is that for common situations, low sensitivity shows up as a Bayes factor near 1. You are not tempted to accept the null hypothesis just because the experiment was insensitive. The Bayes factor also penalizes vague theories; in that case, data significantly different from the null may actually support the null. Further, you can combine experiments together or continue to collect data until the Bayes factor for all the data is extreme enough for you to make your point.

A disadvantage of the Bayes factor is shown by the somewhat arbitrary way we settled on p(population effect|MR) and hence on $p(D|MR)$. $P(D|MR)$ reflected not only the data but also our subjective judgments about what is likely, given both morphic resonance and other things we know. In that sense, $p(D|MR)$ did not reflect just the data and the theory of morphic resonance per se; so it was not a true likelihood. Unfortunately, a logical analysis of morphic resonance, or almost any theory in psychology, together with relevant past studies, does not yield a definitive unique distribution for p(population effect|theory). One solution is to report how the Bayes factor varied with assumptions, for example, how it varied with different assumed standard deviations for the p(population effect|theory) distribution. Figure 4.14 shows how the Bayes factor varies for non-word data for the first experiment. People can then choose the Bayes factor based on the assumptions that they endorse. Most simply, one could report just the maximum value of Bayes factor the analysis allows and the associated assumptions (in this case, the peak in Figure 4.15 is a Bayes factor of 12 for a standard deviation of p(population effect|theory) of around 3).

Figure 4.15

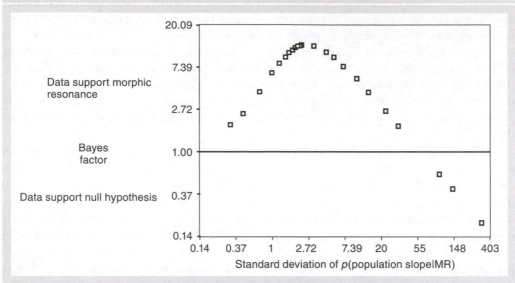

Relation of Bayes factor to distribution of *p*(population slope|MR) (Note: The axes use 'log scales': Each labelled point is 2.72 times higher than the previous point, and 2.72 is an arbitrary number for this purpose.).

Stopping rules

Likelihoods (and hence posterior distributions, credibility intervals and Bayes factors) are insensitive to many stopping rules. For example, in the previous chapter, we considered a hypothetical study to determine the proportion of women who experienced G Spot orgasm. One could decide to stop collecting data when a certain sample size has been reached (e.g. 30 women in total) or alternatively one could decide in advance to stop when a certain number of women who experienced G Spot orgasm had been reached (say, 6). Even if in both cases one ended up with six women claiming to experience G Spot orgasm out of 30 asked in total, on a classic Neyman–Pearson analysis, one estimates the population proportion differently in the two cases (6/30 vs 5/29). A Bayesian analysis produces the same answer in both cases. In both cases, what is important is the exact data obtained in asking successive women. They answer: no, no, no, yes, no and so on for 30 answers. Those are the exact data. The probability of obtaining those data given a hypothesis, for example that the population proportion = 0.3, is the *same* regardless of the stopping rule. The probability is $0.7 \times 0.7 \times 0.7 \times 0.3 \times 0.7 \times \ldots$ and so on for 30 answers for both stopping rules. The likelihood is unaffected by which stopping rule is used; thus, the posterior, credibility interval and Bayes factor are unaffected as well.

Remember we cannot use a stopping rule like 'Stop when my *t*-test is significant at the 5% level' in the Neyman–Pearson approach. For example, consider a one-sample *t*-test, which is mean/SE (for the null hypothesis that population mean = 0). For a reasonable number of subjects, the critical value of *t* is 2; that is, the test is significant at the 5% level when the mean is about two standard errors from zero. As more subjects are run, the standard error gets smaller and smaller, and the sample mean will vary more and more tightly around zero. Even given the null is really true, sooner or later the sample mean will randomly sneak out to two standard errors from zero. At this point, the sample mean may be very very close to zero, but because the standard error is so small, we still get a *t*-value of 2. Sooner or later that is guaranteed to happen. (In fact, sooner or later the mean will sneak out to any number of standard errors from zero as you wish; you just have to wait long enough.) As we shall see, the Bayes factor behaves very differently.

The Bayes factor is the likelihood for the alternative theory (e.g. morphic resonance), $p(D|MR)$, divided by the likelihood for the null, $p(D|null)$. As more and more subjects are run and the sample standard error shrinks, and, assuming the null is true, the sample mean will hover around zero more and more closely. But $p(D|MR)$ remains pretty constant as more subjects are run, given that the theory allows a range of population values covering the area around zero. The probability density of these values will not change just because you run more subjects. Now, what about $p(D|null)$? As more subjects are run, the standard error shrinks, so the $p(D|null)$ distribution has to become more peaked, higher around zero, in order that the area under the curve remain unity. This is illustrated in Figure 4.16, which shows $p(D|null)$.

In Figure 4.16, the curve of crosses corresponds to when four times as many subjects are run as in the curve of filled circles (say $4n$ vs n subjects). Thus, the $4n$ curve has a smaller standard error than the n curve (half the size in fact). Compare the height of the line (i.e. $p(D|null)$ for a mean two standard errors away from zero for the $4n$ curve with the n curve. It is higher for the $4n$ curve.

Assuming the null is true, as more data are collected, the mean will vary around zero, mostly keeping within about two standard errors from zero, but sometimes reaching two standard errors or beyond. When the mean reaches two standard errors out, $p(D|null)$ will be higher after many subjects are run rather than after only a few. This is true for any number of standard errors out. That is, as more subjects are run, $p(D|null)$ is expected to just keep increasing. As $p(D|null)$ increases, so the Bayes factor decreases. Assuming the null is true, with increasing subjects the *t*-value does a random walk around zero, going up and down randomly; the Bayes factor is, by contrast, driven closer and closer to zero with increasing

Figure 4.16

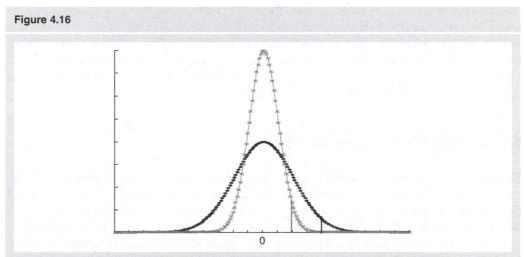

0

$p(D|null)$ for data collected with *n* subjects (filled circles) and *4n* subjects (crosses). The tall vertical line indicates the height of the *4n* curve two standard deviations out and the small vertical line indicates the height of the *n* curve two standard deviations out. Notice the lines are of different heights.

subjects. There is no guarantee that the Bayes factor will ever exceed a certain value, like 4, even after an infinite number of subjects. If you run 'until I get a significant result', you are guaranteed to, sooner or later, even assuming the null is true. Neyman–Pearson statistics are sensitive to the stopping rule; Bayesian statistics are relatively insensitive. That is a distinct advantage of the Bayesian approach. All that matters is the data you actually obtained, not what intentions you may or may not have had about when to stop. In commenting on the insensitivity of Bayesian analyses to the stopping rule, Savage (1962, p. 72) said 'it is impossible to be sure of sampling until the data justifies an unjustifiable conclusion, just as it is impossible to build a perpetual motion machine. After all, whatever we [i.e. classic and Bayesian statisticians] may disagree about, we are surely agreed Bayes' theorem is true where it applies'.

The relative insensitivity of the likelihood to stopping rules gives Bayesian statistics an advantage over conventional significance testing. If journals ever adopted, say Bayes factors as the standard statistical tool, they would probably introduce a criterion for publication like 'The Bayes factor should be 4 for supporting a theory or 1/4 for confirming a null'.[4] This provides a perfectly good stopping rule 'Stop when the Bayes factor is 4 or 1/4'. If you collected 30 participants and were not quite there yet, just collect some more. On the other hand, if you collected 30 participants and the results were not quite significant, you could not collect some more until you made it at the 5% level; yet the current system makes the former practice almost inevitably wide spread. If you had collected 30 subjects and just missed out, binning all that work would be a tragic waste, and where is the virtue in that. The current system invites cheating.

Running until the confidence interval is a preset width also avoids common wicked temptations (compare with the previous chapter). If you decided to run until the 95% confidence interval excluded zero, you are guaranteed to always succeed even if the null is true, for exactly the same reasons just noted above. So running until a confidence interval excludes zero is not a valid stopping rule for Neyman–Pearson statistics. Similarly, if you decided to run until the 95% *credibility* interval excluded zero, you are also guaranteed to succeed. The implication for Bayesian inference is different than for classic inference, however (contrast Mayo, 1996). With the Neyman–Pearson approach the exclusion of zero from the confidence interval corresponds to a decision to reject the null hypothesis. With the Bayesian approach, given the prior and posterior are probability density functions, the null before and after any amount of data collection has zero probability. We are entitled to use the posterior to calculate the probability that the true population value lies in any *interval*. If the true population value is zero, then the bulk of the area of our posterior will become contained in an interval closer and closer to zero, no matter what the stopping rule.

Weakness of the Bayesian approach

The strengths of Bayesian analyses are also its weaknesses. Its strengths lie in directly addressing how we should update our personal probabilities and in the insensitivity of the statistical conclusions to various apparently arbitrary circumstances. As we will see, these two points define its greatest weaknesses.

First, are our subjective convictions really susceptible to the assignment of precise numbers? And are they really the sorts of things that do or should follow the axioms of probability?

4. Jeffreys (1961, p. 432) suggested that Bayes factors between 1 and 3 were 'barely worth mentioning'; those between 3 and 10 were 'substantial'; those above 10, strong.

Should papers worry about the strength of our convictions in their result sections, or just the objective reasons for why someone might change their opinions? Our convictions can seem like will-o'-the wisps. A small comment by someone, an analogy, a random thought, spotting a connection or a stylistic incompatibility in what you believe can shift the plausibility of a theory completely in the absence of any data. If you are uncomfortable with trying to assign precise numbers to your convictions, one solution is just to focus on the likelihood. After all it is the likelihood that tells you everything you need to know about the relative support the data gives different hypotheses. People who only use likelihoods are called likelihood theorists. It gives you many of the advantages of Bayesian statistics and avoids any issues concerning nailing down slippery subjective probabilities (see next chapter and Oakes, 1986, for further discussion; and Royall, 1997, for a sustained defense of likelihood inference). On the other hand, a Bayesian might ask a likelihood theorist, "If you are going to go part way down the Bayesian path, is it not half hearted not to go all the way?". Given that the likelihood will come to dominate the posterior, assuming that the likelihood is only some-what more precise than the prior, a reasonable approximation to most people's beliefs in many scientific cases can be obtained by assuming a uniform or uninformative prior so that the likelihood dominates completely (people who by default use uninformative priors are called 'objective Bayesians'). In the next chapter, we will discuss uniform priors and consider likelihood inference in more detail.

The second (at least apparent) weakness of Bayesian statistics is that they are not guaranteed to control Type I and Type II error probabilities (Mayo, 1996), especially with multiple testing. Whether this is a weakness is at the heart of the debate between Bayesian and classical approaches. I will motivate intuitions on both sides and leave you to decide if there is a weakness.

Neyman–Pearson statistics are designed to control Type I and Type II error probabilities in an optimal way. Any other method for making acceptance and rejection decisions will not be so optimal. Bayesian statistics do not give you black and white decisions; but life forces such decisions on us. At some point, we have to act on our knowledge one way or another. A journal editor may say he will only publish papers with Bayes factors above 4 or less than 1/4. Now we have a decision routine and we can ask about its long-term Type I and Type II error rates.

Imagine 10 measures of early toilet training are correlated with 10 measures of adult personality. Out of these 100 correlations, three are found to be significant at the normal 5% level: that is, for these three, their 95% confidence intervals exclude zero. A Neyman–Pearson user of statistics would say: 'One expects about 5 to be significant by chance alone; these are weak data and do not lead one to accept any hypothesis about toilet training affecting personality.' How might a Bayesian proceed? If we are really interested in evaluating point null hypotheses, we can calculate Bayes factors for each of the 100 hypotheses. I ran a simulation calculating 1000 Bayes factors by sampling 1000 times from a population with a mean of zero.[5] The alternative hypothesis in each case allowed positive and negative population values symmetrically (normal distribution centred on zero). Of course, some Bayes factors will exceed a given threshold by chance alone. For example, 78 of these 1000 Bayes factors,

5. Each sample was a random draw from a normal population with a mean of zero and a standard deviation of 0.1. The prior for the alternative hypothesis had a mean of zero and a standard deviation of 0.2. (If we had determined the maximum Bayes factor for each sample allowed by varying the standard deviation of the prior independently for each sample to find the optimal one, the proportion of Bayes factors above 4 would be a bit higher.) The standard deviation of sample means depends on the number of data points in each sample. If we had collected more data in each sample so that each sample was drawn from a population with a standard deviation of .01, then the error rate decreases: For example, the proportion of Bayes factors above 2 in a simulation of 1000 studies was only 4.4%.

that is, 7.8%, were above 2. Further, 2.8% were above 4. Thus in 100 tests, we might expect 2 or 3 Bayes factors to be above 4 by chance alone (this is not a fixed error rate; it depends on the exact alternative hypothesis considered). According to the Bayesian, in interpreting any one of these Bayes factors, unlike the Neyman–Pearson statistician interpreting significance tests, we would take no account of the fact that we ran 100 tests in total. Mayo (1996) presents this as a case against Bayesians: Bayesians are highly likely to generate support for experimental hypotheses when the null is true.

A Bayesian does not ignore all the other 97 results in evaluating a grand theory concerning toilet training and personality. For example, if a Freudian theory predicted ALL tested relationships, its Bayes factor in the light of the 100 correlations would be very low! BUT, the critic continues, the Bayesian can still run a lot of tests and pick out one result for which the Bayes factor is above some threshold. SHOULD not one's confidence in the alternative hypothesis supported by this one test be reduced because of all the other tests that were done (albeit they were tests of different hypotheses)? But why should what else you may or may not have done matter? The other tests were not, as such, relevant to the one hypothesis under consideration; the other tests tested different hypotheses. How can they matter?

If you were an editor would you publish the paper because there was 'substantial' support (e.g. Bayes factor = 4) for one of the 100 specific hypotheses? What if the author just reported testing that one hypothesis and constructed a plausible theory for it to put in his introduction. He did not even mention running the other tests. According to the Bayesian, there is nothing wrong with that (assuming the other tests really did not bear directly on the theory). According to classical statistics, that is clearly cheating. What do you think?

We can motivate the intuition that multiple testing without correction involves cheating more strongly with another example. This will also enable us to see how the Bayesian can respond in detail – and show that while failing to correct for multiple testing is cheating when using classical statistics, our intuitions may not see it quite that way when Bayesian methods are used!

Box 4.6   Which theory to test

In a *Nature* editorial, John Maddox (1981) said of Sheldrake's first book that 'the book is the best candidate for burning there has been in many years . . . Sheldrake's argument is pseudo-science . . . Hypotheses can be dignified as theories only if all aspects of them can be tested.' While this last comment is naïve (contrast Popper 1934, who recognized good science will include metaphysical elements), Lewis Wolpert (1984) argued '. . . it is possible to hold absurd theories which are testable, but that does not make them science. Consider the hypothesis that the poetic Muse resides in tiny particles contained in meat. This could be tested by seeing if eating more hamburgers improved one's poetry.'

One way of capturing the notion that not all testable theories are actually worth testing is in terms of the prior probability of the theory, as illustrated in Figure 4.17. One wants to test theories that will have high impact, that are simple, and have other desirable characteristics. For example, the theory that my pen will drop to the ground if I let go of it now will have no impact on anyone if found to be true. On the other hand, it will not be worth putting in effort to test a high-impact theory if you find it outrageously implausible. Morphic resonance is a theory that if confirmed would have an enormous impact in all areas of science. But some, like Wolpert, find it is so implausible it is not worth testing. Despite arguments (e.g. by Popper) that all theories have essentially a zero probability (after all, only a miniscule fraction of all theories are true), we certainly treat some theories as more probable than others, as the morphic resonance debate demonstrates. We take into account a theory's plausibility in deciding whether to pursue it. Figure 4.17 represents a space personal to each individual; a plot of impact versus prior probability. Theories will pepper this space. The line represents a decision bound. Theories that are sufficiently implausible or

Box 4.6 *continued*

Figure 4.17

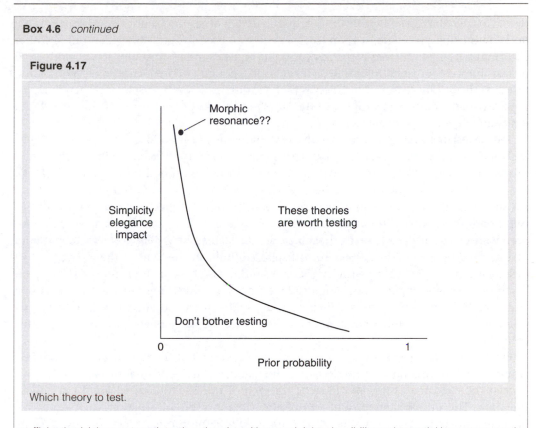

Which theory to test.

sufficiently trivial are not worth testing; theories with enough joint plausibility and potential impact are worth testing. Remember this is a personal space, a space each individual configures for themselves. Only you can say what your odds are in favour of different theories, and where your decision bound is. What are your subjective odds in favour of morphic resonance? Where would morphic resonance be for you in the space of Figure 4.17?

A Tibetan monastery wishes to find the reincarnation of a recently departed lama. The monks will test a child's ability to pick a favourite object of the old lama amongst a collection of similar objects. They put the old lama's walking stick in a collection of 20 other walking sticks of other monks from the monastery. Field testing at a nearby school (which the monks are sure does not contain the reincarnation) shows that the probability of a child picking the old lama's stick from the collection of 21 sticks is indeed 1/21. Now they have their test. If a given candidate child does pick the old lama's stick, then $p = 1/21 < 0.05$. That is, using the classical approach, if a candidate child passes the test, we can reject the null hypothesis that the child chose at random. Assuming we are happy we have excluded other possible hypotheses (like the testers gave conscious or unconscious cues), we can then accept the hypothesis that the child is the reincarnation. The old lama had said before he died that he would be reborn in a certain area. Various omens narrow the search down to 21 candidate children in that area. The monks test all the children and one child passes the test. Can the monks conclude that this child is the reincarnation? No. The test controlled Type I error to a satisfactory degree only when conducted as a single one-off test. With 21 tests, the probability of at least one of the tests giving a positive result assuming all children chose at random is $1 - (20/21)^{21} = 0.64$. That is, the probability of a Type I error for the tests considered as a family is 0.64. Clearly, the family of tests does not constitute a reliable decision-making procedure; it cannot legitimately be used for indicating that one or other child in a set of 21 children is the reincarnation. This example illustrates the obvious need to take into account multiple testing. If one tests enough children, sooner or later a child will pass the test by chance alone. Yet, as we have discussed, the Bayesian approach does not have any corrections for multiple testing. Does not this sort of example therefore show the Bayesian approach *must* be wrong?

The Bayesian disagrees. A null hypothesis is that none of the children were reincarnations and all chose randomly. The likelihood of this null hypothesis is the probability of observing the exact sequence of data obtained given the null is true, likelihood(null) = $(20/21)^{20}(1/21)$. Let us say that the 10th child was the one who chose the stick. Assuming that the reincarnation will definitely choose the stick, the likelihood of the hypothesis that the 10th child is the reincarnation, likelihood(10th), is $(20/21)^{20} \times 1 = (20/21)^{20}$. Thus, whatever your prior odds were on the 10th child being the reincarnation against the null hypothesis, they should be increased by a factor likelihood(10th)/likelihood(null) in the light of these data, that is, by a factor of 21. 'Ha!' the classical statistician smirks, 'you have manufactured evidence out of thin air! By ignoring the issue of multiple testing, you find strong evidence in favour of a child being the reincarnation just because you tested many children!' Indeed, the fact that we have tested all the other children does not change the value of the Bayes factor for this child – it stands at 21.

But the Bayesian just patiently continues. The likelihood of the hypothesis that the first child is the reincarnation is zero because if he had been the reincarnation, he would have chosen the old lama's stick, and likewise for each of the 20 children who did not choose the stick. The probabilities of any one of them being the reincarnation go to zero. We have also just seen the probability of the 10th child being the reincarnation increases by a factor of 21. You can think of it as the probability associated with each of the 20 children who did not choose the stick being passed onto the probability associated with the child who did choose the stick. That is, the probability of *one or other* of the children being the reincarnation does not change one wit in the light of these data. Let us say before we collected the data the probability of one or other of the children being the reincarnation was π (read as 'pi'). Thus, the probability of the null, that none of the children were the reincarnation, was $(1 - \pi)$. If the prior probabilities of each of the 21 children being the reincarnation were equal, they would have been each $\pi/21$. After collecting the data, 20 of these probabilities go to 0, and the remaining one goes to π. They still sum to π. The posterior probability of the null is still $(1 - \pi)$. If you were convinced before collecting the data that the null was false, then you could choose the reincarnation with confidence (he is the 10th child); conversely, if you were highly confident in the null before collecting the data, you should be every bit as confident afterwards. And if you think about it, this is just as it should be. The Bayesian answer does not need to correct for multiple testing, the Bayesian explains, because if an answer is already right, it does not need to be corrected.

The example illustrates how the Bayesian can consider families of tests. In fact, as you run more tests of true nulls, the posterior probability of all nulls being true will typically increase (compared to the prior) because while the probability of some nulls decrease, most will increase (Box 4.7 considers an example). And it may be that we feel multiple tests need correction precisely because we sense that the probability of all nulls being true should increase as we collect more data (test more true nulls). The Bayesian approach respects this intuition.

Box 4.7   A Bayesian analysis of a family of tests

You gather together 20 famous psychic superstars, all of whom claim to have a particular paranormal ability. You test the psychic who claims special ability to see what other people see by having a sender look at a picture and the psychic choose one of 20 pictures. Similar tests are devised for each psychic such that the probability of passing by chance alone is 1/20. The psychics do not claim to be able to respond 100% of the time; but given the test conditions, and the claimed extent of their abilities, you work out that the probability of passing given they have psychic abilities is 0.90 (coincidentally the same for each person). So for each person we have a test with alpha = 0.05 and power = 0.90. We conduct 20 tests so we would expect one psychic to pass the test by chance alone. Thus, on the classical account, finding one pass and 19 fails provides no grounds for asserting any paranormal activity happened. What does a Bayesian analysis say?

Let us say it was the 15th psychic who passed her test. Your prior odds on that psychic having powers against the null should be changed by the ratio of the likelihoods, that is by $0.90/0.05 = 18$. We have strong evidence that this psychic has paranormal powers. If we regard the fact that 19 other psychics were tested is irrelevant to the claim that *this* psychic has powers, then no account is taken of the 19 failures. The strong evidence stands as it is. Again, as in the reincarnation case, it seems we can capitalize on chance (testing lots of people) in *creating* evidence. As a whole the situation is exactly as we would expect by chance, yet by using Bayes we have strong evidence that one person is a psychic superstar. Surely Bayes has got it wrong!

But the reason we wish to treat the set of tests as a family in this case is precisely because we regard the tests as addressing in some sense the same issue. We do not like to take one test in isolation because all tests bear on the issue. For a psychic that failed, the likelihood of the null is 0.95 and the likelihood of the hypothesis that they have powers is 0.10. Whatever your prior odds were on the null, they should be increased by a factor of $0.95/0.10 = 9.5$ for this psychic. So whatever your prior odds were on the null that *none* of the psychics had powers, they should be increased in the light of these data by an amount $9.5^{19}(1/18) = 2 \times 10^{17}$. The data provide astronomically high support for the null over the hypothesis that they all had powers. In fact, the data also provide support for the full null over the hypothesis that psychic powers exist and only 1/20 of psychic superstars really have such powers.

In sum, when one views the family of tests as a whole, one test passing out of 20 increases the probability of the complete null being true. This analysis shows that it is both true that your odds against the null for the one individual test passed should increase and that your odds on all the nulls jointly being true should increase. This may at first sound contradictory but in fact the statements are consistent, as the Bayesian analysis shows. This analysis may explain the apparently contradictory pull of our intuitions in dealing with cases of multiple testing. On the one hand, we recognize that classical statisticians are right to insist that when thinking of a set of tests as a family, the total number of tests is important. On the other hand, many users of classical statistics do not always correct for the number of tests because they feel evidence for a hypothesis is still evidence for that hypothesis regardless of being part of a family (as just one example, consider the common practice of placing asterisks in a correlation matrix to indicate $p < 0.05$, with no correction for multiple testing). The Bayesian analysis respects both intuitions. In our example, your probability for the complete null should increase yet your probability for the one particular null should decrease.

Our intuitive need for corrections for multiple testing in some circumstances may sometimes reflect additional implicit assumptions that can be analyzed in a Bayesian way. In a study that seems to be data dredging (e.g. analysing the correlation of religiosity with 20 other variables with no strongly motivating theory given) the presence of many weak results may change our prior probability that the procedure used for selecting variables was good at filtering out null hypotheses. In this case, a large number of weak results may affect our posterior probability of any given null being true: We may increase our probability that the variables were selected in a thoughtless way.

Finally, bear in mind that issues to do with multiple testing often arise when the prior probability of the nulls is very high. Data dreading means precisely that one expects most nulls to be true. In motivating corrections for multiple testing, the classical statistician asks us to imagine all nulls are true, that is, we are certain that the nulls are true. Of course, if we are certain the nulls are true before collecting the data, a Bayesian analysis indicates we should be certain they are true afterwards as well. Even if we are not completely certain in a null, an only moderate Bayes factor may still not leave the posteriors for the nulls high enough for us to want to treat them as true.

Is this enough to assuage you that the problem of multiple testing has been dealt with?

Using the Bayesian approach to critically evaluate a research paper

From reading the introduction to the paper, identify the key main prediction the paper makes that follows from the substantial theory. For now we will stick to a prediction that could be tested with a t-test. Sketch your personal prior probability distribution for the effect predicted, assuming a normal distribution does not violate your intuitions. From the data, determine the likelihood function and hence, using your personal prior, the posterior probability function. Make a good sketch of your posterior. Consider the author's theory. The author may just predict that there should be some difference between conditions, but he does not specify what size difference. Both your prior and posterior will give a 100% probability for there being *some* difference: In most cases, the prediction of there being some difference is so obvious it scarcely counts as a prediction at all. The author is probably being lazy. He may really mean there will be a difference larger than some minimal amount. If the author does not state what that minimal amount is, estimate it yourself based on the sort of effect typically found in that literature. Let us say the minimal interesting effect is more than 5 ms either side of zero. In your prior how much area is under the curve from −5 to +5 ms? That is, your prior probability for there being an effect so small, the author's theory is rendered false or irrelevant. What is your posterior probability for the effect lying between −5 and +5 ms? Has it increased or decreased? If the probability has increased, the data do not support the author's theory; if decreased the data support it. No categorical decisions in accepting or rejecting any hypotheses need be made, however. How do your conclusions compare with the author's?

Another approach is to use the Bayes' factor. Assume you believe the author's theory absolutely. Sketch your prior again, assuming the theory (call it theory A for Author's theory) – this is p(population effect|theory A). In the previous paragraph, we assigned zero probability to any particular effect size, including zero, because you assumed a normal for your prior. Do you wish to assign a non-zero probability to the null hypothesis of no effect? If you do, you can calculate the Bayes' factor using the provided program. The Bayes' factor tells you how much to increase your probability in the theory over the null given the data. How does this conclusion compare to the author's?

Now whether not you are willing to assign a non-zero probability to the null, you can use the Bayes' factor to compare the author's theory to the substantial theory which the author or you consider to be the main competitor. Identify this theory (call it theory B), assume it absolutely and sketch the prior assuming this theory: p(population effect|theory B). Calculate the Bayes' factor for this theory. When you do this, the program tells you what 'Likelihoodtheory' is. Divide the likelihood for theory A (which you will have obtained by following the exercise in the last paragraph) by the likelihood for theory B. This is the

Bayes' factor for the author's favoured theory over the main competitor. By how much does the data support the author's theory over the competitor theory? How does this compare to the author's own conclusions?

Sometimes a Bayesian analysis will support the instincts of an author in interpreting Neyman–Pearson statistics as a way of updating their personal convictions. But sometimes the Bayesian analysis will give very different answers because only the Bayesian approach requires personal probabilities be updated coherently, that is, according to the axioms of probability. Often people should be penalized more severely for the vagueness of their theories than they realize.

Summary: Neyman–Pearson versus Bayes

Table 4.1 summarizes the contrasts between Neyman–Pearson and Bayesian statistics. In classic statistics, it matters in what context a test was done (as part of a family of 100 other tests, 5 other tests, or just done by itself?); in Bayesian statistics, the support for a hypothesis depends *only* on the data directly relevant to that hypothesis. In classic statistics, it matters whether you invent your explanation for an effect before conducting the test or afterwards (planned vs post hoc tests). In Bayesian statistics, it is irrelevant whether you invented the hypothesis on Wednesday or Friday, the *timing* of an explanation is irrelevant to how good an explanation it is of the data, and to how much the data support it. Contrast the common idea, for example supported by Popper and Lakatos (see Chapters 1 and 2), that the novelty of a prediction is important for how much confirmation supports a theory. From the Bayesian perspective, timing and novelty are clearly irrelevant for the magnitude of the likelihood, and the likelihood tells you everything you need to know about the support the data has for a theory. Therefore, the timing of data relative to explanation is irrelevant.

Table 4.1   Neyman–Pearson versus Bayes

	Meaning of probability	Aim	Inference	Long-run error rates	Sensitive to
Neyman–Pearson	Objective frequencies	Provide a reliable decision procedure with controlled long-term error rates	Black and white decisions	Controlled	Stopping rule; what counts as the family of tests; timing of explanation relative to data
Bayes	Subjective	Indicate how prior probabilities should be changed by data	Continuous degree of posterior belief	Not guaranteed to be controlled	Prior opinion

In sum, in the Neyman–Pearson approach, it is assumed that what the scientist wants is a generally reliable procedure for accepting and rejecting hypotheses, a procedure with known and controlled long-term error rates. According to the Bayesian, the scientist wants to know the relative amount of support that data provided for different hypotheses so she knows how to adjust her convictions.

What do you want from your statistics?

We established in the previous chapter that you were probably an unwitting closet Bayesian. Now you know the issues, do you want to come out of the closest? Or do you want to renounce your old tacit beliefs and live a reformed life?

Before you draw any final conclusions, consider the final major school of inference, likelihood inference, discussed in the next chapter.

Review and discussion questions

1. Define the key terms of probability, probability density, prior probability, likelihood, posterior probability, credibility interval, Bayes factor.
2. State the likelihood principle. In what ways does Neyman–Pearson hypothesis testing violate the likelihood principle?
3. Think of some null hypotheses that have been tested in a journal article you read recently. To what extent does it make sense to give them a non-zero prior probability?
4. How does a credibility interval differ from a confidence interval? Calculate both for the same set of data and compare and contrast the conclusions that follow from each.
5. Discuss whether the Neyman–Pearson or Bayesian approach gives more objective conclusions.
6. Discuss whether it makes sense to correct for multiple testing in the Bayesian approach.

Further reading

One of the few textbooks of statistics providing a Bayesian perspective suitable for people with the mathematical abilities of the average psychology undergraduate is Berry (1996). Berry provides the equivalent of a first-year undergraduate course in statistics for psychologists, building up step by step to determining credibility intervals for normal data and also for proportions. Bayes factors are not considered.

For an excellent introduction to both objective and subjective probabilities, and the logic of statistical inference that follows from each, see Hacking (2001).

The standard philosophical treatment advocating Bayes with unshakable conviction is Howson and Urbach (1989, see especially Chapters 1, 10 and 11). A defence of Neyman–Pearson and criticism of Bayes is provided by Mayo (1996), especially pp. 69–101 and Chapters 9 and 10. Howard, Maxwell and Fleming (2000) is a readable short comparison of Bayes with Neyman–Pearson. Oakes (1986) is an excellent overview of different approaches to statistics (though unfortunately now out of print). If you want to explore Bayesian analyses for a range of research designs, McCarthy (2007) takes the reader through how to use the free online software WinBUGS which allows great flexibility in data analysis.

Finally, if you have some mathematical background, even if just very good high school level, I strongly recommend Jaynes (2003), for a forceful argument for the 'objective Bayesian' approach.

Matlab program for calculating Bayes factors

To use the program to calculate a Bayes factor for your data you need to enter your sample mean and standard error. You also need to decide: Does my theory predict a rectangular distribution for the population effect (as in Figure 4.11) or a normal distribution? If rectangular, what are the limits? If a normal, what is its mean and standard deviation? If a normal, does the theory allow both positive and negative effects or only effects in one direction? Answers to these questions will enable the program to calculate: The likelihood of the obtained data given your theory, the likelihood of the obtained data given the null and the Bayes factor.

Notes

1. If the theory allows only effects in one direction, and you want to specify a normal for the distribution of the population effect given the theory, enter zero as the mean of the normal. The program will also presume that the theory predicts positive effects in this case.
2. The null hypothesis is assumed to be that the population mean is zero.
3. It is assumed your likelihood can be represented by a normal distribution (and the prior by normal or rectangular). The adequacy of the results depends on the plausibility of that assumption. Note you can test hypotheses relevant to the contrasts described in Box 4.8.

Box 4.8   What about ANOVA? (for readers already exposed to the analysis of variance)

The statistical tool psychologists use most often is analysis of variance (ANOVA). This box will briefly indicate a possible Bayesian approach to various ANOVA designs. In the Neyman–Pearson approach, if there are more than two conditions, an F test can be conducted to answer the question of whether any one condition is different from any other. I hope it strikes you that this question is not really the question you typically want answered. What you want to know is by how much does *this* condition differ from *that* condition, or by how much does the average of these two conditions differ from the average of those three, or some other equally specific question. The only reason one conducts an overall F test is to protect against the inflated Type I error rate that results from multiple testing. With three groups, there are three t-tests that could be conducted comparing each group with each other. In classical statistics, one has to worry about the fact that three tests are conducted at once. So a typical procedure is to first conduct an overall ('omnibus') F, testing if one can reject the null that all group means are equal. If and only if that is significant does one continue with a post hoc test for pair-wise comparisons. But from a Bayesian point of view, one can adjust one's prior beliefs in the size of any difference without regard for multiple testing. There is no need for the omnibus F, one can just get straight down to asking the questions one is interested in.

Given a set of independent variables, a specific question (including a main effect or interaction) can generally be formulated as a contrast, i.e. a difference between averages of groups, as described in Box 3.7. Comparing group 1 with group 2 is a contrast. Comparing the average of groups 1 and 2 with the average of groups 3 and 4 is a contrast. If the design is completely repeated measures (all subjects have a score for all conditions), then you can already perform a Bayesian analysis on any contrast that interests you.

For each subject, calculate the contrast of interest (e.g. average of conditions 1 and 2 minus the average of conditions 3 and 4). Now for each subject you have a number. The mean of this set of numbers is the mean of your likelihood and the standard deviation is the standard deviation of your likelihood. So you can determine prior, likelihood and posterior just as we have done in Boxes 4.3–4.5. Perform as many contrasts in this way as address questions you are interested in.

Box 4.8 *continued*

For a between-subjects design, we can use the formulae in Box 3.7. Say we have four groups with means m_1, m_2, m_3 and m_4. We can represent our contrast as a set of numbers, a_i. For example, the difference between groups 1 and 2 is a contrast, $C = (1)m_1 + (-1)m_2 + (0)m_3 + (0)m_4 = m_1 - m_2$. In this case, $a_1 = 1$, $a_2 = -1$, $a_3 = 0$ and $a_4 = 0$. If we wanted to compare the average of groups 1 and 3 with the average of groups 2 and 4, we have the contrast $C = (0.5)m_1 + (0.5)m_3 + (-0.5)m_2 + (-0.5)m_4 = \frac{1}{2}(m_1 + m_3) - \frac{1}{2}(m_2 + m_4)$. In this case, $a_1 = 0.5$, $a_2 = -0.5$, $a_3 = 0.5$ and $a_4 = -0.5$. For roughly normally distributed data within each group, C is roughly normally distributed with standard error given by $\sqrt{(\sum a_i^2)}SD_p/\sqrt{n}$ where n is the number of subjects in each group and $SD_p = \sqrt{(1/4(SD_1^2 + SD_2^2 + SD_3^2 + SD_4^2))}$. Now you can work out priors, likelihoods and posteriors for any contrast of interest in a between-subjects design.

As a Bayesian, you can kiss ANOVA goodbye forever. Do you feel sad?

A compiled version will be available at
http://www.lifesci.sussex.ac.uk/home/Zoltan_Dienes/inference/

```
normaly = @(mn, variance, x) 2.718283^(- (x - mn)*(x -mn)/(2*variance))/
realsqrt(2*pi*variance);

    sd = input('What is the sample standard error? ');
    sd2 = sd*sd;
    obtained = input('What is the sample mean? ');

    uniform = input('is the distribution of p(population value|theory)
uniform? 1= yes 0=no ');

    if uniform == 0
        meanoftheory = input('What is the mean of p(population value|
theory)? ');
        sdtheory = input('What is the standard deviation of p(population
value|theory)? ');
        omega = sdtheory*sdtheory;
        tail = input('is the distribution one-tailed or two-tailed?
(1/2) ');
    end

    if uniform == 1
        lower = input('What is the lower bound? ');
        upper = input('What is the upper bound? ');
    end

    area = 0;
    if uniform == 1
        theta = lower;
    else theta = meanoftheory - 5*(omega)^0.5;
    end
    if uniform == 1
        incr = (upper- lower)/2000;
    else incr = (omega)^0.5/200;
```

```
        end
    for A = -1000:1000
            theta = theta + incr;
            if uniform == 1
                dist_theta = 0;
                if and(theta >= lower, theta <= upper)
                    dist_theta = 1/(upper-lower);
                end
            else %distribution is normal
                if tail == 2
                    dist_theta = normaly(meanoftheory, omega, theta);
                else
                    dist_theta = 0;
                    if theta >0
                        dist_theta = 2*normaly(meanoftheory, omega, theta);
                    end
                end
            end

        height = dist_theta * normaly(theta, sd2, obtained);
        %p(population value=theta|theory)*p(data|theta)
        area = area + height*incr; %integrating the above over theta
    end


    Likelihoodtheory = area
    Likelihoodnull = normaly(0, sd2, obtained)
    Bayesfactor = Likelihoodtheory/Likelihoodnull
```

Appendix Getting personal odds directly

Say somebody is willing to pay you 1 unit of money if a theory is found to be true. If you wish to take the bet, you must reciprocate by paying them a specified amount if the theory is found to be false. What is the maximum specified amount which you are just willing to pay? This maximum amount is called your odds in favour of the theory. I will assume that you are a betting person and you will always bet if you think the bet either favourable or indeed simply fair. Consider the theory that the next toss of this coin will be heads. I will pay you a pound if the next toss is heads. Will you play with me if I want 50p if the next toss is tails? Most people would, but there is not a right answer; it is up to you. Will you play with me if I want 90p if the next toss is tails? £1? £1.50? Assuming the highest amount you would just be willing to accept paying is £1, then your personal odds in favour of next toss being heads is 1 (i.e. 1:1, 50:50, or even odds).

You can convert odds to probability by bearing in mind that

$$\text{odds(theory is true)} = \text{probability(theory is true)}/\text{probability(theory is false)}.$$

Hence

$$\text{probability(theory is true)} = \text{odds}/(\text{odds}+1).$$

Thus, in this case, with odds of 1, probability(next toss is heads) = $1/(1+1) = 0.5$.

Now consider the theory that there is a two-headed winged monster behind my office door. I will pay you a pound if we open the door and find a monster. Will you play if I want 50p if there is no monster? No? How about 25p then? 0p? Assuming you picked 0 as the highest amount, your odds in favour of the theory being true are 0. So your personal subjective probability of the theory being true is also 0.

Now consider the theory it will snow tomorrow. I will pay you a pound if it does snow tomorrow. Will you play if I want you to pay me 50p if it does not snow? If you think it is very likely to snow, this is a very good bet for you. Chances are it will snow, I pay you a pound and you pay me nothing. Will you play if I want a pound if it does not snow? That is still a good bet if you think it is very likely to snow. Will you play if I want £2 if it does not snow? This may be your cut-off point. In that case your odds are 2 (in other words, 2 to 1), and your personal probability that it will snow tomorrow is $2/(2+1) = 0.67$.

Finally, to consider an extreme, consider the theory that there will be traffic in London tomorrow. I will pay you a pound if there is traffic. Will you play if I want you to pay me £1 if there is no traffic? Presumably, you will find this an attractive proposition, a good way of fleecing some idiot out of a pound. How about if I want £10 if there is no traffic? Presumably, you are so certain that there will be traffic in London that you will still unflinchingly accept the game. In fact, you would presumably be willing to play the game even if you have to pay some arbitrarily high number if there is no traffic; your personal odds in favour of the theory that there will be traffic in London tomorrow are very large. Thus, your personal probability that there will be traffic in London tomorrow is (a very large number)/(a very large number +1), which is very close to 1.

5 Fisher and the likelihood: the Royall road to evidence

Royall (1997) suggested there are three quite different questions one could ask in the light of data:

(1) What should I do now?
(2) What should I believe now?
(3) How should I treat the data as evidence for one theory rather than another?

The questions are different. Sometimes you should act as if a theory were true (answer to question 1) even if you do not believe the theory (answer to question 2). Imagine, for example, you have been bitten by mosquitoes deep in the jungle in Thailand. The mosquitoes in that part of the world sometimes carry malaria although most people who get bitten there do not contract the disease. You might take anti-malarial medicine even though it is unlikely you have the disease, especially given malaria is potentially fatal and the medicine has few side effects. Sometimes you should act as if a theory were true even if you believe the theory to be false.

The Neyman–Pearson approach is an attempt to answer what you should do: In the light of the data, which theory should you accept or reject? According to Neyman, such acceptances and rejections are just 'behavioural' decisions, binary events for which we can work out long-run relative frequencies, and which need not reflect beliefs. In contrast, the Bayesian approach is an answer to what you should believe: It tells you how strongly you should believe in different theories. We saw in the previous chapter that the answers provided to these different questions can be radically different. Sometimes the Bayesian analysis shows that data imply you should believe the null hypothesis more strongly even as the Neyman–Pearson approach indicates one should reject the null. Of course, the approaches are answering different questions; so it is no wonder they can give seemingly different answers. One cannot use the Neyman–Pearson approach to answer what you should believe or how confident you should be in a belief.

The question of the evidential force of the data is also a different question from what you should believe. Just because some evidence points a certain way, it does not mean you should believe that way. You may have other prior reasons for believing the opposite. According to the Bayesian schema, Posterior belief = likelihood × prior belief. Your belief in the light of given data depends on both the likelihood and your prior. According to the Bayesian schema, the likelihood determines the evidential weight of the data. Your posterior belief reflects both that evidential weight AND your prior. If you had strong prior reasons for disbelieving pyramid power, one experiment providing evidence in favour of the theory could still legitimately leave you still strongly disbelieving the theory.

Readers of a paper may not be especially interested in the beliefs, prior or posterior, of the paper's author. Arguably, they are more interested in whether the data is evidence for one theory rather than another. So one approach to statistical inference is to base inference on likelihoods (without priors or posteriors and without significance tests). Such a manoeuvre also neatly side-steps the whole debate on whether probabilities should be objective

(Neyman–Pearson long-run frequencies of behavioural outcomes) or subjective (Bayesian degrees of belief) as the likelihood can be used in either case. In this chapter we will discuss the likelihood school of inference. First, we will indicate why the existing schools do not provide an answer to the question we might really want to know the answer to, namely, how strong is the evidence for one theory rather than another?

Why significance does not indicate evidence

Currently scientists use p-values to indicate the strength of evidence against the null, a practice suggested by Fisher (though not by Neyman nor by Pearson). The smaller the p-value, the greater the evidence there is said to be against the null. Often the conclusions used by this practice are sensible, which is no doubt why scientists have continued using p-values in this way. Nonetheless, Royall (1997) argues that significance levels are not in general good measures of the strength of evidence. They confuse the strength of evidence with the probability of obtaining that evidence and these two things are different. The probability is determined by factors that are separate from the strength itself, as we will now argue.

The probability calculated in a p-value depends on the set of things that could have happened but did not. What could have happened depends on subjective factors like the intentions of the experimenter. For example, if the experimenter had intended stopping at 30 subjects, but the p-value at this point is $p = 0.07$, she might decide to top up with another 20 subjects. To calculate the significance for this experiment we need to take into account that the experimenter could have stopped at 30 subjects, even though she did not. Let us say the experimenter would have stopped after 30 subjects if p had been less than 0.05. Then in an indefinite number of replications of the decision procedure 'Run 30 subjects, test; if not significant at $p = 0.05$ run 20 more and test again', 5 % of the time Type I errors would be made when $n = 30$. On the remaining 95 % of the time that the experimenter continues running, there is another opportunity for Type I errors. So the overall long-run Type I error rate must be more than 5 %. *No matter how many subjects are later run, no matter how strong the evidence for and against different hypotheses, having tested once at the 5 % level, the significance level can never be below 0.05.* Significance as an indication of the long-run Type I error rate is not in general the same as the strength of evidence.[1] Clearly one can always in principle obtain stronger evidence by taking more observations even when this stronger evidence cannot be reflected in the significance level.

You may suggest that while significance levels obviously do need to be adjusted for stopping rules to control overall Type I error rate, perhaps one can use unadjusted p-values as a measure of strength of evidence. That is, one could just use the p-value SPSS gives you when all 50 subjects are entered. But p-values do not allow you to do this. A $p < 0.05$ is no evidence against the null at all if it were obtained by using the stopping rule 'Stop when the p-value is less than 0.05'. A $p < 0.05$ is guaranteed to be obtained eventually under this rule, so it means nothing. To be meaningful p-values must be adjusted according to stopping rule. They also need to be adjusted for multiple comparisons.

Consider a test of whether a therapy (consisting of recounting a painful event while rapidly moving the eyes) improves recovery from psychological trauma; the p-value is 0.04.

---

1. This is a point Fisher recognized. He did not think the concept of Type I error rate was relevant to most of science. However, current practice is to associate p-values with both Type I error rate and strength of evidence. Further, if one rejects an interpretation of p in terms of long-term error rates, one needs a coherent account of what a p-value is the probability of.

However, another test was made in the same experiment involving another group of patients given a variant therapy (recounting a painful event while simultaneously generating random numbers). We have a family of two tests. Now our set of possible outcomes over which we calculate the probability for the first comparison includes the outcomes for the other comparison in order to protect family-wise Type I error rate. With a Bonferoni correction, the first p is no longer significant at the 5 % level. You might think the outcome data for the eye-movement therapy is evidence for the therapeutic effectiveness of specifically *that* therapy independently of whether you happened to test *other* therapies. If so, then you should reject significance as a measure of evidence.

Similarly p-values depend on whether they are two-tailed or one-tailed. A one-tailed test means if the mean difference had come out the other way you would have reported it as non-significant no matter how large the difference was. Would you really have reported a very large mean difference as non-significant if it had come out the other way? Who is to say whether you would or you would not? Royall remarks (p. 117) p-values "are not determined just by what the experimenter did and what he observed. They depend also on what he would have done had the observations been different – not on what he says he would have done, or even on what he thinks he would have done, but on what he really would have done (which is, of course, unknowable)."

Does a given p-value, say $p = 0.04$, always indicate the same amount of evidence against the null? Or is the strength of the evidence dependent on how large the sample is? Some statisticians have argued $p = 0.04$ is always the same amount of evidence regardless of sample size. Others have argued that the evidence is stronger if the sample is smaller. Others have argued that the evidence is stronger if the sample size is bigger. The moral is that p-values are not a principled way of measuring strength of evidence (see Royall, 1997, Chapters 2, 3 and 5).

Here we provide an example where the same p-value is obtained along with intuitively different strengths of evidence. Imagine you are testing whether a pill for men to take just before having sex is 100 % effective in preventing conception during the female's fertile period. We use as a null the hypothesis that the probability of conception is zero and an alternative that the conception rate is the same as with unprotected sex (which is, let us say for the population sampled from, 20 %). One man takes the pill and has sex with his partner in her fertile phase. No conception results. What is the p-value for these data? If the probability of conception is 0, then the probability of seeing no conception in one trial is 1. That is, assuming the null, the probability of obtaining a result as extreme as this or more extreme is clearly 1. (There are no results more extreme.) The p-value is 1. How much evidence do you feel there is for the null hypothesis over the alternative? Now imagine we repeated the procedure with 500 different couples and in all cases there were no conceptions. By any reasonable account of evidence, surely the evidence has increased for the null over the alternative. But the p-value has remained the same, that is 1.[2]

Why Bayesian posteriors do not indicate evidence

We saw in the previous chapter how to calculate your posterior distribution for the value of a parameter. Your posterior will depend partly on the idiosyncrasies of your prior that readers of a scientific journal will scarcely be interested in. One Bayesian response is to use

2. If we used as the null the hypothesis that the probability of conception is 0.2 when the pill is taken, then the p-value changes in the two scenarios (being 0.8 after observing one couple and 0.8^{500} after observing 500). Strangely, the amount of evidence changes for one null but not the other.

uninformative priors, that is, priors that reflect a state of complete ignorance. Then the posterior will be determined just by the likelihood, that is, it will reflect only the evidence. The problem is that there is no such thing as an uninformative prior. Consider a study to determine the ratio of atheists to religious people in Brighton. You might suggest a state of ignorance could be indicated by giving all ratios an equal probability density, that is, a uniform prior, as shown in Figure 5.1a. Thus, the probability that the ratio lies between 0 and 1 is the same as the probability that the ratio lies between 1 and 2. Now consider the implications for the inverse ratio, the ratio of religious people to atheists. When the former ratio lies between 0 and 1, the latter lies between 1 and infinity. When the former lies between 1 and 2, the latter lies between $\frac{1}{2}$ and 1. So if we accept the uniform prior for the ratio (number of atheists)/(number of religious people), it follows that the probability that the inverse ratio (number of religious people)/(number of atheists) lies between $\frac{1}{2}$ and 1 is the same as the probability it has any value greater than 1 (see Figure 5.1b). The prior for the inverse ratio now scarcely reflects a state of ignorance. The point is general. If a prior gives equal probabilities or probability densities for a variable, then any non-linear transformation of that variable (e.g. converting a ratio to its inverse, a reaction time to a speed or a length to an area) will not have a uniform prior. Thus, the prior for the transformed variable reflects definite prejudices. Hence, the prior for the original variable must also reflect definite prejudices and not the state of an ideal ignoramus. Royall (1997) argued that being ignorant about the possible values of a variable cannot be reflected in assigning any particular numbers to the probabilities; it means being unable to assign any such numbers at all. Of course, with enough data the likelihood comes to dominate the prior and the exact shape of the prior becomes less and less relevant. But if this is the argument of the Bayesian, why not just deal with the likelihood and not worry about priors and posteriors at all?

Figure 5.1

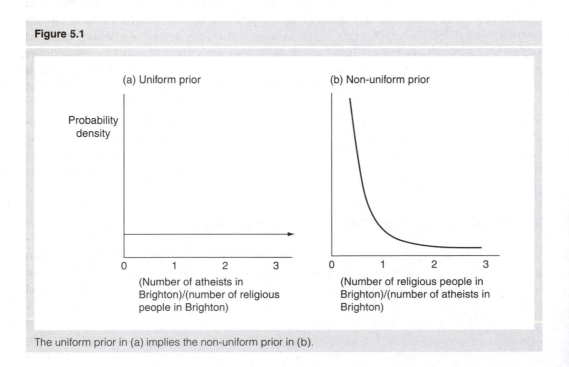

(a) Uniform prior

(b) Non-uniform prior

Probability density

0   1   2   3
(Number of atheists in Brighton)/(number of religious people in Brighton)

0   1   2   3
(Number of religious people in Brighton)/(number of atheists in Brighton)

The uniform prior in (a) implies the non-uniform prior in (b).

Sir Harold Jeffreys (1891–1989) from Cambridge and Edwin Jaynes (1922–1998) from Washington, both mathematical physicists as well as statisticians, made important advances in specifying priors such that transforming a variable does not produce contradictions. A ratio and its inverse cannot both have flat priors, because that is a literal contradiction, as Figure 5.1 shows. However, there is a prior one can assign a ratio such that the prior for the inverse of the ratio will have the same form and both priors are mutually compatible. The development of the mathematical tools to do this has been a great step forward, defining a distinctive and compelling "objective Bayesian" approach (see Jaynes, 2003), where priors are meant to reflect only information that can be clearly specified. Yet while these tools can produce well behaved priors in certain cases, the general problem of specifying a prior reflecting minimum prejudice, or indeed only reflecting whatever objective constraints we want to put in, has not been solved.

Why likelihood ratios indicate evidence

Fisher coined the term 'likelihood' in 1921, and thereafter in various publications briefly indicated a basis for inference using it. But the likelihood as such never formed the main core of Fisher's approach to inference. The examples in his textbooks were replete with significance tests and thus these were what scientists focused on. Several authors developed Fisher's use of the likelihood, such as Edwards (1972), and likelihood inference became a distinct minority approach, albeit one with staunch supporters. Likelihoods as mathematical entities are in fact widely used by statisticians and applied scientists, but typically in the context of techniques in the Neyman–Pearson and Bayesian traditions. Likelihood theorists, however, see likelihoods as providing an alternative to the other traditions, not simply as providing a tool within error probability or Bayesian schools of inference. Richard Royall, a statistician from John Hopkins University, presented a particularly clear case for likelihood inference per se in his 1997 book. Indeed, much of this chapter has been inspired by Royall's book. Royall's work also inspired a series of symposia involving ecologists, statisticians and philosophers to discuss the nature of scientific evidence, resulting in the Taper and Lele (2004) edited volume. That volume illustrates the growing appeal of the likelihood school to some (though not all) scientists. It also illustrates that the nature of scientific and statistical inference is a topic scientists can and should take an informed stand on.

Royall (1997) used a simple example to explain and motivate likelihood inference. Consider two urns of balls, one urn containing only white balls and the other urn containing an equal mixture of white and black balls. Your beautiful assistant flips a coin to choose an urn and draws a number of balls from it. The prior probability that the pure white urn was chosen is 0.5, and the prior odds in favour of the pure urn are thus p(pure urn)$/p$(mixed urn)$ = 0.5/0.5 = 1$. Let us say your assistant draws three balls and they are all white. The likelihood of the mixed urn is given by the probability of drawing three whites given the urn is mixed, p(3 whites/mixed urn)$ = \frac{1}{2}^3$. The likelihood of the pure white urn is given by the probability of drawing three whites given the urn is pure white $= 1^3 = 1$. So the likelihood ratio in favour of the pure urn $= p$(3 whites/pure urn)$/p$(3 whites/mixed urn)$ = 1/(1/2^3) = 2^3 = 8$. From the previous chapter, by Bayes' theorem, Posterior odds in favour of pure urn $=$ likelihood ratio $\times$ prior odds in favour of pure urn. From the mathematics of probability theory, the impact of the data in updating probabilities depends only the likelihood ratio; further the likelihood ratio tells us precisely how much to update our probabilities. If we take the likelihood ratio to be a measure of strength of evidence, it will never tell us that the evidence goes one way, while probability theory tells us to update our probabilities in another way. As a measure of evidence it has the desirable property of being consistent with probability theory.

Of course, it is controversial whether theories in general can be assigned probabilities. The urn case was set up so that objective probabilities could be assigned to the theory that a particular urn was chosen (because which urn was chosen depended on a coin toss). But whether we can assign probabilities to the theory that 'the mean difference between ginseng and placebo conditions is 50 milliseconds' is another matter. In the Bayesian tradition you can and in the Neyman–Pearson (and Popperian) tradition you cannot. Likelihood theorists suggest making the issue irrelevant by treating the likelihood ratio as the relative evidence for one theory rather than another as a general 'law' – the so-called 'law of likelihood', a term coined by Hacking (1965). Then the likelihood ratio provides a consistent measure of relative evidence both in cases where one thinks theories have probabilities and where they do not. It would be odd if the meaning of relative evidence for two theories changed simply because for other reasons one thought one could or could not meaningfully assign a probability to the theories.

The law of likelihood respects the intuition that a result most strongly supports the theory that most strongly predicted it. In the limit, if one theory says an outcome must happen and another forbids it, finding the outcome clearly supports the first theory over the second. The law of likelihood generalizes this to probabilities between 0 and 1. Conversely, it is reassuring for the law of likelihood that in the limit of 0 and 1 it produces the obviously sensible conclusion.

Neither of these arguments entail that the law of likelihood must be right. But Royall points out the law has the further desirable consequence that strength of evidence can be separated from the probability of obtaining such evidence. Moreover in certain respects these probabilities behave in more desirable ways than the α and β of Neyman–Pearson, a point we discuss in the next section. While evidence can be misleading, it turns out it will not be misleading very often and, moreover, the probability of misleading evidence goes to zero as the sample size increases.

The two-urn example of Royall's enables us to get a feel for what the strength of evidence is that a given likelihood ratio signifies. Three white balls give a likelihood ratio of 8, as we saw; fairly strong evidence in favour of the pure over the mixed urn. In general, n white balls drawn consecutively gives a likelihood ratio of 2^n. If you had drawn just one white ball (and no black), the likelihood ratio would be 2. I am sure you agree, while it is some evidence it is not very compelling evidence for the pure over the mixed urn. Two white balls gives a likelihood ratio of 4, which maybe you agree is still not very strong evidence. Royall suggests taking a ratio of 8 as 'fairly strong' evidence in general, and 32 (2^5, corresponding to drawing 5 white balls in a row) as 'strong' evidence. These are of course arbitrary conventions he is suggesting. You can calibrate yourself for different numbers by considering how strong the evidence would feel to you for the pure over the mixed urn for different numbers of white balls drawn consecutively.

Neyman–Pearson statistics are inconsistent with the law of likelihood. Likelihood depends only on the data obtained, not on what else might have been obtained, whereas significance depends on the latter. For example, imagine you want to know whether Sam resides in England or Scotland. You manage to find out that Sam's height is six foot. According to the likelihood principle, the only facts of relevance are the probability of someone in England being six foot and the probability of someone from Scotland being six foot. On the other hand, in the Neyman–Pearson approach, the probabilities of the other heights, like the probability of being six foot five, are also needed (because Sam's measurement might have been six foot five, even though it was not). Whether or not there was a wave of immigration of

American basketball players over six foot tall into Scotland would change the calculations on the Neyman–Pearson approach, but the likelihood ratio is unaffected by such irrelevancies. Conversely, if a freak job opportunity arose in a television company making soap operas in Sydney needing six-foot tall Scots as actors, depriving Scotland of all people of exactly six-foot tall, then the important fact for likelihood inference is that $p(6'|$ comes from Scotland$) = 0$. For significance testing the relevant fact is that $p(6'$ or taller$|$comes from Scotland$) = 0.21$, which is inferentially irrelevant.

To illustrate further how the Neyman–Pearson approach violates the likelihood principle, Figure 5.2 shows the distribution of an outcome expected on a null hypothesis and on an alternative hypothesis. The distributions happen to be normal. The vertical line is our decision criterion; any sample mean greater than the line results in us accepting the alternative and

Figure 5.2

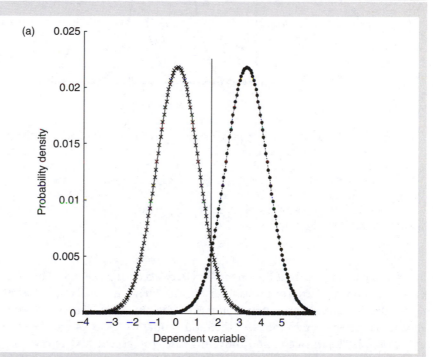

(a) The curve made of crosses is the probability density for data assuming the null hypothesis that the population mean is zero and the curve made of circles is the probability density for data assuming an alternative hypothesis that the population mean is 3.28. The standard error is scaled to be 1. The curves cross at 1.64 standard errors from the mean of each distribution. A criterion, represented by the vertical line, is placed where the curves cross. A sample mean observed to the right of the line will lead to rejecting the null and a sample mean to the left will lead to accepting the null. α is the area under the curve for the null to the right of the criterion; β is the area under the curve for the alternative to the left of the line. α and β are both 5 % in this example. The likelihood ratio is the ratio of the heights of the curves for the mean sample value of the dependent variable. In this case, the accept/reject decisions will always coincide with the direction of evidence indicated by the likelihood ratio. However, categorical decisions will be made for sample means near the criterion in which region the likelihood ratio indicates only weak support for one hypothesis over the other.

Figure 5.2 *continued*

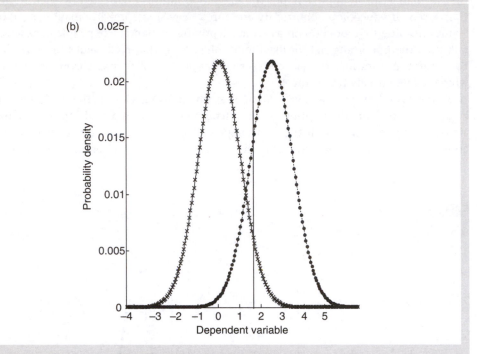

(b) This time the alternative hypothesis is that the population mean is 2.48. The criterion is still placed at 1.64, so that α remains controlled at 5 %. Because the mean of the alternative is closer to the null distribution than in (a), now more of the area of the curve for the alternative is to the left of the criterion; this time β is 20 %. Because the criterion is no longer where the curves intersect, in this case decisions can be made that are opposite to the way the evidence points (as indicated by the likelihood ratio). Just to the left of the criterion, evidence supports the alternative even though the null is accepted. At the criterion, the likelihood ratio in favour of the alternative is 2.7.

any sample mean less than the line results in us accepting the null. The location of the line is chosen to control the error probabilities α and β. Figure 5.2a illustrates setting α at 0.05 and β at 0.05. The likelihood ratio is the ratio of heights of the curves for the observed sample mean. Where the curves intersect the ratio is one, which is where the criterion is placed in this example. In this case, and only this case, the accept and reject decisions will always correspond to the direction of the likelihood ratio; acceptances of the alternative will always correspond to the likelihood ratio favouring the alternative, and similarly for accepting the null. Notice, however, that categorical decisions will sometimes be made on the basis of likelihood ratios very close to 1. If a result is just significant, the evidence favouring the alternative is very weak. Similarly, if a result just misses out on significance, the evidence favouring the null is very weak. Yet Neyman–Pearson produces categorical decisions in these cases. But it gets even worse when β is more than 0.05 (i.e. power is less than 0.95), which it almost always is in practice. Figure 5.2b illustrates setting α at 0.05 and β at 0.20, a typical recommendation. Now the likelihood ratio could favour the alternative by as much as 2.7 when the experiment is taken as confirming the null. In fact, setting β at 0.20 is a recommendation, not a typical state of affairs. Cohen (1977) estimated that in an arbitrarily chosen issue of a top psychology journal, the β was on average 0.5. In this more typical scenario, the likelihood ratio could be as high as 3.9 in favour of the alternative even when on the Neyman–Pearson approach one would reject the alternative. The figure illustrates a one-tailed decision procedure. For the more typical two-tailed test case, the likelihood ratio could be as high as 6.8 in favour of the alternative while by Neyman–Pearson the alterative is rejected in favour of the null! In sum, significance testing can lead to decisions in opposition to the direction the evidence is pointing, even for reasonably strong evidence.

The possible contradiction between acceptance decisions in Neyman–Pearson and the direction of evidence occurs because of the relative costs of Type I and II errors presumed in setting α and β. The typically smaller value of α than β reflects the presumption that Type I errors are more costly than Type II, so their errors need to be controlled more strictly. The problem is that in practice no experimenter thinks through the costs and makes an informed choice of α and β. She just follows conventions. Even if she did think through the costs, there is no reason to think every reader of the paper would choose the same costs. Surely what the reader wants to know is the direction and strength of evidence, not a decision that reflects the subjective costings of another researcher (nor even a decision that reflects poorly thought out conventions). The likelihood ratio reflects relative evidence; decisions based on significance tests in general do not.

Probabilities of misleading and weak evidence

You want to know which of two types of meditation is better for lifting mood. So you ask each subject to meditate on the image of helping others for half an hour on the morning of one day and meditate with an empty mind for half an hour on the morning of another. The outcome is a binary choice by the subject indicating the day on which they felt happier: with an image of helping or an empty mind. Imagine a previous study has found that people expect both sorts of meditation to work equally well. If results just depend on expectation, then the expected proportion of 'image' days indicated (call this θ) would be 0.5. On the other hand, maybe a pilot study based on the theory that helping others is particularly useful for becoming happier, indicated the proportion θ might be 0.8. You wish to be able to discriminate these views by providing fairly strong evidence for one of them over the other.

If one person was tested and chose 'image' meditation as the happier day, the likelihood for the hypothesis $\theta = 0.8$ based on this single observation is given by p(obtaining exactly that result$| \theta = 0.8) = 0.8$. A useful property of likelihoods is that the likelihoods for successive independent data points can simply be multiplied to get the overall likelihood.[3] When the second person is tested, the likelihood for the hypothesis that $\theta = 0.8$ is thus given by p(observing outcome of second subject$| \theta = 0.8) \times p$(outcome of first subject$| \theta = 0.8)$. So if m people are tested and n of them indicate being happier on the image day (and $m - n$ of them happier on the 'empty mind' day), then the likelihood of the hypothesis that $\theta = 0.8$ is given by. $0.8^n 0.2^{m-n}$. For example, if out of 20 people 14 preferred the image day and six the empty mind day, the likelihood is $0.8^{14} 0.2^6 = 2.8 \times 10^{-5}$. On the expectation theory, the probability of each observation, no matter which choice is made, is 0.5. The likelihood of the hypothesis that $\theta = 0.5$ after m subjects is 0.5^m. For our example, the likelihood of the hypothesis that $\theta = 0.5$ is $0.5^{20} = 9.5 \times 10^{-7}$. (In general, the likelihood for design with binary independent trials with fixed probability is $\theta^n(1 - \theta)^{m-n}$.) In this case of $m = 20$ and $n = 14$, the ratio is 2.95, only weak evidence in favour of $\theta = 0.8$ rather than 0.5.

---

3. By the axioms of probability, the probability of a conjunction of independent events is the product of their probabilities.

Fairly strong evidence would be indicated by a likelihood ratio of 8. After n subjects, we have achieved our aim if the likelihood ratio, (likelihood of $\theta = 0.8$)/(likelihood of $\theta = 0.5$), is equal to or more than 8 OR equal to or less than 1/8. In either case, we have strong evidence for one hypothesis over the other. Conversely, the results could be problematic in two ways. First, the results may provide only weak evidence because the likelihood ratio lies between 1/8 and 8. We will of course know if this is the case. But a second way the results could be problematic is if the evidence is misleading because the ratio gives strong evidence not for the true hypothesis but for the false one. This is obviously possible; if evidence were never misleading, we would always know the truth with certainty based on a single observation. As Royall puts it, in the likelihood approach we will always interpret the evidence correctly, but the evidence itself can be misleading. Now we come to a crucial feature of likelihood inference, the probability of misleading evidence. An early important result (e.g. Birnbaum, 1962) was that the probability of obtaining a likelihood ratio of k in favour of the wrong hypothesis is no greater than $1/k$ even for an infinite number of trials. (This is an upper limit; in fact, the probability is often considerably less than $1/k$, as we will see.) This is remarkable, especially for those of us brought up in the tradition of significance testing. Even more strongly, if an unscrupulous investigator sets out to run subjects until the ratio is k, the probability he will be successful is at most $1/k$, even in an infinite number of trials. Notice how different the result is to the probability defined by a p-value: If I run until I get a certain p-value, it is guaranteed that I will do so eventually.

Royall (1997, Chapter 4) shows how to plan how many subjects to run in order to control the probabilities of weak and misleading evidence. For example, if we planned 20 subjects in our meditation study, we will get strong evidence in favour of $\theta = 0.8$ over $\theta = 0.5$ if the number of people, n, choosing the image day is 15. The likelihood ratio is then greater than 8, whereas for $n = 14$, the ratio is only 2.95. The probability of n being greater than or equal to 15 given the hypothesis that $\theta = 0.5$ is 0.02. That is, given the expectation theory is true the probability of misleading evidence is only 0.02. Similarly, given $\theta = 0.8$, the probability of misleading evidence with 20 subjects is only 0.003. The bigger the difference between the hypotheses, the fewer subjects we need to keep the probabilities of misleading and weak evidence low. If we wished to compare the hypothesis that $\theta = 0.2$ with the hypothesis that $\theta = 0.8$, then with only eight subjects the probability of misleading evidence is 0.01. Further, the probability of weak evidence is only 0.046.

The probabilities of weak and misleading evidence behave differently than the probability of a Type I error. The probability of a Type I error remains constant at its set level no matter how many subjects are planned for the experiment. Conversely, the probabilities of weak and misleading evidence tend to zero in the limit as more subjects are run (Royall, 1997).

The probabilities of misleading and weak evidence are only important in initially planning the study. Once the data are collected the probabilities are irrelevant: We can simply look at the evidence, which is quite independent of the probabilities. If the evidence is weak, we can run more subjects until it is strong enough for our liking.

Likelihood intervals

While we might have planned the study considering the hypotheses $\theta = 0.2$ and 0.8, we can look at the likelihood for all values of θ, as shown in Figure 5.3, in an imaginary case where we found 14 out of 20 people indicate they were happier on the day they meditated on the

Figure 5.3

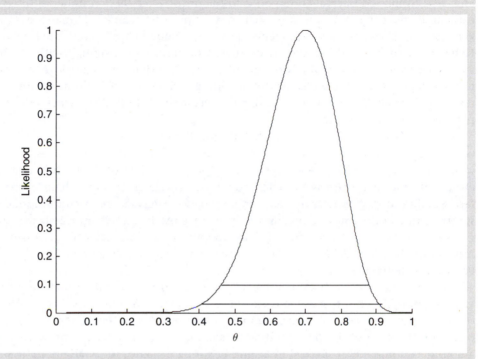

Likelihood function for population proportion θ, having observed 14 successes out of 20 trials. The maximum likelihood value of theta is 0.70. The bottom horizontal line gives the 1/32 likelihood interval, from 0.41 to 0.91. The next line up is the 1/8 interval, from 0.48 to 0.87.

image of giving rather than with an empty mind. The graph was constructed by calculating $\theta^{14}(1-\theta)^6$ for each θ. The likelihood is proportional to this number but the number can be scaled by any constant we want: By the law of likelihood it is only the ratio of likelihoods that tell us relative evidence, and the constant falls out in taking the ratio. So for convenience the figure is scaled so that the highest likelihood is 1.

Figure 5.3 illustrates how one can calculate the likelihood equivalent of the confidence or credibility interval: the likelihood interval. All the likelihood values of more than 1/8 ($= 0.125$) define the 1/8 likelihood interval, marked on the figure (given the highest likelihood is scaled to be 1).[4] The 1/8 likelihood interval in our example runs from $\theta = 0.48$ to $\theta = 0.87$. The value with the highest likelihood is $\theta = 0.7$. But this value does not have even fairly strong evidence supporting it over any other value in the 1/8 interval. So we can treat the values in the interval as roughly equally well supported in the precise sense none has fairly strong evidence for it over any other value in the interval. Defined in this way, the interval is not a probability interval: not an interval of subjective probability (unlike credibility intervals) nor a long-run relative frequency of capturing the true population value (unlike confidence intervals). The meanings of the three intervals are radically different though in fact their numerical widths often agree closely. The 1/8 likelihood interval corresponds to

4. Royall (1997) recommended the 1/8 and 1/32 intervals. Edwards (1979) suggested as a convention taking two units of the natural log of the likelihood ratio, which would give the 1/7.4 interval, close to Royall's 1/8.

the 96 % confidence interval for a normal distribution (uncorrected for stopping rules, etc.); and 1/32 likelihood interval corresponds to the uncorrected 99 % confidence interval for a normal distribution. Thus, the suggested conventions of 1/8 and 1/32 match existing conventions for Neyman–Pearson inference quite well. Nonetheless, confidence intervals have to be corrected for anything that affects their probabilities of covering the true population value; the likelihood interval is a statement of relative evidence (defined by the likelihood ratio) independent of the probability of obtaining such evidence. We now comment on the relation of the likelihood interval to stopping rule, multiple testing and whether the test was planned or post hoc.

We saw in the previous section that the likelihood is the product of likelihoods for each independent observation. Thus, the likelihood, that is the evidence, is independent of stopping rule: The likelihood depends only on the product of the probabilities for each event. This product is clearly not changed by the experimenter, in the light of the data so far, deciding to stop or not. By contrast, confidence intervals are of course influenced by stopping rule; for example, stopping when one has reached a certain number of successes gives a different confidence interval than stopping when one has reached a certain total number of observations for the same data (see Chapter 3). The likelihood interval is exactly the same in both cases.

We saw in Chapter 3 that a confidence interval can be made to exclude any particular value by running until that value is excluded. Eventually the chosen value will lie outside the interval. We also saw above that if one picks two particular possible population values, one cannot run until the likelihood ratio favours one value over the other by a specific amount: You may never succeed in acquiring strong evidence for a false hypothesis over a true one. Nonetheless, you can run until a likelihood ratio favours some unspecified value over a particular one, for example, until *some value or other* is better supported than $\theta = 0.5$. That is, a likelihood interval behaves like a confidence interval in that one can run until some particular value is outside its limits. You could decide to run until the likelihood ratio excludes $\theta = 0.5$, for example, and you would eventually succeed, even if $\theta = 0.5$ is the true value. On the face of it, this point presents a challenge for likelihood inference (Mayo, 1996).

One could argue that choosing to stop when the interval excludes $\theta = 0.5$ does not undermine the meaning of the resulting likelihood interval: the current best evidence simply does, for example, strongly favour $\theta = 0.506$ over $\theta = 0.5$. If $\theta = 0$ is true, the likelihood interval will bunch more and more closely around $\theta = 0$ as data is accumulated, just as it should, no matter what the stopping rule. Nonetheless, if the experiment were, for example, investigating the paranormal, one could always claim to have any amount of evidence in favour of some small paranormal effect by use of a suitable stopping rule (so long as one did not care in advance about the size of the effect).

The point to remember is that likelihood inference is about *relative* evidence for one hypothesis over another, and in this respect it differs from both Fisherian and Neyman–Pearson inference. On Fisherian evidence one gets evidence against the null (according to *p*-value), full stop. On Neyman–Pearson if a confidence interval excludes zero, one rejects zero, full stop. On likelihood inference, since it is the likelihood ratio that is used for inference, evidence is always for one hypothesis *relative to another*. So a likelihood interval excluding the null is not evidence against the null, full stop. In fact, the evidence will support the null as compared to some other hypothesis. 0.504 may be better supported than 0.500, but the evidence for 0.500 may be overpowering compared to 0.55. So the likelihood interval excluding a value is not in itself reason to reject that value, in contrast to confidence intervals.

If researchers move to using likelihood inference, they will need to shift how they think – and not use likelihood results as if they were corresponding Fisherian or Neyman–Pearson results.

Likelihood intervals are not adjusted for the number of related comparisons conducted. The evidence favouring one therapy over a control obviously remains the same no matter how many other different therapies have been tested. What if you compared 100 therapies with a control, would not some of the likelihood intervals show strong evidence against the null just by chance? And should one do anything about that? Of course, sometimes evidence will be misleading, but the job of statistics in the likelihood approach is to interpret what the evidence itself is saying. For those therapies where the evidence indicated strong evidence for some effect of treatment over no effect, that is what the evidence is. It would be possible to report likelihood intervals together with an estimate of error probabilities for those intervals (as recommended by Evans, 2000, for example). But if you were tempted to use those error probabilities to influence the evidential interpretation of the data you would be back with the problems of using p-values as evidence that we started with.

Any temptation you might feel to modulate the evidential interpretation of likelihoods by their error probabilities motivates questioning whether one really can conceptually separate the strength of evidence from the probability of obtaining it (cf Mayo, 1996, 2004). But the evidence is still the evidence even when it points wrongly. Any criterion of strong evidence will sometimes point the wrong way for a given comparison. That comparison exists as part of all other different comparisons assessed in the world, past and future. Why should it matter to you which of the other different comparisons a particular investigator is mentally grouping together? Surely it should make no difference to what the strength of evidence is. Comparisons which actually bear on the same question can be combined in the likelihood approach, as we will see later.

The likelihood does not depend on whether a test is planned or post hoc. The probability of an observation given a hypothesis does not depend on whether the hypothesis was formulated before or after making the observation. In Popper's terms, the objective (world three) relation between evidence and data does not depend on when a person was first aware of either (such awareness belonging to a separate world, world two). Curiously though, Popper thought that the timing of the observation relative to the theory was important for assessing theories. As we noted in Chapter 2, the novelty of a prediction is often felt to be important in assessing theories. Otherwise pejorative terms like data dredging, snooping, fishing and trawling are used. The likelihood theorist should feel such insults are irrelevant to her. We return to the issue below in the context of more general philosophies of science.

In sum, in constructing likelihood ratios and intervals, we need pay no attention to stopping rules, the number of other analyses we are doing, nor whether the analysis was planned or post hoc. In this sense likelihood inference is less subjective than classic Neyman–Pearson procedures. In likelihood inference we just look at what the data are; the experimenter's personal and unknowable intentions are irrelevant.

The likelihood has a further desirable property. The likelihood of a variable remains the same under any one-to-one transformation of that variable (Edwards, 1979). For example, if the 1/8 likelihood interval for time (T) between button presses goes from 2 seconds to 3 seconds, you can find the interval for speed ($1/T$) simply by directly transforming the limits: The 1/8 likelihood interval for speed goes from 1/3 to $1/2$ presses per second. Confidence and credibility intervals do not behave like this. Having found the confidence interval for time, you do not directly know the confidence interval for speed. But surely strong evidence that reaction time lies between 2 and 3 seconds per press is also precisely equally strong evidence that speed lies between 1/3 and ½ presses per second. The fact that confidence and credibility intervals do not respect this truism is a telling sign they do not measure quite what we want.

We will now illustrate the application of likelihood inference to specific simple cases you are likely to come across. Because the strict application of the law of likelihood to inference has a minority following compared to Neyman–Pearson and Bayesian approaches, the future will certainly bring more detailed techniques and different solutions as the philosophy is more thoroughly explored.

Example with categorical variables

We have already provided an example of the simplest case of a categorical variable: a binary outcome variable with identical independent trials (called 'Bernoulli trials'; e.g. the meditation study). A common complication on the simplest case is cross-classification. We may want to know, for example, not just the extent to which one form of meditation is better than another, but whether its effectiveness depends on, for example, whether the person has vivid imagery or poor imagery. Imagine people were classified according to a binary code, as good or bad imagers, and received the two types of meditation as before. The person indicates on which day they felt happiest. We obtain data as shown in the table below:

	Preferred meditating on giving	Preferred empty mind meditation
Poor imagery	5	10
Vivid imagery	14	6

We can conceive of the problem as comparing two population proportions: The proportion of poor imagers θ_{poor} who prefer meditating on giving rather than an empty head and the proportion of vivid imagers θ_{vivid} who prefer meditating on giving rather than an empty mind. We can construct likelihood functions for each proportion separately, as we did above. We can also construct a likelihood function for an explicit comparison between the two. Royall (1997, p. 165) provides an equation for the likelihood function of the ratio γ (gamma) $= \theta_{poor}/\theta_{vivid}$ that has been converted to Matlab code in the Appendix. The program will construct a likelihood function with 1/8 and 1/32 intervals, and provide a likelihood ratio for any two specified gammas. Figure 5.4 shows the likelihood function for γ for the example data.

The maximum likelihood value of γ is about 0.5, that is, the most likely hypothesis is that poor imagers are half as probable as vivid imagers to benefit from giving meditation over empty mind meditation. However, this value does not receive even fairly strong support over any other value in the interval from 0.18 to 0.94, so the data do not yet strongly distinguish values reasonably close to 1 (little difference between poor and vivid imagers) and reasonably small (striking differential preference between the two imager groups). For comparison with a null hypothesis testing analysis, $\chi^2 = 4.64$, $p < 0.05$, so the null hypothesis of equal preference between poor and vivid imagers is rejected. If you had a practical interest in meditation as a therapy for depression, would you prefer to know 'the null was rejected' or to see the whole likelihood curve with 1/8 and 1/32 intervals indicated on it?

Figure 5.4

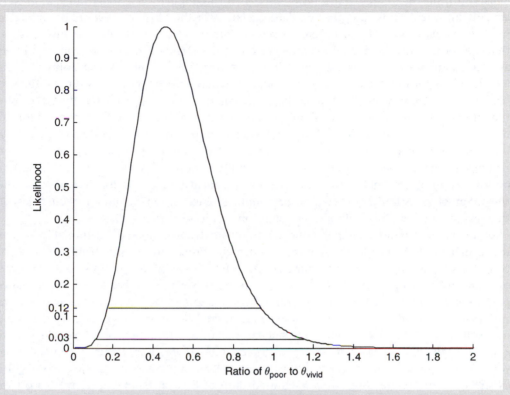

The likelihood function for $\gamma == \theta_{poor}/\theta_{vivid}$. θ_{poor} is the probability that poor imagers prefer giving rather than empty mind meditation and θ_{vivid} is the probability that vivid imagers prefer giving rather than empty mind meditation. The data indicate a maximum likelihood gamma of 0.46, with a 1/8 likelihood interval from 0.18 to 0.94 and a 1/32 likelihood interval from 0.12 to 1.14.

Examples with approximately normal data

A more sensitive design for testing which style of meditation most increases happiness is not to ask subjects to make a binary choice but to ask them to rate their happiness on a scale, for example from 1 to 9, where 5 is 'neutral', 1 is 'deepest depression' and 9 is 'bliss'. Each subject provides us with two ratings, one for each day on which they practiced a certain type of meditation (or an average over a number of days for each meditation type). We can find for each subject the difference (happiness with giving meditation) − (happiness with empty mind meditation). Our data consist of these difference scores. If we can assume the mean of successive samples would be distributed approximately normally, then the appropriate likelihood function is the normal. But there is a problem. A normal distribution has two parameters, mean and standard deviation. We do not know the population standard deviation in order to calculate the likelihood for the mean. This is known as the problem of nuisance parameters: We are interested in the evidence for different values of one parameter (the mean in this case) but the likelihood function depends also on another (the standard deviation in this case). There is no general solution to this problem.

One solution is to produce an *estimated likelihood*: Find the best estimate for the standard deviation from the sample and then proceed as if the population standard deviation were actually known. In this case, the standard deviation of the likelihood would be estimated by the standard error of the difference scores. But this leads to likelihood distributions that are too narrow, because it assumes we know the standard deviation when really we are uncertain, we have only estimated it. This uncertainty should be transmitted to the likelihood. Bayesian inference has a solution. In the previous chapter, we used the estimated likelihood for convenience, but noted how one could set up a prior for our uncertainty in the standard deviation and use this prior to transmit its uncertainty to the likelihood for the mean. In fact, that is an elegant solution a Bayesian can use with all nuisance parameters: set up priors for them and 'integrate them out' (we did this for the Bayes factor). The likelihood theorist, however, does not want to use probability distributions that rely on a subjective interpretation of probability. He wants real likelihoods: those that reflect just the data and the assumed statistical model (whose probabilities reflect actual sampling frequencies) so that, given a model, the likelihood represents only objective evidence.

Unfortunately, it turns out that if one uses the estimated likelihood in likelihood inference, it can make a difference to the degree to which the probability of misleading evidence is controlled. Recall that one of the selling points of likelihood inference is the control it gives over the probability of misleading evidence: there is a universal bound of at most a $1/k$ chance of finding a likelihood ratio of size k in the wrong direction. Indeed, for a normal with known variance this bound is much lower: for example, there is at most a 0.021 chance of finding misleading evidence for $k = 8$ and at most a 0.004 chance of finding misleading evidence for $k = 32$ (Royall, 2004). That is, we could, with probability 0.98, sample forever from a normal with known variance and *not once* find evidence concerning means in the wrong direction as strong as that represented by a likelihood ratio of 8. That is an impressive reason for using likelihood methods. Things change with estimated likelihoods. The maximum value of the probability of misleading evidence with estimated likelihoods can be as large as 0.5. (Similarly, Bayesian likelihoods, where priors are used to integrate out nuisance parameters, are also not guaranteed to respect the universal bound on the probability of misleading evidence; Royall, 2000, p. 779.)

We need to find another solution to the problem of nuisance parameters. One solution is the *profile likelihood*. In this case, for each value of the parameter we are interested in (the population mean in our current discussion) we explore all possible values of the nuisance parameter (e.g. the population standard deviation) and choose the maximum likelihood value of the nuisance parameter. Thus, for each possible population mean value we find whatever standard deviation has maximum likelihood for that mean. It turns out that the standard deviation we should use for each mean is then the standard deviation of the sample data about that mean. It also turns out in this case that the profile likelihood becomes the t-distribution[5]: Conveniently, in this case we can specify a formula for the profile likelihood of the mean (in some other cases profile likelihoods have to be calculated by brute number crunching). Importantly, while profile likelihoods are not real likelihoods, they turn out to respect the same bounds on misleading evidence when sample sizes are adequate (Royall, 2000). Further, while not all profile likelihoods are robust to model failure, the Student's t likelihood is also robust to violations of normality (Royall and Tsou, 2003). These considerations strongly motivate using a profile likelihood for sampling from a normal with unknown variance.

---

5. Which coincidentally is of course exactly the distribution used in classical statistics for tests of means when the standard deviations are only estimated (t-tests).

The Appendix provides Matlab code for calculating the profile likelihood for cases where we want to estimate the population mean but the population standard deviation is unknown. Given sample mean and sample standard error, the program gives the 1/8 and 1/32 likelihood intervals and a likelihood ratio for any two possible population means. The maximum likelihood mean is just the sample mean.

We may be interested in being able to distinguish *no* difference between the two types of meditation from a difference of *three* units in favour of giving meditation. We test 30 subjects on the two types of meditation, producing a mean advantage of giving meditation over empty mind meditation of 1.9 rated units of happiness and a standard error of 1.2. The likelihood ratio for three units over zero units is 2.1, so the evidence does not strongly favour one hypothesis over the other. The 1/8 likelihood interval runs from −0.7 to 4.5. Clearly, insufficient data have yet been collected to draw interesting conclusions. We do not just conclude 'there is a null effect therefore I do not think there is any difference between the conditions'; we conclude that we need to collect more data in this case. If the true difference were two units, as more subjects were run support would accumulate for a difference of three over a difference of zero, because three is closer to two, the true value, than zero is. (If the true difference were by fluke exactly half way between the two theories, that is 1.5 in this case, then the likelihood ratio would not be expected to show substantial support for either theory over the other, no matter how many subjects were run. The likelihood interval would reveal why to the experimenter.)

The program can be used generally whenever you have the same subject participate in several conditions. You may want to compare all of several meditation conditions with all of several drug conditions. Then for each subject take the difference between the average of the meditation conditions and the average of the drug conditions, and analyse these difference scores as above. Or you might want to know if the effectiveness of meditation is changed when a drug is used at the same time. Just analyse the relevant contrast between conditions (see Box 3.7 for further detail on contrasts).

In Box 3.7 you were also introduced to contrasts between the means of different groups of subjects and given the formulae for calculating a contrast for different questions that may interest you with its standard error. In Chapter 4 you were told how credibility intervals could be calculated for any such contrast and in so doing you could do away with ANOVA as traditionally understood. Likewise, you can also calculate likelihood intervals (and relevant likelihood ratios) for between-subjects contrasts. In this way you can now answer by likelihood methods any question about main effects, interactions or simple effects in an ANOVA design. Because the likelihood is insensitive to multiple comparisons, you can assess as many contrasts as answer interesting questions, without further corrections. The appendix provides a program for using the t-distribution as a likelihood for such contrasts.

You can also now produce likelihood intervals and ratios for correlations using the formulae given in Box 3.7. The Fisher transformed correlation is roughly normally distributed, so you can use normal tables to determine the likelihood – the height of the normal is the likelihood.

Cumulating evidence

We noted above that the likelihood for a design with binary independent trials with fixed probability is $\theta^k(1-\theta)^l$ where k is the number of successes and l the number of failures. If one study finds $k = 10$ and $l = 5$ and another study finds $k = 19$ and $l = 13$, the likelihood based on all the data (29 successes and 19 failures) is $\theta^{29}(1-\theta)^{18}$, that is $\theta^{10+19}(1-\theta)^{5+13} = \theta^{10}(1-\theta)^5 \; \theta^{19}(1-\theta)^{13}$ which is the likelihood for the first study times the likelihood for the second. In general, for different data sets (using same design and variables), the likelihoods from each can be multiplied to obtain the likelihood for all the data. Cumulating evidence is simple in the likelihood paradigm (at least in principle; much work remains dealing with the nitty gritty of real data). Contrast the situation with null hypothesis testing. Typically, people quite wrongly presume that two null results constitute twice the evidence against the null as one null result. This habit of thought is sufficiently ubiquitous it is depressing to imagine just how many wrong decisions concerning research direction or the status of a theory have followed such faulty reasoning. Of course, meta-analysis based on Neyman–Pearson principles provides tools for correcting these habits, but the habits are so tempting they remain ingrained. It must be an advantage of the likelihood paradigm that it does not even invite these errors.

The Bayes factor we considered in the previous chapter is a sort of likelihood ratio, but it is not a 'true' likelihood. Its construction depended on integrating over prior beliefs in order to construct a likelihood not just for the value of a parameter (mean slope) but for a theory (morphic resonance). Thus, we needed to know the probability distribution of slope values predicted by morphic resonance. Using this prior probability distribution had advantages: we could, for example, say something about our belief in morphic resonance as a direct result of the analysis. On the other hand, the Bayes factor is not guaranteed to cumulate evidence in the same way as a real likelihood. The Bayes factor for a data set need not be the product of the Bayes factors calculated on each half of the data. In a Bayesian analysis, care must be taken in updating information to ensure internal consistency.

The likelihood analyses we have considered so far concern only the evidence for a parameter in a model having one value rather than another. This begs the question: How can we determine the evidence for one *model* over another (for example, a normal over some other distribution of slopes, or one computational model of a psychological phenomenon over another)? Further, we could, as likelihood theorists, work out the relative evidence for one slope *value* over another, but not for morphic resonance over the null. How does the evidence for a value or a model relate to evidence for a substantial theory (e.g. morphic resonance)?

Choosing models[6]

In calculating likelihoods above we assumed a statistical model, such as the data were independent binary trials or the data were continuous and normally distributed. The likelihood ratios provided evidence for one value of a model parameter rather than another only in the context of this model. Such a procedure does not assume that the model is absolutely true. If the model were true, then in the limit as sample size increases the likelihood function would peak over the true parameter value. But if the model were only an approximation to reality, then the likelihood function would still peak over that parameter value which enabled the model to best approximate reality (in a precise mathematical sense of 'approximate' not developed here, but see Royall and Tsou, 2003). Nonetheless, we always want to know how good our model is as an approximation to reality. In a statistical sense, the probability of making various sort of errors depends on the goodness of the model in approximating reality.

6. This section may be difficult; you may skip without loss of continuity.

And importantly, in a scientific sense our aim in collecting data is often precisely to tell us what model we should have of the phenomenon.

A model specifies the structural relation between variables. For example, a linear model says the variables are related by a straight line and a quadratic model says one variable is related to the square of another. For a relatively good model, the obtained data are relatively likely given some parameter values; that is, the model will be able to fit the data. So at first glance one way of determining the relative evidence for *model one* versus *model two* would be to consider the likelihood ratio p(data | model one with best fitting parameter values)/ p(data | model two with best fitting parameter values). This would be exactly analogous to the methods we have been using for determining the evidence for one parameter value over another for a given model. But a simple example illustrates a problem. Figure 5.5a shows three observations generated from an underlying linear relation with some random noise added to each observation. The best fitting straight line naturally comes close to matching the reality that generated the data. To fit the line we need to find values for two parameters: the intercept and slope of the line. Of course, the straight line does not fit the data perfectly because there is noise in the relationship between the two variables. The fit is not perfect, so the likelihood, the probability of producing these data given the linear model with best fitting parameters, is less than one. Figure 5.5b shows we can fit the points perfectly with a quadratic, which has three parameters (intercept, linear and quadratic terms). Of course, with three parameters we can fit three data points perfectly. The fit is perfect and thus the likelihood is one. The likelihood ratio favours the quadratic over the linear model.

Figure 5.5

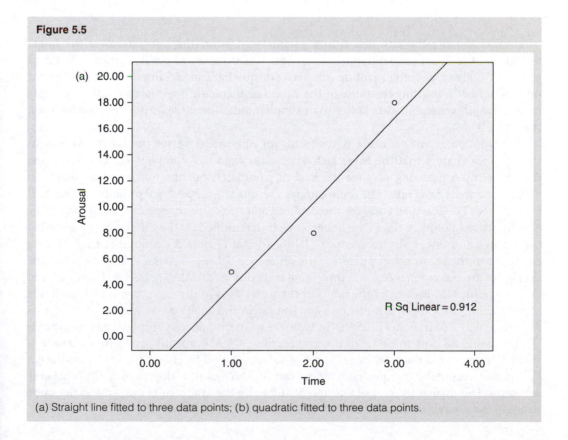

(a) Straight line fitted to three data points; (b) quadratic fitted to three data points.

Figure 5.5 *continued*

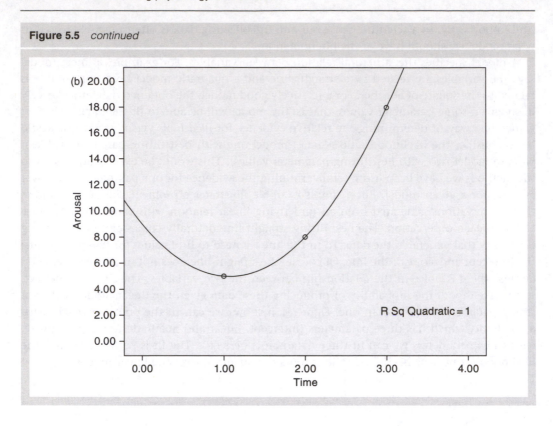

The likelihood ratio with best fitting parameters favours the quadratic over the linear model but the linear model happens to reflect the structure of reality better. The linear model will generalize better to future data sets. The quadratic model fitted the data better but only because it was fitting the noise in the data: The quadratic *over-fitted* the data. Complex models can in general fit data better than simple models even when they are further from the truth.

One solution is to calculate a Bayes factor for one model versus the other. We saw in the previous chapter that the Bayes factor penalizes vague (or complex) models. We assess the model by considering not just the best fit parameters but the full range of parameter values the model *could* take. The more different results the model *could* produce, the more it is penalized. For example, consider the data in Figure 5.5, the change of arousal over three equally spaced points in time. The linear slope is determined by the difference in arousal at times three and one. Call this contrast LIN (= arousal at time 3 – arousal at time 1). Any curvature in the relationship will affect the difference between arousal at time two and the average of arousal at times one and three. Call this contrast QUAD. Figure 5.6 shows a plot of QUAD against LIN. Because of the limits of the scales used in the experiment, LIN has limits of ±20 and QUAD also has limits of ±20. The linear model allows any value of LIN in its full range. The linear model produces only linear relations between arousal and time, that is QUAD should be close to zero. But because of noise, QUAD can still deviate from zero by a small amount in the linear model. The set of values allowed by the linear model are shown by the dark rectangle. The quadratic model can fit ANY point in the space of the large grey rectangle. The smaller the area of a rectangle the more the model rules out, and so the more strongly the model predicts the data to be in any point in its rectangle.

Figure 5.6

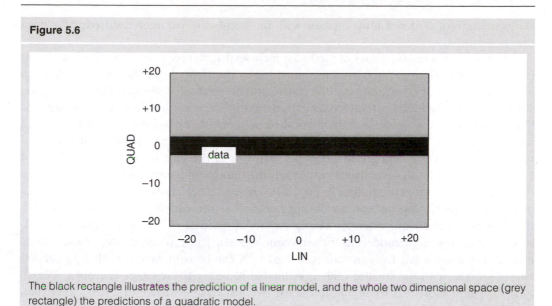

The black rectangle illustrates the prediction of a linear model, and the whole two dimensional space (grey rectangle) the predictions of a quadratic model.

The obtained data are also shown. Both models can closely *fit* the data. But because the linear model rules out more, the data are more strongly predicted by the linear model than the quadratic model. In fact the Bayes factor, the likelihood ratio (considering all possible parameter values) in favour of the linear model over the quadratic, is roughly the area of the grey rectangle divided by the area of the black rectangle. Notice how the logic here is the same as that we used for assessing models of learning in Chapter 1 when discussing Popper (see Figures 1.4–1.7).

The above analysis follows the likelihood intuition that data most strongly supports the model that most strongly predicts it. Considering all parameter values, the linear model more strongly predicted the data than the quadratic model did. Notice we implicitly assumed in this analysis that all parameter values of LIN were equally probable for the linear model, and all parameter values of LIN and QUAD equally probable for the quadratic model. We used uniform priors, but subjective priors nonetheless. It is because of the subjective priors that Bayes factors are eschewed by pure likelihood theorists. If you are happy with using priors, Bayes factors can be used flexibly for assessing a full range of models across the sciences. But if you are shy of using any sort of prior in calculating likelihoods, what can you do?

In this simple case, we can also use likelihood methods already considered above. If the evidence for QUAD having a value zero over a minimally interesting value is strong enough, one could treat QUAD as negligible and hence focus work on the linear model. This is a possible strategy because the models are *nested*: The linear model is a special case of the quadratic model when its quadratic parameter is set to zero. However, we are often faced with choosing between models which are not nested. Further, in nested models, a model with 10 parameters will always fit the data better than a model with one parameter (assuming the latter does not fit perfectly). How strong should the evidence be for the 10 parameter model over a one parameter model before we prefer the more complex model? We cannot use our normal criteria of strength of evidence (8, 32, etc.), because every parameter we add allows a better fit even if only because of over-fitting. Somehow the required likelihood ratio for a given strength of evidence must increase with the number of parameters differing between the models.

A very general method (or set of methods) for assessing the relative evidence for different models in the likelihood framework was provided by the Japanese mathematician Hirotugu Aikake. His 1971 paper became a citation classic, and his method, developed in various papers since then, has been used extensively in both the natural and social sciences. Akaike showed that the distance (in a precise mathematical sense) between an approximating model and the true model of reality can be estimated by finding the parameter values that maximize the probability of the data given the model (call this L, the likelihood of the model) and calculating: $-\log(L) + K + a$ constant, where K is the number of parameters that are estimated from the data (and logs are to base e, i.e. 2.718). If we do not know the true model, which of course in general we do not, we do not know what the constant should be. However, the constant is the same when we evaluate different models on the same data (i.e. measure the distance of the models to the same true model). Thus, in comparing models we do not need to know what the constant is. $-\log(L) + K$ can be compared for different models and the model with the smaller value is estimated to be relatively closer to reality. (We do not know how close it is in an absolute sense; we just have evidence that it is closer than the other models under consideration.) For historical reasons, Akaike multiplied the distance measure by 2 (which obviously makes no difference for comparisons between models) to get:

$$\text{Akaike's Information Criterion (AIC)} = -2 \log(L) + 2K$$

We have been assessing relative evidence by a ratio of likelihoods, $L1/L2$. Notice that $\log(L1/L2) = \log(L1) - \log(L2)$. So taking a difference between logged likelihoods is equivalent to taking a ratio of raw likelihoods. Because AIC involves logs, one compares models by taking the difference between the AIC scores for the different models. If we were comparing models with the same number of parameters, AIC reduces to the log of the likelihood ratio. Previously, we took a likelihood ratio of 8 as fairly strong evidence and 32 as strong evidence. Likelihood ratios of 8 and 32 correspond to AIC differences of 4.1 and 6.9 between models with equal numbers of parameters. Indeed, according to convention, AIC differences of 4 to 7 are regarded as considerable evidence for one model over another (e.g. Burnham and Anderson, 2002). If model one had one more parameter than model two, by the AIC, a likelihood ratio of 8 would no longer constitute fairly strong evidence for model one over model two. We need to apply a penalty for the extra parameter. Instead, a likelihood ratio of 20 is now needed! (See if you can work this out from the formula for AIC.) In sum, Akaike provided a principled way of trading off likelihood ratios against differences in parameter numbers in evaluating relative evidence for one model over another.

The AIC is a measure of relative evidence. Thus, the recommended criteria (e.g. an AIC difference of 4 is fairly strong relative evidence for one model over another) are not meant as strict acceptance and rejection criteria: They simply indicate relative strength of evidence which one can act on as suits one best. The AIC method is general in that it can apply to nested models or non-nested models. Since the original papers there has been a growth industry in determining different criteria that could be used (see e.g. Burnham & Anderson, 2002; Taper & Lele, 2004). The AIC or its variants can be used in determining the relative evidence for the distribution of one's data being normal versus some other distribution, for determining the relative evidence for one multiple regression equation over another, or for one computational model over another. Null hypothesis testing is neither needed nor desirable in these situations if one's interest is in relative evidence for different models.

Note that in practice AIC and the Bayes factor will largely give similar results in comparing two models, but they can differ. For example, imagine two models that have the same number of parameters and that can fit a data set perfectly with some parameter values. AIC provides no means of choosing between them. The Bayes factor will support the model which over all parameter values tended to concentrate its predictions in the area of the data (compare Figure 5.6).

Finally, statistical models need to be kept separate from substantial theories. Likelihood methods may show that there is more evidence for one model than another, but there is still an inferential step in going from this claim to claiming there is evidence for one psychological theory rather than another. One mean value may have strong evidence over another, but whether this supports a theory (e.g. cognitive dissonance theory) depends on the validity of the variables as measures of what they say they measure, of how well controlled the experiment was, on what other explanations are possible. Similarly, one computational model may be supported over another, but a model instantiates both psychological princi-ples (e.g. perhaps the principle that forgetting takes place) and arbitrary decisions needed to make the model run at all (e.g. maybe the precise form of the forgetting function). What enables a model to fit the data depends on all its operating assumptions, from the principled to the arbitrary. Yet evidence needs to be somehow channelled to target spe-cific assumptions, either core or auxiliary, in order to influence what theories to work on. And so ultimately we are led back to the issues we started this book with, for exam-ple to the ideas of Popper and Lakatos on the more general bases of theory choice and progress.

Knowing the truth

Models are in general approximations to the truth. Indeed, often we like to work on models we know are false just because they are simple yet approximate well. A simple model may apply reasonably well in many apparently disparate situations even if it fits none perfectly. Often we work on simple models in order to understand general principles more clearly, that is, in order to explore the world 3 properties of our theories (in Popper's sense). We still want to know where such simple ideas break down in explaining the details of par-ticular data sets because we will certainly want to eventually explore those details in fuller models.

Popper urged scientists to search for theories that made predictions unlikely on the basis of other knowledge in order to pursue better approximations to the truth. Popperian corrob-oration of one model over another thus consists in many cases of one model having greater evidence over the other in the likelihood sense (at least in those cases where likelihoods can be calculated). There is a further analogy in that relative likelihood is an estimate of distance between probability distributions and the true distribution, that is of verisimili-tude in a very particular sense. Verisimilitude is a more general notion but it is interesting that Popper's ideas and likelihood ideas correspond in a number of areas (Taper & Lele, 2004).

Likelihood theory and the ideas of Popper and Lakatos differ in their treatment of novelty. Both Popper and Lakatos valued novel predictions. The likelihood is not sensitive to the relative timing of being aware of the data and thinking of a model or theory. Yet the intuition that it makes a difference is strong amongst scientists. Burnham and Anderson (2002) in their textbook on likelihood methods for assessing models warn against data dredging, an activity they regard as perhaps merely 'venial' but in some cases 'mortal': 'Grevious data dredging is endemic in the applied literature and still frequently taught or implied in statistics courses without the needed caveats concerning the attendant inferential problems' (p. 41). But there is nothing in the evidential measures recommended by Burnham and Anderson for model assessment that reflect the number of models considered or how you thought of them. The AIC has no term for the number of comparisons conducted nor for whether a model was post hoc. Is AIC therefore incomplete? Of course, family-wise error rate is inflated by data dredging, so Neyman–Pearson statistics should be and are sensitive to it (though quite how they handle the issue remains arbitrary in detail). Likelihood measures are not sensitive to whether data were dredged or not, because the evidence is simply the evidence. A dead body with a knife in its back is surely evidence of murder whether netted out of the lake by some fishermen or located by a prior police inquiry.

You may remember from Chapter 2 that Lakatos himself gave up on the importance of temporal novelty per se and adopted the notion of use novelty: Evidence supports a theory to the extent it was not used in constructing it. The likelihood does not acknowledge the relevance of even this sort of novelty. One might be able to reconcile the views of Lakatos and likelihood theorists by regarding likelihood theory as applicable to strictly statistical hypotheses (e.g. the mean amount of opinion change for this experiment is 2 rather than 0 units) and Lakatos' ideas as applicable to the substantial theory (e.g. cognitive dissonance theory) that generated the statistical hypothesis. Then the ability of cognitive dissonance theory to generate novel statistical hypotheses contributes to its progressiveness, but the evaluation of statistical hypotheses is independent of the timing of the data and their conception. This position may be tempting but the distinction in methods of assessing statistical hypotheses and substantial theories does not seem principled. Perhaps there is a Bayesian account based on personal probabilities: In general, the relationship between statistical hypotheses and the data is so tight, the relevance of the one to the other is immediately obvious to us, so novelty is irrelevant; but the relation of substantial theories to different data typically needs work in exploring. Realizing that some previously unconsidered evidence is relevant for a theory may boost our personal probability in the theory (Howson and Urbach, 2006). Of course, already considered evidence, because it was used in constructing the theory, is already reflected in our personal probability. This is one account of the importance of use novelty, though not one either Popper or Lakatos would like. Thagard (1992) argued novelty only appears important because novel as opposed to post hoc predictions typically rely on simple auxiliaries. The novelty of data relative to explanation and what to do about it will surely remain a topic of continued controversy.

Randomization

The different schools of inference have clashed not only over data analysis but also over experimental design, in particular on the role of randomization. Fisher proposed the random assignment of subjects to conditions as a means for dealing with extraneous variables. The proposal has been regularly praised as one of Fisher's greatest contributions. In an experiment to test, for example, the effectiveness of different memorization strategies, subjects may be assigned one of two different strategies for memorizing a list of romantic words. There will be some subject characteristics relevant to their ability to memorize the words regardless of the strategy they are assigned. Maybe gender makes a difference, for example, with women being better at remembering romantic material than men. One can control such a variable by ensuring an equal number of men and women in each group. But there are numerous variables that could influence the results, such as IQ and imagery vividness and many others we cannot even think of. We cannot control them all. But if we randomly assign subjects to groups, we do not need to control them all, nor even know what they are. Here is why. These variables sum to create a given pattern of differences between individuals even before we have given the groups their different treatments. If we randomly assign people to groups, so that each person has an equal probability of going into each group, the expected difference between the groups in memory ability is zero. Any difference that does arise can arise only by chance. The chance of that is exactly what we calculate in our *p*-value. And the significance level is precisely our prior commitment to the size of such risk we are willing to take. In that sense, we have accounted for all the variables that might be relevant whether we know of them or not! No one can fault our study because, for example, there may have been a difference in IQ levels between the groups and maybe this explained the results. (A typical formulaic manoeuvre made in undergraduate practical reports: Think of an uncontrolled extraneous variable as a criticism of the practical.) The criticism is not a valid explanation of a significant result because all such extraneous variables have been accounted for by the beauty of randomization.

Randomization gets around the problem of experimenter bias. If the experimenter assigns subjects based on conscious or unconscious beliefs about some subjects being more appropriate for one condition rather than another, then there will be a systematic difference between conditions in the type of subjects. The difference in subject type rather than treatment might explain a significant result. When Fisher recommended random assignment he meant literal random assignment, not arbitrary assignment based on the whim of the experimenter. Even if the experimenter assigns subjects always in the order group one then group two, then assignment is not random but systematic, and this can allow systematic bias. For example, maybe subjects tend to come to the experimenter in pairs with a tendency for the more extroverted to be in front. For random assignment, the experimenter could have two cards labelled one and two, shuffle them before each pair of subjects and run in the resulting order.

Randomization is recognized as being so important that it defines the difference between a true experiment and a merely observational study: Only in a true experiment are subjects randomly assigned to conditions. Clinical trials are often regarded as completely invalid if random assignment has not been used.

But from the perspective of Bayesian and likelihood inference life is not so simple. Something can be random in two senses. One is it that it was generated by a random process; the other is that it has intrinsic properties that make it random. A random process will sometimes generate 10 heads in a row, and that sequence, as a product of random process, is in a sense random. Yet it would not pass some tests of randomness around. The logic for randomization given above relied on the first sense of randomness. It was because each subject *could* just as well have been assigned to each group that we could calculate *p*-values. But Bayesian and likelihood theorists are not concerned with what could have happened and did not; they are concerned only with what happened. If exactly the same assignments of subjects to conditions were made by an experimenter carefully choosing which condition was 'appropriate' for each subject, on the one hand, and by another experimenter with a flip of a coin, on the other, then for classical statisticians the first experiment is invalid and the second beyond reproach. For Bayesian and likelihood theorists the evidential import of the data is exactly the same in both cases because the data are the same.

Bayesians and likelihood theorists argue that randomization can be desirable but is not the sine qua non of good evidence. Randomization is desirable because it *tends* to balance out extraneous variables across conditions. It is a convenient way of *approximately* balancing out variables when we do not know what most of the relevant variables are. But it is not guaranteed to do this. The Bayesian statistician Savage (1962) asks us to imagine randomly assigning 32 fur-bearing animals to two groups to test the effect of a pelt-conditioning vitamin. Of these animals, some were junior and some senior, some black and some brown, some fat and some thin, some wild and some tame and so on. One can construct an example whereby any random assignment into two groups of 16 contains all animals from one side or the other of one of the dichotomies. In this small sample, random assignment *guarantees* an imbalance on an extraneous variable! 'Thus contrary to what I think I was taught, and certainly used to believe, it does not seem possible to base a meaningful experiment on a small heterogeneous group' even with the magic of randomization (p. 91).

Savage revealed 'My doubts were first crystallised in the summer of 1952 by Sir Ronald Fisher. "What would you do", I had asked, "if drawing a Latin Square at random for an experiment, you happened to draw a Knut Vic square?" Sir Ronald said he thought he would draw again' (p. 88). That is, randomization does not guarantee extraneous variables have been best dealt with. If one were to 'draw again' until satisfied with the draw, the assignment would no longer be based on a random process. Nonetheless, Savage acknowledged the usefulness of randomization if the experiment is rather large because then 'randomisation will almost always lead to a layout that does not look suspicious' (p. 89).

In an ensuring discussion, Good suggested that the purpose of randomization is 'to simplify the analysis by throwing away some of the evidence deliberately' (p. 90). We do not need to know all the extraneous variables; they can be regarded as accounted for by the act of random assignment. Savage retorted 'That is a terrible crime to throw away evidence.' Indeed, if one found out in retrospect that the random assignment had put all the males in one group and all the females in another, then no matter what one's statistical persuasion, there is no excuse for ignoring that information. There is no reason to raise gender as a confound in the absence of measuring it; but no reason to ignore it having measured it (see Senn, 2005, for a clear account of these issues). Likewise, Royall (1976) chastised those, like Good, who follow what Royall called the 'closurisation' principle that randomizing means one does not need to look at the actual properties of the sample: First you randomize then you closurize. (Say the last word out loud.) Better to keep your eyes open and look at what the data actually are. To Bayesian and likelihood theorists, the evidence is contained in the actual data.

Using the likelihood approach to critically evaluate a psychology article

From reading the introduction of the paper identify a key main prediction of the author's theory. You should be able to reduce the prediction to a specific contrast (e.g. something that could be tested with a *t*-test in the Neyman–Pearson tradition) rather than a vague statement

In the 1920s during afternoon tea at Cambridge, a lady made a claim that Fisher thought needed randomization to test properly. The example of the lady tasting tea appeared in his 1935 book

like 'at least one of these means will be different from one other'. What value of the contrast in question is minimally interesting on the author's theory? What value is expected on the null hypothesis? Construct a likelihood interval for the contrast. Is the maximum likelihood value consistent with the author's theory? How strong is the support for the maximum likelihood value compared to the null? If the author rejects the null, how strong is the evidence supporting a value consistent with her theory over the null? Note that nulls can be rejected on the Neyman–Pearson approach when the evidence is very weak. Conversely, if the author gets a non-significant result, how strong is the evidence for the null over the minimally interesting value on the author's theory? If the evidence is weak, more subjects should be run – until the evidence is strong enough one way or the other for everyone to be satisfied.

What value of the parameter would be expected assuming the author's theory is false but other relevant background knowledge is true? How strong is the support for the parameter value expected on the author's theory compared to background knowledge? According to Popper, a test is severe and the theory strongly corroborated only if this support is high. The prediction of the theory should be unlikely not just given the null hypothesis but all other relevant background knowledge. Exactly how this intuition should be fleshed out will depend on individual cases – for example, on the range of values allowed by the respective theories.

Remember you can increase sensitivity of your analyses if there is a set of experiments using the same design and variables by combining evidence across experiments by multiplying likelihoods together. That is, the likelihood that the parameter has value x over all experiments is the likelihood obtained from experiment 1 × the likelihood obtained from experiment 2 × ... and so on.

If you criticize someone's work using likelihood analyses, they may counter that the official approach is Neyman–Pearson, so your criticisms are not relevant. Ask them if they are interested in how strongly the data support their conclusions.

Summary of Neyman–Pearson, Bayesian and likelihood inference

We present the three major schools of statistical inference, whose properties are summarized in Table 5.1. In sum, in the Neyman–Pearson approach, it is assumed that what the scientist wants is a generally reliable procedure for accepting and rejecting hypotheses, a procedure with known and controlled long-term error rates. According to both the Bayesian and Likelihood theorists, the scientist wants to know the relative amount of support data provide for different hypotheses. The Bayesian uses the support to adjust her convictions, and may also use her convictions in order to calculate the support (for example, in working out a Bayes factor). The likelihood theorist wants to know simply the relative evidence for different hypotheses.

The differences can be illustrated by considering confidence, credibility and likelihood intervals. Mostly these intervals agree with each other very closely. But they aim for different goals and this can make a difference in detail. The 95 % confidence interval will include the true population value 95 % of the time in the long run, but says nothing about the probability of the current interval including the population value. In fact, one might be quite sure the current interval does not include the population mean even while the confidence interval

Table 5.1 The three schools of inference

	Meaning of probability	Aim	Inference	Long-run error rates	Sensitive to
Neyman Pearson	Objective frequencies	Provide a reliable decision procedure with controlled long term error rates	Black and white decisions	Controlled at fixed values	Stopping rule; what counts as the family of tests; timing of explanation relative to data
Bayes	subjective	Indicate how prior probabilities should be changed by data	Continuous degree of posterior belief	Not guaranteed to be controlled	Prior opinion
Likelihood	Can be used with either interpretation	Indicate relative strength of evidence	Continuous degree of relative evidence	Errors of weak and misleading evidence controlled	None of the above

is perfectly legitimate as a confidence interval. Imagine you start running a reaction time experiment and find the first person has an average reaction time of 600 ms and the second person 602 ms. The estimated standard deviation is thus 1.4 ms. The 50 % confidence interval is (600, 602) and the 95 % confidence interval is (588, 614). Given your prior knowledge of reaction time experiments you may know what typical standard deviations are for this type of data. You might in fact be very sure that the standard deviation has been underestimated by these data: It was clearly just a fluke that the first two subjects scored closely together. Then you would not have 95 % confidence in the 95 % confidence interval, not this one. Even though the procedure is accurate, an interval calculated in this way will include the true mean 95 % of the time, it does not require you have any confidence in a particular interval, least of all this one. The credibility interval would be different. Bayesians point out that it is in exactly such situations – limited data but strong prior knowledge – that incorporating prior knowledge is very useful. Because of your prior knowledge of credible values for the pop-ulation standard deviation, your posterior standard deviation would be larger than 1.4 ms, perhaps considerably. The 50 % and 95 % credibility intervals would therefore also be larger than the corresponding confidence intervals, as they should be if they are to reflect what is credible. Or consider another example. Maybe you have very good reasons for believing the population mean cannot be negative, but much or all of your confidence interval extends below zero. A Bayesian credibility interval could take into account that the population value could not be negative and produce an interval that more closely reflected what you thought reasonable in this case: one only or mainly covering positive values. The likelihood interval avoids either trying to cover the population mean with a certain long run probability or to reflect final opinion. It just reflects what the evidence indicates. Evidence may be misleading sometimes, as it is in the above two examples, but it is always the evidence.

In sum, if you want decision procedures with good long-term error probabilities (which you certainly will in quality control settings) then choose Neyman–Pearson; if you want to know what to believe (as you would, for example, in a court case), choose Bayes; and if you want to know what the evidence is (I often do), choose likelihood infer-ence. I hope you now appreciate the goals of all approaches and can use them all where appropriate.

Review and discussion questions

1. Define the key terms of: likelihood, likelihood ratio, law of likelihood, likelihood interval, estimated likelihood and profile likelihood.
2. For the same set of data calculate a confidence interval, a credibility interval and a likelihood interval. Compare and contrast the interpretation of each.
3. Think of an empirical problem of interest to you. Distinguish a substantial theory relevant to that problem, a statistical model, and a statistical hypothesis. What is the role of likelihood inference in assessing substantial theories, statistical models and statistical hypotheses?
4. How if at all would the stopping rule used affect your interpretation of a likelihood interval and any decision you base on that interval?
5. If you believe one medical treatment is more effective than another, is it ethical to ran-domly assign patients to treatments to test the difference in effectiveness of the treatments? Are any other valid options available? (See Royall, 1991, for further discussion.)

6. Consider an empirical problem of interest to you. Would you like your inferences concerning that problem be guided by the Neyman–Pearson, Bayesian or likelihood approach? Why?

Appendices

A Program for proportion
B Program for 2×2 cross classification
C Program for mean of normal with unknown variance
D Program for between-subjects contrasts

A. Program for proportion

The program asks for the number of successes and the number of failures. The variable likelihood is the likelihood function, which can be plotted against θ (theta) (the possible population proportions). The limits of the 1/8 interval are given by begin8 and end8, and limits of the 1/32 likelihood interval by begin32 and end 32. The maximum likelihood value is θ_{max} (thetamax). The program also asks you to input the θ assumed by two hypotheses; it returns the likelihood ratio for these two values. This ratio could be used as a stopping rule: Collect data until the ratio is greater than 8 or less than 1/8, for example.

```
suc = input('What is the number of successes? ');
fail = input('What is the number of failures? ');
thetamax = 0;
likelihoodmax = 0;

  for B = 1:1000
     theta(B) = B/1000;
     likelihood(B) = theta(B)^suc*(1 - theta(B))^fail;
     if likelihood(B) > likelihoodmax
         likelihoodmax = likelihood(B);
         thetamax = theta(B);
     end
  end
  for B = 1:1000
      likelihood(B) = likelihood(B)/likelihoodmax;
  end
  begin8 = 99;
  begin32 = 99;
  end8 = 99;
  end32 = 99;
  for B = 1:1000
     if begin8 == 99
         if likelihood(B) > 1/8
             begin8 = theta(B);
         end
     end
```

```
  if begin32 == 99
      if likelihood(B) > 1/32
          begin32 = theta(B);
      end
  end
  if and(begin8 ~= 99, end8 == 99)
      if likelihood(B) < 1/8
          end8 = theta(B);
      end
  end
  if and(begin32 ~= 99, end32 == 99)
      if likelihood(B) < 1/32
          end32 = theta(B);
      end
  end
end
  thetamax
  begin32
  end32
  begin8
  end8
```

B. Program for 2×2 cross classification

For the general case with cell counts a, b, c and d:

	Success	Fail
Type X	a	b
Type Y	c	d

We are interested in the extent to which θ_1 (theta1) (the probability of success for type X individuals) is different from θ_2 (theta2) (the probability of success for type Y individuals), as measured by the ratio γ (gamma) $= \theta_1/\theta_2$. The program asks for the values of each of a, b, c and d: Make sure you enter them in that order. The variable likelihood is the likelihood function, which can be plotted against γ. The limits of the 1/8 interval are given by begin8 and end8, and limits of the 1/32 likelihood interval by begin32 and end32. The maximum likelihood value is γ_{max} (gammamax). The program also asks you to input the γ assumed by two hypotheses; it returns the likelihood ratio for these two values. This ratio could be used as a stopping rule: Collect data until the ratio is greater than 8 or less than 1/8, for example.

```
a = input('What is a? ');
b = input('What is b? ');
c = input('What is c? ');
d = input('What is d? ');
m = a + b;
n = c + d;
```

```
k = a + c;
l = b + d;

gammamax = 0;
likelihoodmax = 0;
 for B = 1:10000
    gamma(B) = B/100;
    likelihood(B) = 0;
    for A = b:(m+n-d)
        likelihood(B) = likelihood(B) + nchoosek(A-1, b-1)*nchoosek
           (m+n-A-1,d-1)*gamma(B)^(A-m);
    end
    likelihood(B) = likelihood(B)^(-1);
    if likelihood(B) > likelihoodmax
        likelihoodmax = likelihood(B);
        gammamax = gamma(B);
    end
 end
for B = 1:10000
    likelihood(B) = likelihood(B)/likelihoodmax;
end
begin8 = -99;
begin32 = -99;
end8 = -99;
end32 = -99;
for B = 1:10000
    if begin8 == -99
        if likelihood(B) > 1/8
            begin8 = gamma(B);
        end
    end
    if begin32 == -99
      if likelihood(B) > 1/32
          begin32 = gamma(B);
      end
    end
    if and(begin8 ~= -99, end8 == -99)
        if likelihood(B) < 1/8
            end8 = gamma(B);
        end
    end
    if and(begin32 ~= -99, end32 == -99)
        if likelihood(B) < 1/32
            end32 = gamma(B);
        end
    end
end
```

```
gamma1 = input('What is the gamma assumed by the first hypothesis? ');
gamma2 = input('What is the gamma assumed by the second hypothesis? ');
likelihoodratio = likelihood(gamma1*10)/likelihood(gamma2*10)
```

```
    gammamax
    begin32
    end32
    begin8
    end8
```

C. Program for mean of normal with unknown variance

The program asks for the sample standard error, mean and number of subjects. The variable likelihood is the likelihood function, which can be plotted against θ (theta) (the possible population means). The limits of the 1/8 interval are given by begin8 and end8, and limits of the 1/32 likelihood interval by begin32 and end 32. The program also asks you to input the theta assumed by two hypotheses; it returns the likelihood ratio for these two values. This ratio could be used as a stopping rule: Collect data until the ratio is greater than 8 or less than 1/8, for example.

```
SEd = input('What is the sample standard error? ');
meand = input('What is the sample mean? ');
n = input('How many subjects were run? ');

Vard = n*SEd^2;
SSd = Vard*(n-1);

likelihoodmax = 0;
theta(1) = meand - 5*SEd;
inc = SEd/100;

for B = 1:1000
    theta(B) = theta(1) + (B-1)*inc;
    likelihood(B) = (SSd + n*(meand - theta(B))^2)^(-(n-2)/2);

    if likelihood(B) > likelihoodmax
        likelihoodmax = likelihood(B);
    end
end
for B = 1:1000
    likelihood(B) = likelihood(B)/likelihoodmax;
end

outofrange = meand - 6*SEd;

begin8 = outofrange;
begin32 = outofrange;
end8 = outofrange;
```

```
end32 = outofrange;
for B = 1:1000
    if begin8 == outofrange
        if likelihood(B) > 1/8
            begin8 = theta(B);
        end
    end
    if begin32 == outofrange
        if likelihood(B) > 1/32
            begin32 = theta(B);
        end
    end
    if and(begin8 ~= outofrange, end8 == outofrange)
        if likelihood(B) > 1/8
            end8 = theta(B);
        end
    end
    if and(begin32 ~= outofrange, end32 == outofrange)
        if likelihood(B) < 1/32
            end32 = theta(B);
        end
    end
end

theta1 = input('What is the population mean assumed by the first
  hypothesis? ');
theta2 = input('What is the population mean assumed by the second
  hypothesis? ');
B1 = int16((theta1 - theta(1))/inc + 1);
B2 = int16((theta2 - theta(1))/inc + 1);
likelihoodratio = likelihood(B1)/likelihood(B2)
    begin32
    end32
    begin8
    end8
```

D. Program for between-subjects contrasts

Imagine you have k groups of subjects each with mean m_i and standard deviation SD_i of a roughly normally distributed variable. The contrast, $C = \sum a_i m_i$, where a_i are the contrast weights. For roughly normally distributed data and equal variances within each group, the mean contrast value C has a standard error $\sqrt{(\sum a_i^2)} SD_p / \sqrt{n}$, where n is the number of subjects in each group and $SD_p = \sqrt{(1/k \sum SD_i^2)}$. The degrees of freedom are $\sum(n_i - 1)$. If the number of subjects in each group are unequal, use the harmonic mean for n ($= k/(\sum 1/n_i)$). See Box 3.7 for explanation of what a contrast is.

The program asks for the standard error of the contrast, mean of the contrast and the degrees of freedom. The variable likelihood is the likelihood function, which can be plotted against θ (theta) (the possible population contrast means). The limits of the 1/8 interval are given by begin8 and end8, and limits of the 1/32 likelihood interval by begin32 and end 32. The program also asks you to input the θ assumed by two hypotheses; it returns the likelihood ratio for these two values. This ratio could be used as a stopping rule: Collect data until the ratio is greater than 8 or less than 1/8, for example.

```
SEd = input('What is the standard error of the contrast? ');
meand = input('What is the contrast mean? ');
nu = input('what are the degrees of freedom of the contrast? ');
likelihoodmax = 0;
theta(1) = meand - 5*SEd;
inc = SEd/100;

  for B = 1:1000
     theta(B) = theta(1) + (B-1)*inc;
     likelihood(B) = (1 +(meand - theta(B))^2/(nu*SEd^2))^(-(nu+1)/2);

     if likelihood(B)> likelihoodmax
         likelihoodmax = likelihood(B);
     end
  end
  for B = 1:1000
      likelihood(B) = likelihood(B)/likelihoodmax;
  end


  outofrange = meand - 6*SEd;


  begin8 = outofrange;
  begin32 = outofrange;
  end8 = outofrange;
  end32 = outofrange;
  for B = 1:1000
      if begin8 == outofrange
          if likelihood(B) > 1/8
              begin8 = theta(B);
          end
      end
      if begin32 == outofrange
          if likelihood(B) > 1/32
              begin32 = theta(B);
          end
      end
      if and(begin8 ~= outofrange, end8 == outofrange)
          if likelihood(B) < 1/8
              end8 = theta(B);
          end
      end
```

```
        if and(begin32 ~= outofrange, end32 == outofrange)
          if likelihood(B) < 1/32
              end32 = theta(B);
          end
      end
end


theta1 = input('What is the population contrast mean assumed by the first
  hypothesis? ');
theta2 = input('What is the population contrast mean assumed by the
  second hypothesis? ');
B1 = int16((theta1 - theta(1))/inc + 1);
B2 = int16((theta2 - theta(1))/inc + 1);
likelihoodratio = likelihood(B1)/likelihood(B2)
    begin32
    end32
    begin8
    end8
```

References

Abelson, R. P. (1995). *Statistics as principled argument*. Erlbaum.

Andersson, G. (1994). *Criticism and the history of science: Kuhn's, Lakatos's and Feyerabend's criticisms of critical rationalism*. Brill.

Armitage, P., Berry, G., & Matthews, J. N. S. (2002). *Statistical methods in medical research*. (4th ed.). Blackwell.

Baker, R. R. & Bellis, M. A. (1994). *Human sperm competition: Copulation, masturbation and infidelity*. Kluwer.

Baker, R. & Oram, E. (1998). *Baby wars: Familyhood and strife*. Diane Pub Co.

Barker, P., Chen, X., & Andersen, H. (2003). Kuhn on concepts and categorisation. In T. Nickles (Ed.), *Thomas Kuhn*. Cambridge University Press (pp. 212–245).

Bechtel, W. (2008). *Mental mechanisms: Philosophical perspectives on the sciences of cognition and the brain*. Routledge.

Berkson, W. (1976). Lakatos one and Lakatos two: An appreciation. In R. S. Cohen, P. K. Feyerabend, & M. W. Wartofsky (Eds.), *Essays in memory of Imre Lakatos*. D. Reidel Publishing Company (pp. 39–54).

Berry, D. A. (1996). *Statistics: A Bayesian perspective*. Duxbury Press.

Birnbaum, A. (1962). On the foundations of statistical inference (with discussion). *Journal of the American Statistical Association, 53*, 259–326.

Boden, M. (2006). *Mind as machine*, volumes I and II. Oxford University Press.

Boucher, L. & Dienes, Z. (2003). Two ways of learning associations. *Cognitive Science, 27*, 807–842.

Brooks, L. (1978). Non-analytic concept formation and memory for instances. In E. Rosch & B. B. Lloyd (Eds.), *Cognition and categorisation*. Erlbaum (pp. 169–211).

Burnham, K. P. & Anderson, D. R. (2002). *Model selection and multimodel inference: A practical information-theoretic approach*. (2nd ed.). Springer.

Chalmers, A. F. (1999). *What is this thing called science?* Open University Press.

Cheng, P. C.-H. & Simon, H. A. (1995). Scientific discovery and creative reasoning with diagrams. In S. Smith, T. Ward, & R. Finke (Eds.), *The creative cognition approach* (pp. 205–228). MIT Press.

Chow, S. L. (1998). Précis of statistical significance: rationale, validity, and utility. *Behavioral and Brain Sciences, 21*(2), 169–194.

Churchland, P. M. (1988). *Matter and consciousness: A contemporary introduction to the philosophy of mind*. MIT Press. A Bradford book.

Cohen, J. (1977). *Statistical power analysis for behavioral sciences*. Academic Press.

Cohen, J. (1994). The earth is round ($p < 0.05$). *American Psychologist, 49*(12), 997–1003.

Cohen, R. S., Feyerabend, P. K., & Wartofsky, M. W. (1976). *Essays in memory of Imre Lakatos*. D. Reidel Publishing Company.

Dennett, D. (1987). *The intentional stance*. MIT Press.

Diamond Jr, A. M. (1992). The polywater episode and the appraisal of theories. In A. Donovan, L. Laudan, & R. Laudan, R. (Eds.), *Scrutinizing science: Empirical studies of scientific change*. John Hopkins University Press (pp. 181–198).

Donovan, A., Laudan, L., & Laudan, R. (1992). *Scrutinizing science: Empirical studies of scientific change*. John Hopkins University Press.

Dracup, C. (1995). Hypothesis testing – what it really is. *The Psychologist, 8*, 359–362.

Dunbar, K. (1997). How scientists think: On-line creativity and conceptual change in science. In T. B. Ward, S. M. Smith, & J. Vaid (Eds.), *Conceptual structures and processes: Emergence, discovery, and change*. American Psychological Association Press.

Edmonds, D. & Eidinow, J. (2001). Wittgenstein's Poker. Faber & Faber.

Edwards, A. W. F. (1972). *Likelihood*. John Hopkins University Press.

Edwards, A. W. F. (1979). *Likelihood, expanded edition*. The John Hopkins University Press.

Edwards, W., Lindman, H., & Savage, J. (1963). Bayesian statistical inference for psychological research. *Psychological Review, 70*, 193–242.

Erdelyi, M. H. (1985). *Psychoanalysis: Freud's cognitive psychology*. W. H. Freeman and Company.

Evans, M. (2000). Comment on Royall, 2000. *Journal of the American Statistical Association, 95*, 768–769.

Feyerabend, P. K. (1970). Consolations for the specialist. In Lakatos, I. & Musgrave, A. (Eds.), *Criticism and the growth of knowledge*. Cambridge University Press (pp. 197–230).

Feyerabend, P. K. (1975). *Against method*. Humanities Press.

Feynman, R. P. (1965). *The character of physical law*. MIT Press.

Feynman, R. P. (1998). *The meaning of it all*. Penguin Books.

Fisher, R. A. (1921). On the 'probable error' of a coefficient of correlation deduced from a small sample. *Metron, 1*(4), 3–32.

Fisher, R. A. (1935). *The design of experiments*. Oliver and Boyd.

Fisher, R. A. (1955). Statistical methods and scientific induction. *Journal of the Royal Statistical Society, Series B, 17*, 69–78.

Fodor, J. A. & Pylyshyn, Z. (1988). Connectionism and cognitive architecture: A critical analysis. *Cognition, 28*, 3–71.

Giere, R. N. (1999). *Science without laws*. University of Chicago Press.

Gigerenzer, G. (1993). The superego, the ego and the id in statistical reasoning. In G. Keren & C. Lewis (Eds.), *A handbook for data analysis in the behavioural sciences: Methodological issues*. Erlbaum.

Gigerenzer, G. (2000). *Adaptive thinking: Rationality in the real world*. Oxford University Press.

Gigerenzer, G. (2004). Mindless statistics. *Journal of Socio-Economics, 33*, 587–606.

Gigerenzer, G., Swijtink, Z., Porter, T., Daston, L., Beatty, J., & Kruger, L. (1989). *The empire of chance: How probability changed science and everyday life*. Cambridge University Press.

Gray, J. (2002). *Men are from Mars, Women are from Venus: How to get what you want in your relationships*. Harper Collins.

Greene, B. (1999). *The elegant universe: Superstrings, hidden dimensions, and the quest for the ultimate theory*. Vintage Books.

Grünbaum, A. (1984). *The foundations of psychoanalysis: A philosophical critique*. University of California Press.

Grünbaum, A. (1986). Précis of the foundations of psychoanalysis: a philosophical critique. *Behavioral and Brain Sciences, 9*, 217–284.

Hacking, I. (1965). *Logic of statistical inference*. Cambridge University Press.

Hacking, I. (2001). *An introduction to probability and inductive logic*. Cambridge University Press.

Harlow, L. L., Mulaik, S. A., Steiger, J. H. (Eds.) (1997). *What if there were no significance tests?* Erlbaum.

Howard, G. S., Maxwell, S. E., & Fleming, K. J. (2000). The proof of the pudding: An illustration of the relative strengths of null hypothesis, meta-analysis, and Bayesian analysis. *Psychological Methods, 5*, 315–332.

Howell, D. C. (1987). *Statistical methods for psychology.* (2nd ed.). Duxbury Press.

Howell, D. C. (2001). *Statistical methods for psychology.* Wadsworth.

Howson, C. & Urbach, P. (1989). *Scientific reasoning: The Bayesian approach.* Open Court.

Howson, C. & Urbach, P. (2006). *Scientific reasoning: The Bayesian approach.* (3rd ed.). Open Court.

Hunter, J. E. & Schmidt, F. L. (2004). *Methods of meta-analysis: Correcting error and bias in research findings.* Sage.

Jaynes, E. T. (2003). *Probability theory: The logic of science.* Cambridge University Press.

Jeffreys, H. (1961). *The theory of probability.* (3rd ed.). Oxford University Press.

Ketelaar, T. & Ellis, B. J. (2000). Are evolutionary explanations unfalsifiable? Evolutionary psychology and the Lakatosian philosophy of science. *Psychological Inquiry, 11*, 1–21.

Kitcher, P. (1982). *Abusing science: The case against creationism.* MIT Press.

Koertge, N. (1998). *A house built on sand: Exposing postmodernist myths about science.* Oxford University Press.

Kuhn, T. S. (1962). *The structure of scientific revolutions.* (2nd ed. 1969). University of Chicago Press.

Kuhn, T. S. (1970a). Logic of discovery or psychology of research. In I. Lakatos & A. Musgrave (Eds.), *Criticism and the growth of knowledge.* Cambridge University Press (pp. 1–24).

Kuhn, T. S. (1970b). Reflections on my critics. In I. Lakatos & A. Musgrave (Eds.), *Criticism and the growth of knowledge.* Cambridge University Press (pp. 231–278).

Kuhn, T. S. (1974). Second thoughts on paradigms. In F. Suppe (Ed.), *The structure of scientific theories.* University of Illinois Press (pp. 459–482).

Kuhn, T. S. (1977). *The essential tension: Selected studies in scientific tradition and change.* University of Chicago Press.

Kuhn, T. S. (2000). *The road since structure.* University of Chicago Press.

Lakatos, I. (1970). Falsification and the methodology of scientific research programmes. In I. Lakatos & A. Musgrave (Eds.), *Criticism and the growth of knowledge.* Cambridge University Press.

Lakatos, I. (1978). Edited by J. Worrall & G. Currie. *The methodology of scientific research programmes, Philosophical Paper, Volume 1.* Cambridge University Press.

Lakatos, I. & Feyerabend, P. (1999). Edited by M. Motterlini. *For and against method.* University of Chicago Press.

Lakatos, I. & Musgrave, A. (Eds.) (1970). *Criticism and the growth of knowledge.* Cambridge University Press.

Lanczos, C. (1974). *The Einstein decade (1905–1915).* Elek Science.

Larvor, B. (1998). *Lakatos: An introduction.* Routledge.

Laudan, L. (1977). *Progress and its problems.* University of California Press.

Lloyd, E. A. (2005). *The case of the female orgasm: Bias in the science of evolution.* Harvard University Press.

Lynch, M. P. (2005). *True to life: Why truth matters.* MIT Press.

MacKenzie, D. A. (1981). *Statistics in Britain, 1865–1930: The social construction of scientific knowledge.* Edinburgh University Press.

Maddox, J. (1981). A book for burning? *Nature* editorial 24 Sept 1981.

Magee, B. (1997). *Popper.* Fontana.

Mayo, D. (1996). *Error and the growth of experimental knowledge.* University of Chicago Press.

Mayo, D. G. (2004). An error statistical philosophy of evidence. In M. L. Taper & S. R. Lele, *The nature of scientific evidence: Statistical, philosophical and empirical considerations*. University of Chicago Press (pp. 79–96).

McCarthy, M. A. (2007). *Bayesian methods for ecology*. Cambridge University Press.

McDougal, W. (1938). Fourth report on a Lamarckian experiment. *British Journal of Psychology, 28*, 321–345.

Meehl, P. (1967). Theory-testing in psychology and physics: A methodological paradox. *Philosophy of Science, 34*, 103–115. http://www.tc.umn.edu/~pemeehl/074TheoryTesting Paradox.pdf.

Miller, D. (1994). *Critical rationalism: A restatement and defence*. Open Court.

Murphy, K. R. & Myors, B. (2004). *Statistical power analysis: A simple and general model for traditional and modern hypothesis tests*. (2nd ed.). Erlbaum.

Oakes, M. (1986). *Statistical inference: A commentary for the social and behavioural sciences*. Wiley.

Perner, J. & Dienes, Z. (forthcoming). Representation. In *Oxford companion to consciousness*. Oxford University Press.

Perrin, C. E. (1992). The chemical revolution: Shifts in guiding assumptions. In A. Donovan, L. Laudan, & R. Laudan (Eds.), *Scrutinizing science: Empirical studies of scientific change*. John Hopkins University Press (pp. 105–124).

Plunkett, K., McLeod, P., & Rolls, E. T. (1998). *Introduction to connectionist modelling of cognitive processes*. Oxford University Press.

Pollard, P. & Richardson, J. T. E. (1987). On the probability of making type I errors. *Psychological Bulletin, 102*(1), 159–163.

Popper, K. R. (1934/1959/1975). *The logic of scientific discovery*. Hutchinson. The original German edition was published in the Autumn of 1934 with the imprint 1935, so Popper always references it 1934. The English translation came out in 1959.

Popper, K. R. (1945/2002). *The open society and its enemies: Volume 1*. Routledge.

Popper, K. R. (1963/2002). *Conjectures and refutations*. Routledge.

Popper, K. R. (1970). Normal science and its dangers. In I. Lakatos & A. Musgrave (Eds.), *Criticism and the growth of knowledge*. Cambridge University Press (pp. 51–58).

Popper, K. R. (1972/1979). *Objective knowledge: an evolutionary approach*. Clarendon Press.

Popper, K. R. (1974). Replies to my critics. In. P. A. Schilpp (Ed.) *The philosophy of Karl Popper*. Open Court (961–1200).

Popper, K. R. (1976). *Unended quest: an intellectual autobiography*. Fontana.

Popper, K. R. (1982). Quantum theory and the schism in physics. Hutchinson.

Popper, K. R. (1983). *Realism and the aim of science*. Hutchinson.

Popper, K. R. (1994). *The myth of the framework: In defence of science and rationality*. Routledge.

Popper, K. R. (2001). *All life is problem solving*. Routledge.

Reichenbach, H. (1938). *Experience and prediction*. University of Chicago Press.

Rosch, E. (1973). Natural categories. *Cognitive Psychology, 4*, 328–350.

Rosenthal, R. (1993). Cumulating evidence. In G. Keren & C. Lewis (Eds.), *A handbook for data analysis in the behavioural sciences: Methodological issues*. Erlbaum.

Roth, W. T., Wilhelm, F. H., & Pettit, D. (2005). Are current theories of panic falsifiable? *Psychological Bulletin, 131*, 171–192.

Royall, R. M. (1976). Current advances in sampling theory: Implication for human observational studies. *American Journal of Epidemiology, 104*, 463–474.

Royall, R. M. (1991). Ethics and statistics in randomized clinical trials. *Statistical Science, 6*, 52–88.

Royall, R. M. (1997). *Statistical evidence: A likelihood paradigm*. Chapmen & Hall.

Royall, R. M. (2000). On the probability of observing misleading statistical evidence. *Journal of the American Statistical Association, 95*, 760–780.

Royall, R. M. (2004). The likelihood paradigm for statistical evidence. In M. L. Taper & S. R. Lele, *The nature of scientific evidence: Statistical, philosophical and empirical considerations*. University of Chicago Press (pp. 119–137).

Royall, R. M. & Tsou, T. S. (2003). Interpreting statistical evidence by using imperfect models: Robust adjusted likelihood functions. *Journal of the Royal Statistical Society B, 65*, 391–404.

Salmon, W. C. (2005). *Reality and rationality*. Oxford University Press.

Salsburg, D. (2002). *The lady tasting tea: How statistics revolutionized science in the 20th century*. Henry Holt & Co.

Savage, L. J. (1962). *The foundations of statistical inference: A discussion*. Methuen & Co Ltd.

Schilpp, P. A. (Ed.) (1974). *The philosophy of Karl Popper*. Open Court.

Searle, J. (2004). *Mind: A brief introduction*. Oxford University Press.

Senn, S. (2005). Baseline balance and valid statistical analyses: Common misunderstandings. http://TinyURL.com/y57n2a.

Sheldrake, R. (1981). *A new science of life*. Paladin.

Sheldrake, R. (1988). *The presence of the past*. Collins.

Shepard, R. N. (2001). Perceptual-cognitive universals as reflections of the world. *Behavioral and Brain Sciences, 24*, 581–671.

Smolensky, P. (1988). On the proper treatment of connectionism. *Behavioral and Brain Sciences, 11*, 1–74.

Sokal, A. & Bricmont, J. (1998). *Intellectual impostures: Postmodern intellectuals' abuse of science*. Picador.

Sutherland, S. (1994). *Irrationality: The enemy within*. Penguin Books.

Taper, M. L. & Lele, S. R. (2004). *The nature of scientific evidence: Statistical, philosophical and empirical considerations*. University of Chicago Press.

Thagard, P. (1992). *Conceptual revolutions*. Princeton University Press.

Thornton, S. (2005). Karl Popper. *Stanford encyclopedia of philosophy*. http://plato.stanford.edu/entries/popper/#Trut.

van Fraassen, B. C. (1980). *The scientific image*. Oxford University Press.

von Mises, R. (1928). *Wahrscheinlichkeit, Statistik und Wahrheit* ('*Probability, statistics and truth*'). Wien: Springer.

von Mises, R. (1957). *Probability, statistics and truth*. Macmillan.

Whewell, W. (1840). *The philosophy of the inductive science founded upon their history*. Parker.

Woit, P. (2006). *Not even wrong: The failure of string theory and the continuing challenge to unify the laws of physics*. Jonathon Cape.

Wolpert, L. (1984). A matter of fact or fancy? *The Guardian* 11 Jan 1984.

Worrall, J. (2003). Normal science and domatism, paradigms and progress: Kuhn 'versus' Popper and Lakatos. In T. Nickles (Ed.), *Thomas Kuhn*. Cambridge University Press (pp. 65–100).

Wright, D. B. (2002). *First steps in statistics*. Sage.

Wright, D. B. (2003). Making friends with your data: Improving how statistics are conducted and reported. *British Journal of Educational Psychology, 73*, 123–136.

Glossary

Ad hoc: Ad hoc literally means in Latin 'to this', and is generally used in English to mean for this particular purpose in hand (but not useful in the long term or more generally). For example, an ad hoc committee is formed for a particular one-off purpose and disbanded afterwards. In science and philosophy, an ad hoc change to a theory is a change that protects the theory from being falsified by a particular finding but the change is a step backwards in terms of the scientific virtues of the theory. For example, in the Popperian approach, a change that decreases the falsifiability of a theory is ad hoc. Changes to theories in the light of evidence are part of the way science progresses; but those changes which are ad hoc are not part of such progress.

Alpha: In the Neyman–Pearson approach, alpha (α) is the long-run relative frequency that a decision procedure will reject the null hypothesis when the null hypothesis is actually true. It is the significance level with which you would be just willing to reject the null. On a given occasion, your test might yield a p-value of 0.009, which is significant at the 1% level. But if you would have rejected the null with a p-value less than 0.05, your alpha level is 5% not 1% nor 0.009.

Auxiliary hypothesis: The hypotheses you need to allow your main theory to make contact with data. For example, your main theory might be that highly hypnotizable people are good at selective attention. To test this theory, you need some hypotheses – auxiliary hypotheses – concerning what hypnotizability and selective attention are and how to measure them. Popper called auxiliary hypotheses 'background knowledge'.

Beta: In the Neyman–Pearson approach, beta (β) is the long-run relative frequency that a decision procedure will accept the null hypothesis when the null hypothesis is actually false. Before running an experiment, a researcher should decide on acceptable levels of both alpha and beta. Such factors as the number of participants and the size of the effect one is interested in determine beta.

Collective: The set of events that an objective probability – understood as a relative long-run frequency – applies to. Technically, the set should be infinite, but this requirement is often relaxed in practice. For example, the probability of a person having black hair depends on whether the collective is all British people or all British people who are ethnically Korean. A collective is also sometimes called a reference class.

Confidence Interval: In the Neyman–Pearson approach, an interval created by a procedure that in the long run will include the population value to be estimated a definite proportion of times. For example, a 95% confidence interval will include the true population value 95% of the time. In estimating the mean effect of visualization training on subsequent speed of performance of a sporting move, the 95% confidence interval may run from 1 to 6 seconds. We can reject an effect of the training speeding up performance more than six seconds or less than one second, but we cannot reject any of the values in between. The confidence interval gives a measure of the sensitivity of the study: We have in this case narrowed down the estimate of the training effect to lie in a 5-s interval. The interval is often numerically very similar to a corresponding credibility or likelihood intervals, but the meanings are very different.

Corroboration: In Popper's approach, the more a theory has survived serious attempts to falsify it, the greater the degree of corroboration (or confirmation) of that theory. That is, the more unlikely the successful prediction of a theory is, given the rest of our background knowledge, the greater the degree of corroboration. Confirming the prediction of a theory that we would expect on our background knowledge anyway only marginally corroborates a theory. Surviving severe attempts at refutation confirms a theory in a sense but it does not render a theory more probable on Popper's account (for Popper all theories have zero probability). However, in a way that requires no further justification for Popper, it is still rational to act on the basis of the most corroborated theories.

Credibility Interval: In the Bayesian approach, an X% credibility interval means there is an X% probability of the true population value falling in the interval. In this approach, probabilities are subjective, that is they reflect degrees of conviction. If a 95% credibility interval goes from 1 to 6 s, then you are 95% sure the true population value lies in the interval [1,6].

Demarcation criterion: The means for distinguishing science from non-science. Popper believed that the demarcation criterion was falsifiability and the application of a falsificationist attitude. He believed that this criterion did not provide a sharp boundary but a useful one nonetheless. Kuhn believed that the criterion was puzzle solving with the aim of understanding nature and Lakatos that it involved working in a progressive research programme. The point of a demarcation criterion is that it indicates an optimal way for knowledge of the world to grow.

Degenerating: In Lakatos' approach, a research programme is degenerating if it is constantly trying to catch up with the data. A degenerating programme either makes no novel predictions or, if it does, such predictions are found to be false. The predictions need to be novel to stop the programme from degenerating; looking at the data in order to scrape together some 'predictions' from your pet theory to put in the introduction of the paper would be cheating (see 'post hoc' below).

Duhem–Quine problem: Pierre Duhem (1861–1916) was a French physicist and philosopher of science and Willard Quine (1909–2000) was an influential American philosopher and logician. They both pointed out an indeterminacy problem in testing theories, namely, that as a whole web of beliefs is bought to bear in making and testing a prediction, if the prediction fails it is not obvious what part of the web of beliefs should be altered.

Hard core: In Lakatos' approach, the hard core of a research programme is the central theories that are protected from falsification; instead, auxiliary hypotheses in the protective belt take the brunt of the falsifying force of data and are modified accordingly, sparing the hard core. For example, the hard core of the dopamine theory of schizophrenia is that schizophrenia results from an imbalance in dopamine systems. Though Lakatos did not elaborate this point, one person's hard core may be another's protective belt: The dopamine theory of schizophrenia could be regarded as part of the protective belt of a research programme whose hard core is that all mental illness can be biochemically explained.

Hypothesis testing: In the Neyman–Pearson approach, a procedure for deciding between two hypotheses, the null and the alternative hypothesis, where the researcher ends up accepting one and rejecting the other. The procedure is designed to control at stated pre-determined levels the probabilities of accepting wrongly either the alternative or the null hypothesis (these probabilities are called alpha and beta, respectively). This is the logic meant to be followed in psychology journals, but most people seem to forget about controlling beta.

Incommensurability: In Kuhn's approach, incommensurability refers to the fundamental difficulty of comparing paradigms. Originally, Kuhn emphasized profound difficulties in rationally comparing two paradigms because each paradigm specified different problems that needed solving, different criteria by which to evaluate whether a solution was a good one, and different ways of observing data. Later Kuhn reserved the term 'incommensurability' to mean precisely one thing: the way in which a set of terms can refer differently before and after a theory change. For example, before Copernicus the term 'planet' included the sun and moon; and only afterwards did it include the earth. Such change of reference means different theories or paradigms may be difficult to compare, but clearly rational comparison is not ruled out.

Induction: Reasoning by drawing a conclusion not guaranteed by the premises; for example, by inferring a general rule from a limited number of observations. Popper believed that there was no such logical process; we may guess general rules but such guesses are not rendered even more probable by any number of observations. By contrast, Bayesians inductively work out the increase in probability of a hypothesis that follows from the observations.

Law of Likelihood: The law of likelihood, a term coined by the philosopher Ian Hacking in 1965, states that the extent to which the evidence supports one value of a population parameter rather than another is equal to the ratio of their likelihoods. The law forms the basis of the likelihood school of inference. Significance testing often violates the law of likelihood: A significance test may indicate that one should accept the null when the likelihood ratio indicates greater evidence for the alternative over the null hypothesis.

Likelihood: The relative probability of the data given a population parameter value, considered as a function of different values of the parameter. The likelihood is a *relative* probability in the sense that all that matters is the ratio of probabilities for different possible parameter values; as long as these ratios are maintained, the absolute size of the likelihood does not matter. For this reason, a likelihood is not actually a probability, just proportional to one.

Likelihood Interval: A $1/n$ likelihood interval is the set of possible population values whose likelihood is no less than $1/n$ of the maximum likelihood value. For example, all the values in a $1/8$ likelihood interval are roughly equally well supported in the sense that none has fairly strong evidence for it over any other value in the interval (none has a likelihood eight or more times greater than any other). A $1/8$ likelihood interval will often be very similar in end points to a 95% confidence interval or a 95% credibility interval.

Likelihood Principle: The likelihood principle, first stated in 1962 in three separate publications by the statisticians Barnard, Birnbaum and Savage, states that all the information relevant to inference contained in data is provided by the likelihood. (The Law of Likelihood tells of a specific way to use that information.) Significance tests violate the likelihood principle because they take into account information not in the likelihood, for example, how many other tests one conducted, when one decided to stop collecting data, and whether or not the test was post hoc. Bayesians and likelihood theorists subscribe to the likelihood principle; Neyman–Pearson theorists do not.

Logical Positivism: A movement in the first half of the 20th century which Popper and Kuhn saw themselves as reacting against. The logical positivists took the term 'positivism' from the French intellectual Auguste Comte (1798–1857), whose positivism emphasized recognizing observable (rather than metaphysical or theological) phenomena. Logical positivists accepted as meaningful both logical definitions and also empirical statements, which could be verified by observation (and induction): All else was meaningless.

Normal Science: In Kuhn's approach, science is normal when scientists try to force nature to fit their basic theories and treat difficulties in these attempts as a reflection of their own competence rather than as a reflection on their basic theories. Normal scientists have an almost religious devotion to their basic theories. Popper saw Kuhnian normal science as not science properly speaking at all, indeed, as a threat to civilisation; Kuhn saw it as a necessary process for the progress of science.

Novelty: A prediction has temporal novelty if it is made before the relevant data are known, and use novelty if it was theoretically motivated without the use of the relevant data. Popper, Lakatos and Neyman and Pearson value novelty, as do many scientists; novelty is irrelevant on the Bayesian and likelihood approaches because it has no logical bearing on the relation between data and hypothesis. One reason temporal novelty may be valued is that it means the choice of auxiliary hypotheses in deriving the prediction was fair or simple. In that case, a careful consideration of the reasons for postulating different auxiliaries should render novelty irrelevant.

Null Hypothesis: On Fisher's approach, a null hypothesis is a hypothesis we seek to nullify, one asserting that a population value is equal to a certain value. Often it is the hypothesis of no effect (the 'nil hypothesis'), for example of no difference or of zero correlation, but it need not be. For example, a null hypothesis could be that the correlation is precisely 0.2. If we obtain a significant result we reject – nullify – the null hypothesis; if we do not obtain a significant result we suspend judgment. By contrast, Neyman and Pearson considered two hypotheses, the null and the alternative, where the null is defined simply as the one most costly to reject falsely. In the Neyman–Pearson approach, we will always end up rejecting one hypothesis and accepting the other.

Paradigm: 'Paradigm' comes from the original Greek meaning 'pattern' or 'example'. Kuhn used the term 'paradigm' in a number of ways of which the following two are paradigmatic. A paradigm in the narrow sense is a specific example of good scientific practice which young scientists are trained on so that they will see future problems by analogy with the model cases. In the broader sense, a paradigm is the whole world view that results from this training on the examples. A paradigm in the broad sense is the entire constellation of beliefs, values and techniques shared by all members of a scientific community. Kuhn later invented the term 'interdisciplinary matrix' for paradigm in a broad sense, but this latter term never took off.

Population: A population is the set of all entities we wish to draw inferences about when often all we have access to is observations of just a sub-set (i.e. a sample). Fisherian, Neyman–Pearson, Bayesian and Likelihood approaches are all ways of drawing inferences from a sample to a population. Just what the population is in many psychology experiments is a moot point. In a strict statistical sense we can only draw inferences about a population from which we have randomly sampled, though random sampling from a stated population is very rare in psychology. Often we wish to draw inferences about people in general. All people living now? What if everyone died except for our two groups, those 10 people who took the Peruvian Natural Viagra™ and those 10 who did not? Would a statistical test be worthless because we have tested the whole population? (So there is no need to generalize from sample to population.) Or is the population we are interested in not the set of all actual people but a set of possible observations? Is it the set of future possible observations these people might allow? Or the set of all people that might have lived with a relevantly similar range of genetics, culture and environment? Or is the population the set of different ways we might have randomly assigned these same people to the groups? These questions are still debated.

Positive heuristic: In Lakatos' approach, the positive heuristic is the set of guidelines on how to change the protective belt in the light of failed predictions in order to protect the hard core. A mature science will have a well-developed coherent positive heuristic. Part of the positive heuristic for people working on the dopamine hypothesis of schizophrenia could be to doubt an animal model giving recalcitrant data as an appropriate animal model of human schizophrenia and to provide principles by which a better animal model could be established. Sometimes the positive heuristic and hard core are difficult to distinguish. For example, the principle that some specific dopamine receptor type or pathway is involved is both part of the hard core and a means for dealing with difficult data (did the drug target the relevant receptor type?).

Post hoc: Post hoc comes from Latin meaning 'after this'. In statistics, post hoc refers to a hypothesis or test of a hypothesis that was not specified in advance of collecting the data. In the Neyman–Pearson approach, the test procedure is different depending on whether the test was post hoc or planned; in the Bayesian and likelihood approaches, it makes no difference. Often when reading papers you may suspect that the predictions in the introduction were written after the data had been scrutinized, thereby making post hoc hypotheses appear planned. Is this common practice cheating (Neyman–Pearson, Lakatos, Popper) or desirable because it makes reading the paper a lot easier (Bayes and likelihood)?

Posterior Probability: Your subjective probability in a hypothesis after collecting data. It is obtained by following the Bayesian schema, posterior = likelihood X prior. Only Bayesian statistics directly tells you how strongly you should believe a hypothesis, significance tests, for example, do not.

Power: In the Neyman–Pearson approach, power is the long-run relative frequency of rejecting the null hypothesis when it is in fact false. That is, power = 1 − beta. Given the statistics that we use have a firm logical basis in the Neyman–Pearson approach, power calculations should be a routine part of planning an experiment but rarely are. And unfortunately, without sufficient power a null result is meaningless. With sufficient power, a null result can be very important. A failure to replicate earlier work with a powerful null result does not necessarily mean the early result was wrong. But it does suggest that the method section of the previous paper specifying how to obtain the result was incomplete. Theory should be modified to specify the contextual conditions that produce the result.

Prior Probability: In the Bayesian approach, the probability of the hypotheses before data is collected. According to the personal Bayesians, the prior probability is exactly how probable you personally feel each hypothesis is. People starting from familiarity with the same previous studies and theories could have very different subjective probabilities for the same hypothesis. By contrast, according to objective Bayesians, people with the same information should have the same prior, say a prior that is maximally uninformative given that the known constraints are satisfied. Exactly how to assign prior probabilities is still a debate amongst Bayesians.

Progressive: On Lakatos' approach, a research programme is progressive if it keeps ahead of the data. It should make novel predictions (theoretically progressive) and at least some of these predictions should be confirmed (empirically progressive). The need for novel predictions might partly explain why scientists are so concerned about how early they had their ideas.

Realism: Realism is the claim that there are real entities that exist independently of our theories about them. We construct theories that attempt to refer to these entities even if we cannot see them with our eyes or otherwise directly observe them. What we can directly observe (objects, emotions, mental states?) is an old philosophical and psychological question. Specifying what exactly in our theories we regard as real (even if not directly observable) is also surprisingly not always self-evident. In applying statistical inference we assume a real population distribution, but also accept that our model of it (e.g. as normal, having perfectly linear relationships, etc.) will be inaccurate and hence not be real as such.

Significance testing: 'Significance' is a term introduced by Fisher and refers to whether a test statistic is sufficiently extreme that we reject the null hypothesis. In Fisherian significance testing only a null hypothesis is considered (not an alternative hypothesis). If the p-value is smaller than certain limits, typically 5 or 1%, we declare the result significant at the most extreme limit the p-value is just smaller than (contrast the related notion of 'alpha'). According to Fisher, the level of significance is some sort of rational measure of the disbelief we can have in the null hypothesis. However, Fisher did not have a fully worked out notion of probability. Neyman and Pearson stuck consistently to a relatively frequency interpretation (probability is no measure of degree of belief) and transformed Fisherian significance testing into 'hypothesis testing' (see entry). The terms 'significance testing' and 'hypothesis testing' are not sharply distinguished in the literature, however. Thus, while Fisher did not use the notion of power, it is normal to talk about the need for power in significance testing, because the latter is understood as the Neyman–Pearson hypothesis testing procedure.

Standard deviation: A measure of spread of a distribution. The variance is the average squared deviation of the observations from the mean, and the standard deviation is the square root of the variance. In a normal distribution about 2/3 of the area is included within one standard deviation from the mean, and 95% within two standard deviations.

Stopping rule: The rule used to decide when to stop collecting data. The most common rules are stop when the typical number of subjects in this area have been collected and/or stop at a slightly later point if another handful of subjects might just make the results significant. Neither stopping rule is satisfactory on a Neyman–Pearson approach. Classically, one should decide in advance the number of subjects to be run by means of a power calculation. When using Bayesian and likelihood methods, the stopping rule is irrelevant so long as it is not used to exclude from analysis observations already made.

Type I and II error: A Type I error is rejecting the null when it is true, and a Type II error is accepting the null when it is false. Further types of error include rejecting the null of no difference but accepting the wrong direction of the effect (for example, accepting that boys are faster than girls when in reality girls are faster than boys) and using the wrong statistical model of the data in the first place (e.g. assuming normality when the data are skewed) so that the right decision may be reached for the wrong reasons.

Index